THE GHOST

Julie Welch is the critically lauded author of *Those Glory, Glory Days*, *26.2: Running the London Marathon* and *Out On Your Feet: The World of Hundred-mile Walking*.

Rob White is a professional photographer. *The Ghost* is his first book.

Contents

Acknowledgements

So many people contributed their memories of John White that it would be invidious to list them here; most, in any case, are named in the book. Special thanks, though, are due to Cliff Jones for his time and enthusiasm, and to the White clan – Eddie and Nan, Janette and Alec Ramsey in Scotland, and Tom in Blackpool – for their kindness and hospitality. The authors are also grateful to Norman Giller, author and publisher of *The Golden Double*, for putting them in touch with Jimmy Greaves, and to Matt Phillips at Yellow Jersey, for his insightful editing.

Thanks, too, to Andy Porter, Spurs historian, for the loan of precious books, notably Julian Holland's *The Double*. Spurs and their players have been the subject of numerous works of football literature, many of which are quoted in the following pages. One not mentioned in the text but which provided a valuable source of inspiration is *The Soccer Syndrome*, by John Moynihan, with its marvellous evocation of the night in 1963 that Spurs beat Slovan Bratislava at White Hart Lane.

Julie Welch would also like to record her gratitude for the work of the late Pat Kavanagh, who encouraged her to develop *The Ghost of White Hart Lane* for publication and was still devoting time on its behalf in the weeks before her death in October 2008.

1
Ghost Hunt
Rob, 1972

What if he appears?

Balanced precariously on a cross-beam, I sit back on my heels. My heart is lurching and I have almost stopped breathing as the familiar feeling of hope and longing gets its elbow round my windpipe.

What if my being here somehow . . . summons him up?

Why not? This loft is a dark, spooky place – just where you'd expect to find a ghost.

And I wallow for a moment in the fantasy I've always cherished, the one in which my dad simply walks through the door one day and explains that he's never been dead at all. It was a misunderstanding caused by some bizarre misidentification. The press got it wrong. He was nowhere near the golf course that day.

That's mad. I am eight years old, far too old to believe in Father Christmas and the tooth fairy and ghosts. Anyway, if he did appear, how would he get in? He wouldn't walk into a *loft*. Not unless he came through the skylight.

I return to what I was originally doing, grubbing around for a cardboard box. It is, I should add, not just any cardboard box. I suspect, rather than know conclusively, that it exists. I believe that after being entombed for years at the back of my nan's wardrobe it has found its way to the attic of our new house. My conjecture is that it contains the cuttings, medals, caps, documents and letters that are the nearest I'm going to get to my dad.

A cloud of dust floats around everything, smothering the already weak light into a series of dim, ineffectual haloes. Junk is piled randomly on top of other junk. I have no idea where to start looking. It's like trying to find your way around a city in the aftermath of an earthquake.

I could use a bit of help here. A sign from heaven that I'm getting warm. A shaft of light from the dusty pane beamed directly onto what I'm looking for.

Or a flash of lightning. Why not? And there it would be in front of me. The box. That's the one.

I wobble uneasily on the balls of my feet, and something shifts and rustles in the shadows.

I freeze.

What if . . . something else appears?

Nightmare visions assail me: dark shapes, clammy ectoplasm caressing my cheek, hints of movement behind the trunks, creatures clanking their chains, bastard children of Satan with cloven hooves, lolling tongues and red eyes. Yet I cannot actually bring myself to move, either backwards to the safety and sanity of the loft ladder, or forwards to the unexplored jungle of bric-a-brac.

I must. I have lain in wait for this opportunity for so long. It's the first time my mum and stepdad have gone out as a couple on their own. My big sister is round at a friend's. I'm alone in the house for the first time.

After what seems like hours but is in fact probably a few minutes I realise I have unearthed something promising. Not a box, but a brown leather briefcase embossed with the initials J.A.W.

That would be for John Anderson White. My dad.

The box isn't far away. And when I do find it, it's just . . . weird. How can something so precious be so ordinary? Why isn't everything lying on a bed of velvet? Instead, inside, it looks like a collection of tat: old newspapers, jumbled-up treasures, a scruffy exercise book, letters in faded ink, cards of condolence. Dad's medals are wrapped in tissue paper, as if they're everyday ornaments. They're stuffed into a silver tankard inscribed *John White honoured guest of The National Sporting Club at Dinner given to The Tottenham Hotspur Football Club Team, Café Royal, Monday 24th June 1961*. He's got to have supped from that! It's the Holy Grail!

I carry on rummaging. His boots are bundled together any old how, one toecap stuck in the toecap of the other. His boots! Black leather, size 6½. They look like ballet shoes. The laces hang as though he's just slipped out of them. I can't resist. How much closer can you get to a footballer than his boots? I try them on, hold his medals to my chest. I put the Scotland cap – blue velvet, gold braid – on my head, trying to feel what it's like to be him.

Think! It's got to be in me somewhere. A trace memory, surely, deep in my unconsciousness. Scoring for Scotland against West Germany at Hampden Park in the first minute of your first international! Being inside Wembley dressing room after winning the Double! Think yourself into being your dad!

It's no good. I remain unchangingly myself.

Never mind. I've got these newspapers to read. Carefully I smooth open the ancient, pinkish-yellow front page of the *Scottish Daily Express* for Wednesday 22 July 1964.

GOLF COURSE TRAGEDY
Scots soccer ace is struck by lightning
John White, brilliant young Spurs and Scotland star, was killed by lightning yesterday as he sheltered under an oak tree at Crews Hill Golf Course, Enfield, Middlesex.

I try to turn over the fragile pages. It doesn't help that my hands are shaking. It isn't fear now but an accumulation of all the wanting and anger and frustration that has built up in me over the years. Having a dad who everybody seems to know about except me. Knowing I'll get a pitying look every time I'm introduced as John White's son. Being a small boy in school assembly, starting with the

Lord's Prayer. Every day when I hear those words, 'Our Father, who art in heaven,' I'll think, 'There you go again.' Seething to myself as the same question darts through my mind: How busy is God that He can't decide not to send a bolt of lightning down to someone who is basically a good person?

Part of me wants to look away. This is my dad they've killed off there. But that's the worst bit finished with. I can do this. And now another, much more insistent, part of me starts ravenously scanning.

'. . . Motherwell offered him £2 a week as a ground staff boy. But as he was earning twice as much as an apprentice and his widowed mother needed the money, he turned it down . . .', says the obituary in the *Scottish Daily Express*. And here's Bill Brown: 'He was a terrific bloke'; Denis Law: 'I loved playing with him'; Jim Baxter: 'He was the one person in the game who was friends with everybody.' 'The greatest days were still to come for John White' – that's the opinion of no less than the great Danny Blanchflower. And though I've no memory of my dad – I was five months old when he was killed – this testament to his greatness and this evidence of his niceness just breaks me up.

So now I'm crying; at least, I can feel tears running down my face but the odd thing is that it can't be classified as grief. This is not sorrow. I have no idea why but I actually feel comforted.

He did exist. He was a brilliant player. That much comes home to me as I scan old match reports: 'the white-shirted magician, Scotland's John White . . .'; 'that great artist, John White . . .'; 'John White, mastermind of the Spurs attack . . .'

He was also a joker: 'I will remember him,' wrote his Scotland teammate Jim Baxter, 'in a false moustache giving a Charlie Chaplin impression . . . He was so full of life, so determined to make it fun for others.' One journalist talked about going to a function and seeing 'John White and his great team buddy, Cliff Jones, doing a very commendable can-can'. 'It's a terrible loss. He will be missed by the players more than they would miss anyone else.' Bill Nicholson said that, so it must be true.

And as I look at the front-page headlines of the national news-papers in front of me, massive proclamations in bold type that demon-strate the shock of his death, I feel a twinge of embarrassment. What kind of chippy little git am I, whining about people giving me pitying looks when there's kids out there who also lost a parent that day, through a heart attack maybe, or through being run down by a car, who have nothing like this to remember their loved one by?

I return to the papers. I think I'll look at more cheerful things now, from his earlier days at Tottenham. A full-page cartoon catches my eye.

It's the *Daily Express* FA Cup Special. May 1962. Burnley v Spurs. The drawing depicts my dad as a skeleton, complete with rattling chains. The caption reads:

JOHN WHITE

THE PALE GHOST OF WHITE HART LANE

The frail phantom steps out on to Wembley's lush battlefield. 20 million will see him flit across the TV screen. 100,000 more will see him with their own eyes.

Now I am bewildered, completely. The ghost. That's just bizarre. They called him that while he was still alive.

I put the newspaper under my jersey and hold it there as I climb back down to the landing. If I calm down and read it carefully, perhaps I'll be able to fathom out the whole nickname thing. The Pale Ghost of White Hart Lane. Why did they call him that?

WHITE HOLDS KEY TO SPURS CHANCES AGAINST THE CZECHS

European Cup Winners' Cup, Tottenham Hotspur v Slovan Bratislava

Without Blanchflower (knee injury), Mel Hopkins, a reserve for most of the last three years, at right-back instead of Peter Baker, and with Frank Saul on the right wing instead of Terry Medwin, much will depend on whether John White, the man who has often turned their attack into a devastating goal-scoring machine, is back to form.

Donald Saunders, Daily Telegraph, 14 March 1963

2

John White – A Beginner's Guide

He's no ghost now. This has got to be the best he's ever played.

The date is 15 March 1963. It's a warm spring night in north London and the floodlight pylons are glowing platinum in the gradually darkening twilight.

The match is the quarter-final, second leg of the European Cup Winners' Cup. Spurs are playing Slovan Bratislava of Czechoslovakia. Two weeks back Spurs lost 2–0 in Bratislava in the cold and snow. It could have been 4–0, could have been 10–0, except Bill Brown guarded his goal like it was the Pentagon. The moment they get back to London Bill Nicholson calls them all in for early training and castigates them.

This time it's different. There's nothing about them tonight that Bill, the great perfectionist, could moan about. Stamping their feet on the wooden floor of the stand, the 60,000 crowd sound as though they're capable of wiping out the Czechs' two-goal advantage all by themselves. Spurs are about to make history in Europe. Six weeks from now they will become the first British side ever to win a European trophy.

Like Spurs, Slovan are a money side, with a £500,000 squad of twenty stars in the days when half a million pounds isn't the kind of loose change you might find down the back of Wayne Rooney's sofa. A conglomerate of massive East Europeans, they're led by their gargantuan centre-half Jan Popluhar and it will take some team to make them bow to the roar of the crowd. But some team is what they're up against. This is the greatest Spurs side since the war. Forget push and run. They're even better than the boys of summer '61, the ones who won the Double.

Spurs, with their beautifully poised control, are sweetly into their game. Bobby Smith, a heavy-lidded, broad-backed Yorkshireman, a centre-forward in the classic bashing mould, is doing his best right now to do in Slovan's World Cup keeper, Wilhelm Shroiff. As he left the pitch after the first leg, he pointed a threatening finger at him. 'Londres!' he growled. And now Bobby makes Shroiff lose his nerve from the first moment, when he thumps into him, shattering the beam from the floodlights into fragments.

Jimmy Greaves and Cliff Jones are smashing in shots: Jimmy, scorer of the world's most idiotically opportunist goals, a man who never had to be taught how but who emerged fully formed the moment he put on his first pair of boots; Cliff, the best winger you'll ever see, only five foot seven, incredibly quick and preposterously brave in the air as he goes crashing in over the heads of five people to get to the ball; the movement seems counter-gravitational, the way a salmon goes up a waterfall.

Yet it's none of these three who start what's coming to Slovan. Dave Mackay has been barrelling back and forth along the left flank for half an hour. Long-bodied, short-legged, Dave is a magnificent being strangely reminiscent of a centaur. There's something about him that leaves the impression of restrained violence which might break out at any moment. He isn't a crude player; he's just very strong, the sort who'll come storming through the mud and fog when Spurs are losing to earn them a point. Commitment alone isn't enough to make him a great player, though; he also has fantastic technique. This is him now, jumping onto a cross that's been headed down by a Czech defender. Dave rams home a big, big shot from twenty yards.

One–nil.

The cross has come from John White. He's slim and pallid, his thighs look pathetically unmuscled, but pinning him down is like trying to nail mercury to the floorboards. That, anyway, is how it must seem to Slovan. With John pulling Slovan apart, here one minute, there the next, it's time for Jimmy Greaves to score one of his precious, individual goals, collecting John's pass in midfield and evading two defenders on the run before beating the keeper.

Two–nil on the night, 2–2 on aggregate. The stands are vibrating. And here's John again, initiating the move that ends in Bobby Smith heading Spurs' third goal in nine minutes. Slovan's Schroiff is in bits, Spurs have cancelled out every bad memory of the first leg and then some, and there's fifty minutes of play still to go.

After the break, more. Spurs are immeasurably on top, controlling the game with quick-passing movements which smother the last whimpers of retaliation from Slovan's suffering defenders. The absence tonight of the ageing, injured Danny Blanchflower, the great playmaker, hasn't proved to be the blow to Spurs' hopes people thought. With the opportunity now not to respond to Danny's prompting but to be the prompter, John has stepped up to the plate.

Sixty-five minutes, Greaves, a chip. Seventy-five minutes, Jones, a header. Once again, John instigates the assaults, a presence of astounding energy who appears from nowhere, through gaps of sheer unfeasibility, to split apart a defensive wall.

How does he do it? How does he find those spaces? How does he know where to go? 'If you're playing against Whitey, you'll think: "He's ten yards away. Over there. I'll watch him,"' says Brian James, one of the best sportswriters of his generation. 'You look again. He's not there. Look at how the greatest boxers operate; they watch the eyes and wait for them to twitch. In a similar way, John is waiting for your inattention. He sees you keeping your eye on the ball, keeping tabs on what the full-back's doing, keeping an eye on the centre-half. John White sees that and, whoosh, he's gone.'

'John can see things before anyone else,' says his team-mate Terry

Medwin. 'He'll be involved *knowing* it's going to happen. He does everything right. I doubt if he'd give a ball away in three matches. Easy. Simple. If the ball's been passed somewhere, within twenty seconds he'll have gone somewhere where he can get it. It's knowledge. You've either got it or you haven't. Johnny Haynes has knowledge. So has Bobby Moore. And Cliff Jones – on your bike, he's gone. But with Cliffie, he's operating in the same place every time. John – he can go anywhere. And he'll have gone there for a reason.'

'Such a lovely little bloke,' offers Mel Hopkins, the defender, fondly. 'Great little footballer. One place one minute, another place the next.'

'John is hard to pin down,' adds the renowned football writer David Lacey. 'If you're the opposition, he can vanish before your eyes.'

Just like a ghost.

Above all, John is relentlessly energetic. Dave Mackay will tell you that very often he and John will return to training after lunch, when the other lads have gone off home, and practise further. Even when Dave leaves, John will stay and continue running, running and running.

He's been like that since boyhood. Ask Tom White, John's younger brother. He'll tell you about the day they couldn't stop him playing keepy-uppy.

'We're in the garden and he's been away for half an hour with the ball still on his foot and we couldn't get him to stop. He'd put it on one foot and do a hundred and then he'd flick it on the other foot and do another and then he'd start again, kicking it higher and higher, with this smirk on his face. I mean, we were waiting to have a go, so Edwin, our brother, had had enough of this and he went in and he got a bucket of water and went to the upstairs window and poured it over him. And John still tried to keep it going. It was just incredible.'

A lot of qualities can be read into that story. There's the focus, the sense that life is a joyous comedy to be enacted as intensely as possible, the revelling in his superiority. 'He was,' says Tom, 'a little bastard sometimes.' There's the talent that stands out in a family where all the brothers can run like racehorses and land twenty-yard passes on tin cans: Eddie, growing up to play for Falkirk; Tom, centre-forward at Hearts. That would be enough for any family to boast about, but then there is John. 'White is perhaps more characteristic of [Bill] Nicholson's concept of the game than any other player in the Tottenham side,' Julian Holland is to write of him later in *Spurs – The Double*. 'He is the key to the Championship-winning side.'

John White just loves football. 'Any ball we had in the house,' says Tom, 'he would keep it up. He kept a tennis ball in his pocket to practise with, it's something he's done all through his life. I've heard people say they bumped into him in Edinburgh, with that tennis ball at his feet.' 'I don't think he set out with any ambition to be a professional footballer,' says Sandra, his wife. 'He just plays because he loves it and he wants to be the best at what he's doing.'

A lot has happened to John since 1959, the year he left Scotland for London, when one reporter described him as 'wispy, with a council house haircut'. He's such a subtle player, the crowd didn't get him at first. There's so much happening on a pitch and people like him are not obvious. The fans took a while to realise. They thought he wasn't pulling his weight.

He was born into a working-class Scottish family and scarred by the loss of his father at an early age. He's Spurs royalty now, with a League championship medal, two FA Cup medals and, as part of a golden generation of Scottish players, a bunch of international caps; with John in the side, who's to say Scotland can't lift the 1966 World Cup?

Yet John is still recognisable as the puny Musselburgh boy who cuts the feet off his socks to get a better feel of the ball. Narrow-faced, slim-shouldered, in those butchered socks he stands 5 ft 7½ in and still weighs barely ten stone, most of which seems to be made up of his thick, blond mop of hair. And all match reports tend to talk of him as 'the fragile genius', 'the frail wizard', 'the pale phantom'.

Described like this, he sounds like the Before photo in one of those old Charles Atlas bodybuilding adverts. And indeed, even if after four years at Tottenham, he's thickened out a bit and grown in confidence, calling him the Ghost remains about right. It's something to do with the way he just drifts around defenders, then pops up behind them. Boo! And then: Goal!

No one, it follows, could accuse John White of being a run-of-the-mill midfielder. He plays football the way no one else plays football. When he makes a pass, the chances are you can't see the value of it till he's done it, and then you'll just gasp at the insight and the skill. As a spectator, you can no more anticipate what he's going to do than an opponent can.

Yet when you consider the demands that the game in the early sixties makes on energy, stamina, speed and strength, together with the constant risk of catastrophic leg breaks from hard tackling and quagmire pitches, it's astonishing that he's remained without injury.

The reason is simple; you can't man-mark him. Even if you are a world-class international, there isn't the slightest possibility of getting near him. That being the case, he never gets injured. Here's Peter Baker, on a torrid day for Manchester United against Spurs at Old Trafford. 'Nobby Stiles staggered over and slumped next to me. I said to him, "I thought you were meant to be marking Johnny White." "I'm fucked," Nobby said, "I can't move. He's run my bloody legs off."'

If you still need convincing, in the handful of games John has missed in his four seasons with Spurs so far, Spurs have won only once. When he loses form – and he does so quite predictably roughly midway through the season, for about six games, when the pitches are like sludge – the whole side falters, apart from Dave Mackay, who by now is conditioned to provide the belly-fire to usher them through the slump. But Mackay, for all his skill and commitment, is no creative director, and Bill Nicholson has in the past kept John in the side, knowing he'll snap out of it sooner or later. This season it has been different – a terrible winter in which John has suffered not just the usual agues but a bereavement so psychologically painful he ended up hospitalised. Earlier this month, for the first time in his career at Spurs, John was briefly dropped.

But now in the press box they're having to think up new adjectives. Unrivalled. Matchless. Magical. Incomparable. You only have to look at the last name on the score sheet: *Tottenham 6, Slovan 0 (White, 76 minutes)*. As a coda to his fabulous evening, John bows out with a goal of his own.

The crowd swarm onto the mud-slicked pitch, hugging their heroes. Newspaper headlines the next morning hail a 'SIX-GOAL "MURDER"'. Weeks later, the final in Rotterdam confirms Tottenham's utter dominance as they beat Atletico Madrid 5–1.

But this night at White Hart Lane is the night everyone knows. It doesn't matter that Blanchflower's career is coming to an end, that Bobby Smith has peaked, that you never can tell what condition Mackay's going to be in. Here's what Bill Nicholson is looking for, the answer to: what happens after Danny? This is the night that tells you John White is the future of Spurs.

JOHN WHITE ALL-STAR GAME IS BACKED

Top Scottish football stars last night whole-heartedly supported a *Daily Record* proposal for an all-star testimonial game in memory of John White, who was killed by lightning on a golf course.

In London Tottenham Hotspur's manager Mr Bill Nicholson said after a board meeting: 'A John White fund is being opened, and we are contributing £1000.'

Daily Record, 23 July 1964

3
Remember the Double-winning Team?
Rob, 2010

A complete account of my search for my father would probably take a lifetime to tell because that's how long I've been looking. The need to find out about him dominated my childhood almost from the time I could think. That was when I was old enough to notice that other children lived with their mum and dad while I lived with Mum, my sister Mandy, my grandmother Alma (she was the widow of Bill Nicholson's right-hand man, Harry Evans) and my uncle Andrew, my mother's kid brother who, bizarrely, was only three years older than me.

The trouble was that nobody at home ever talked about Dad. This made his absence seem like some dark family secret, especially as there was no visual evidence to give me a clue – no wedding photo on the mantelpiece, no family album, not even an envelope of old holiday snaps. They must have been such hard times for Mum, those first years – widowed at twenty-two, my sister and me a constant reminder of what she'd had. I didn't like to upset her by asking about him. What if she burst into tears?

There were other, secondary, weirdnesses as well. For example, when I played with other children, their parents had obviously instructed them not to ask, 'Where's your dad?' On the other hand, when I got taken to football and was ushered into the boardroom, people wouldn't talk about anything else.

'This is John White's son.'

'Ah.' A sorrowful look would be bestowed on me. 'What a great player, though.'

Then my head would be patted and I would feel uncomfortable and increasingly chippy. I was proud of my dad but who doesn't want to be liked for themselves?

So, instead, I tried to cobble together some sort of narrative out of what was available. Peter Baker, the right-back in the Double-winning side, was tall, bronzed and debonair, like the actor who played Tarzan – not Johnny Weissmuller, the original, but the one in the TV series, Ron Ely. He was married to Linda, who had been friends with Mum ever since they were the two youngest of the Spurs wives, and the Bakers and their kids used to come round to us on summer afternoons, when there were kickabouts in the back garden.

Peter was like a fun uncle, a good-looking, sporty guy whose appearance was everything a footballer's should be. For me, though, the main attraction was his aftershave. One day I realised it was the same as the one that lingered on my dad's travelling razor, which had been passed down to me along with a little shaving brush and came in a zipped leather top. So I knew what Dad smelt of – the clean-cut, manly smell of Old Spice. When you have nothing, you'll grasp at anything. Even a whiff of aftershave helps.

Then there was Cliff Jones, the winger in the Double side who everyone said was better than a legendary Real Madrid player called Francisco Gento; I suppose the equivalent these days would be someone like Franck Ribéry. Cliff had packed up playing and was working as a PE teacher at Highbury Grove School, on the other side of Highbury Fields, and he almost looked like a cartoon drawing of a very fit guy – short, with a slightly military bearing, always smart, in a blazer or seventies beige suit with fawn-coloured shirt and brown tie, as if he'd just stepped out of *A Question of Sport*. The day before Christmas Eve every year, Cliff came round laden with presents. It was like seeing Santa in a department store, an indication that Christmas was coming. But it wasn't the presents, it was the fact that Cliff Jones was there, full of joy and spirit and warmth. He'd been Dad's best mate. Cliff was good fun. To me, that was evidence. Dad had been good fun too.

Another set of clues was to be found in Musselburgh, the fishing village six miles outside Edinburgh where Dad grew up. Every summer Mandy and I would stay with Granny White in her two-roomed tenement, which had incredible views of Edinburgh on one side and the Firth of Forth to the other. Musselburgh in the late sixties and early seventies seemed pretty much unchanged from the fifties. The ice-cream parlour frequented by my dad and his brothers was still there, as was the ash pitch at the bottom of Links Street he'd played on. So was the bridge he crossed every day when he ran – always ran – to work. I slept on a camp bed in the front room with Granny White, the cooker, the kitchen table and the glass cabinet with the little Delftware football boots that Dad had brought back from a European trip. It made a nice bond between us that felt really natural.

With her housecoat seemingly permanently fused to her body and her slightly Queen-like hairdo, I suppose you'd call Granny White a matriarch. She'd brought up three sons and a daughter on a widow's pension, and her personality was immense and renowned; all the other women in the neighbourhood would go to her if they wanted cheering up. I was a wiry, fine-boned kid with a blond mop of hair, and my apparent resemblance to my father at the same age must have stirred up painful emotions, but she was a get-on-with-it, have-a-laugh kind of person.

I got to know Dad's siblings. Janette was shy but determined, with a stubborn streak and pawky sense of humour that I suspect Dad shared; years later Mum told me of the time he'd returned from an international with the information that 'Denis [Law] is more mature now. If he's offered you a cup of tea he doesn't keep pouring when you take the cup away.'

My uncle Eddie, the oldest of the White boys, was grumpy and funny. He'd been on Falkirk's books before giving up football in favour of the building trade and betting. Uncle Tom, born two years after Dad, was a considerable player in his own right; his clubs included Aberdeen, Hearts and Crystal Palace. The most academic of the boys, he ended up as a director of Blackpool. From photos of the brothers, I could see enough of a resemblance to show what Dad might have looked like in middle age. Baldness is the curse of the Whites.

As I got older there was, of course, one brilliant perk that came from having a famous footballer for a dad, and one who died in eye-poppingly daft circumstances. It provided some of the greatest chatting-up opportunities a teenage boy could wish for. If you can appeal to a girl's sympathies by saying you were deprived of a father growing up because he got struck by lightning, why not? As an essentially shy person, I was willing to take every advantage I could get.

There have been moments of gallows humour, too. In Scotland once when I went to Gullane for an early round of golf on my own, the elderly female receptionist asked for my mobile phone number. As this seemed rather strange, I asked why. 'It's just in case there's some sort of emergency, like, say, you were struck by lightning,' she explained.

Another time, as a big Mike Leigh fan, I went to see *Life Is Sweet*. Set in Ponders End, close to where I grew up, it all seemed very familiar because of these visual references of places and larger-than-life versions of the types of characters I knew. At one stage of the film, one maudlin Spurs fan in a Victorian pub says to another, 'Remember the Double-winning team?' and even before they reeled off the names I thought, Oh shit. They're going to say –'

'. . . John White.'

'Yeah.'

'What a player. Struck by lightning.'

'Cut down in his prime.'

At which point quite a few people in the audience laughed. My knee-jerk reaction was fury. What the hell, I fumed, is funny about that? That's my dad you're tittering about. Then, on the brink of jumping up, I thought about Dad. What would he have done? By then, I'd read enough about him to know that his deep seam of comic lunacy would have prevailed and far from being enraged he would have appreciated the surreal humour.

It's Tom who has, over the years, worked hard to keep the image of my dad burning bright for my sake. I remain touched by the way even now he and Eddie run upstairs to bring down some photo I've already seen a hundred times. In the process I have learnt many essential milestones of Dad's life, and heard a good many anecdotes that help fill in the picture. But most of these are of the don't-speak-ill-of-the dead variety and tell me little more than I already know. For Eddie, Tom and Janette, the wound of his death, with its merciless unexpectedness, is in some ways as raw and painful as the summer day in 1964 when it was inflicted. The best way for them to deal with it, still, is not to go there.

What I have longed to know, and have never been able to find out, are the real, human, almost primal things about my dad. What did he sound like? Did he have a deep voice? A happy voice? Was he quiet or loud? How did he move? What was he like to touch? What went on in his mind? Who was the man behind the well-polished image of John White, the guy who was always mischievous, popular and helpful, everybody's friend?

This drive to know what he was like, flaws and all, has intensified as the years have gone past and I've become a father. It was brought home to me again around five years ago when I found myself accompanying Peter Baker to a home game against Chelsea.

Normally I would have been in the cheap seats; I've been a season ticket holder in the Park Lane lower end for ten years. That day, I wanted to take Elsie and Martha, my daughters. The plan was to give them their first introduction to football, and Spurs, but three together for Chelsea was harder and more expensive than ringside seats at the Second Coming.

It panned out better than I expected. Peter, who automatically gets a ticket as a genuine, copper-bottomed Spurs Legend, needs someone to go with these days. He's all right with familiar surroundings and people – he's really good with my girls, and plays golf with Bert, my stepdad – but he forgets things. So in exchange for my being Peter's minder, which was a genuine pleasure, he pulled three free tickets out of the hat.

The bad news, as far as I was concerned, was another part of the exchange: I was to go onto the pitch at half-time with the girls and collect a decanter engraved with my dad's name, commemorating the induction of the members of the Double side into the Spurs Hall of Fame.

The atmosphere was fantastic, partly because Spurs had equalised just before half-time. When the moment came for us to go on the pitch, I told myself it was no big deal. It was just a patch of grass which I had to stand on for a few minutes. How scary could that be?

Very, very scary for someone who hates the spotlight. I was on a pitch under the floodlights in the middle of a big game in front of 36,000 people, under a giant image of my dad. I gave a little wave and looked for my mates. The Park Lane lower end seemed *miles* from the halfway line.

What I hadn't bargained for was that everyone in the ground started cheering.

There were going to be no tears. I was determined not to become emotional. But I was so proud.

My dad played at a time when footballers lived in houses provided by the club. During the 1963–64 season he earned £100 a week. He owned two cars throughout his life. Compared to today's footballers, he might as well have been playing on another planet.

Yet I very much doubt that in forty years' time the vast majority of today's footballers will be remembered with so much affection that 36,000 people stand up and cheer them. Or that they'll be spoken of with such warmth and tenderness by their team-mates.

My father died in such a freak event that people know about him even if they're not that into football. Even if they are, the standard response to his name is 'Oh yeah. Killed by lightning', rather than 'Oh yeah, played for Spurs from '59 to '64, with Blanchflower and Mackay part of the best midfield of the twentieth century, essential component in the team which won the Double, part of the golden generation of Scotland players . . .'

Ultimately, I feel that skews things slightly, which is a pity. Because what my dad achieved reveals plenty – not just about his magical genius and his sheer joy in life, but about his modesty, generosity, sense of duty, team spirit and dedication: values which, like him, seem irrevocably lost to football.

That is what has spurred me to look into his life, and tell his story now. Above all, I want people to understand his place in the folklore of Tottenham and Scotland and our family.

I want Martha and Elsie to be as proud of him as I am.

'I can still remember my first pair of boots. One of my aunts saw me having a kickabout with some other lads, and noticed I was the one youngster without football boots. She asked me how much a pair would cost. I told her thirty shillings. So she gave me the money as a birthday present. I rushed to the local store, and ran all the way home still wearing my new boots.'

John Graydon meets cover man John White,
World Sports, April 1962

4

The Musselburgh Boy

'God almighty, when I think what we were like,' says Tom White, a burly, quick-witted man in his early seventies, with the shy, engaging smile shared by all the White boys. 'My poor mother. We had a massive double bay window in our bedroom and when we wanted the toilet we jumped out onto a dirt area and into a toilet that had an opening top and bottom, like a stable door. It must have been horrendous for my mum – we used to come back and jump into bed in our bare feet. Even if it was snowing or raining we would jump out because we never had a pot.'

With Eddie and John, his brothers, Tom grew up in Fisherrow, regarded as the heart of Musselburgh and consisting of a few streets plus fishing harbour separated from the rest of the town by the River Esk. Even on a sharp wintry morning that packs the arteries with crushed ice, the place has a rugged handsomeness that must have stayed unaltered for centuries. John was born here, on 28 April 1937, the second of Edward and Ann White's four children. All three boys went on to become professional players; Musselburgh and its surrounding villages have been a traditional breeding ground for Scotland's footballers. Nearby Wallyford is the birthplace of Jock Wallace, Rangers goalkeeper and later manager. Musselburgh itself produced Bert Slater, goalkeeper for Falkirk, Liverpool and Dundee, and the attacking midfielder Dougie Moran, who before he went to Ipswich Town and Dundee United was a member of the late 1950s Falkirk side for which John and Eddie also played.

Tom grew up to be a centre-forward in the classic battering-ram mould. His career highs include, between 1963 and 1964, an attacking partnership with Willie Wallace at Hearts that had him nicknamed 'Goal-a-game White' by the local papers. A low point was when a youthful wild streak, in the form of a drunken car crash in spring 1964, put paid to his chances of an imminent international call-up.

Like John and Eddie, Tom also played in England; his clubs included Crystal Palace and Blackpool. Later, as the owner of a chain of hotels, he was a director of the Lancashire seaside club – a far cry from the poverty of a Scottish childhood blighted by the premature death of their father. Edward White worked as a clerk in the shunting yards. Tom remembers him as a skinny man with thick, fairish hair and an old-style, collar-and-tie smartness. 'If John had lived, he would always have been angular. He probably took after our dad, whereas Eddie and I were bigger lads, we're maybe more from our mother's side. When John was eighteen his natural weight was nine stone eight and I was two years younger than him and two and a half stone heavier.'

Edward White reputedly had been a skilful, left-sided footballer in his youth. 'I remember two men talking to me about Uncle Edward,' says May Wright, a vivacious octogenarian who is the White boys' cousin. 'They were Whitecraigs lads who played for Musselburgh Union and they said what a beautiful touch he'd had and that it was his health stopped him going on.'

A second tranche of athletic DNA came from John's mother. Ann Anderson hailed from the border town of Hawick, where two of her brothers, Carl and Darcy, played rugby for Linden before the war. Carl died at Monte Cassino, but Darcy, whose pace on the wing was blistering, returned to international honours, scoring two tries in Scotland's historic 11–6 victory against New Zealand in the first post-war international.

There's a touch of wistfulness in the way Tom recalls seeing Darcy play for Scotland at Murrayfield, against South Africa. 'We were very proud of him. I went on a school trip up there and we watched the match. And to be fair that was going to be my game because I loved it.' Instead, he followed John into football because he enjoyed reading little reports about his exploits in Under 18 and juvenile football – a self-styled 'little fat guy with a stutter' forever scampering after his glamorous older brother.

Though Darcy went on to sign as a professional for Huddersfield and later became a pro sprinter, knowingly complicit in illegal betting, it's probably safe to infer that most of the Andersons didn't put living dangerously high on the agenda. They all worked in the woollen mills in Hawick, where Pringle and Lyle & Scott were based; Ann and Darcy were the only two of the family who ever left the border town.

Another Anderson brother, Jimmy, stayed in Hawick till the day he died, in 2007, aged ninety-three. Sandra Hart, John's widow, recalls meeting Jimmy in the early days of their marriage. 'He was little and wiry, whereas his wife, Lizzie, was big and stout, so they looked like a Donald McGill postcard husband and wife. He was such a laugh, a devil. He liked a drink. He used to sing at local festivals – he was a bit of performer, so there might have been something of him in John.'

A fourth brother, Will, was a gentle-natured bachelor who liked to say, 'A day spent out of Hawick is a day in life wasted.' Lively and astringent, Ann's take on the place was the polar opposite. 'She often said to me, "The country's all right for sheep and daft folk,"' confides Sandra. 'She couldn't wait to get away.'

Ann's ticket out came in the form of the busloads of Musselburgh lads who descended on Hawick on Saturday nights. They weren't there to shop for cardigans. Hawick's sole attraction for them was much more basic than that. The ratio of women to men in the town was 7:1. It was at one of its dance halls that Ann met John's father.

'I was nine years old when Ann and Edward got married,' says May Wright. 'The wedding was at the registrar's in Hawick and they came back to Musselburgh in the morning. Their first home was in Cairds Row. It was a rented wee room and kitchen with a range, table, chair and a bed, and a shared toilet outside – that was normal then. I came up to their place with a new shopping bag, Ann's wedding present, and asked, 'Can I take your messages?' – could I do her shopping? I felt so important: 'Is there anything else I can do for you, Auntie Ann?' 'Aye,' she said, 'you could just go and have a pee for me.' I loved her. What a personality she had. She was loads of laughs, the extrovert, whereas Uncle Edward was very shy, a gentle, gentle man. And of all the boys, I think John was most like him – gentle, with lean features and a gaunt look.'

John was so weak at birth that he had to be fed with an eye-dropper, and Eddie, little more than a year older than him, was sent to Hawick for a year while John struggled to thrive. Later, says May Wright, he grew into 'a very little, thin boy, very fine got up, with thin legs and fair hair. You would never say he was a robust boy. But he couldn't just walk – he was always kicking, a tin can, a ball, whatever.'

'Any ball we had in the house, he would keep it up,' confirms Tom. 'And it was embarrassing because he would do a hundred on one foot and a hundred on the other, and then say, "I'll give you ten goes." And I'd have ten goes at trying to keep the ball up and I'd get to six, and it'd bounce all over the place. And he'd add all mine up and then he would just put the ball on his left foot and keep it up past my total, then flick it onto his other foot and start kicking it higher.'

By the time John was eight his father had succumbed to a heart condition and was off work. Tom has a single, tantalising memory of Edward taking them down to the harbour at Fisherrow: 'We were looking across the Firth of Forth and there were loads of waves coming in, and he was saying, "Can you see the white horses?" And then we went to where our aunties Maggie and Cathy lived. It was only a short walk, but he could barely make it. Because it was a struggle to walk upstairs he used to whistle up in a special way, and if anybody came to the window he knew it was worth making the effort.'

Maggie and Cathy were Edward's youngest sisters, and known collectively to the children as the Aunties. His older sister, Mairn, owned a fishmonger's in Edinburgh and they ran it for her. The three sisters lived within the same court. Maggie was married to Tam, a railway shunter from Prestonpans. They were childless, and the unmarried Cathy lived with them.

'The Aunties were so Christian,' says Sandra, John's widow. 'John's mum loved a drink but Cathy and Maggie had been brought up in the old Fisher tradition – not a drop of alcohol ever passed their lips. You couldn't tell them you'd been to the pub. Maggie'd send John aspirins – perhaps she thought they were a Scottish thing you couldn't get in England. 'Auntie Cathy used to come down to London and bring him Ayrshire potatoes, bacon and black pudding in a big bag, and kale to keep his bowels regular. I was, like, "Oh God, what's she doing?" She didn't eat with the family herself. She used to get up in the middle of the night and eat Rice Krispies and custard. But you could never imagine the Aunties saying a bad word about anybody. It must have rubbed off on John. It's one thing everyone says about him – his sheer niceness.'

The increasingly disabled Edward moved with his family to the ground-floor tenement beneath Maggie and Cathy's. Number 14 Links Street had three rooms, lit by gas lamps. Ann and Edward slept in the living room which, with a stove and a table, also served as the kitchen. Janette had her own room but the second bedroom was shared by the three boys. Eddie, as the oldest and biggest, had a bed to himself. John and Tom shared the other bed.

'The day came when Auntie Cathy got the four of us into the hallway of Auntie Mairn's house,' says Tom. 'John would have been eight or nine. I was six and I remember Cathy standing us all there and saying, "I've got to tell you something," and I half anticipated what was coming, because before she got it out I blurted it out before her: "Dad's dead."'

'Mother kept us going,' says Janette Ramsey, John's sister. 'She was marvellous, spirit-wise. She had her widow's pension and worked as a waitress, and had four kids. But we never had free meals and I never had National Health glasses, which there was a stigma about. People who had husbands would come to get cheered up by her.'

'I used to love it when I saw her,' says Myra Livingstone, who grew up to marry John's schoolmate, Jim. 'How she coped with those three boys, I never knew.'

'She was a character,' says Eddie White. 'She'd say to us, "I've got people coming from Hawick, so if I ask you, 'Do you want mince and tatties?', say no."'

'Years later,' says Janette, 'when John's children were growing up, she'd teach them dirty songs in the back of the car on the way to Hawick.'

'I remember her standing in a long queue at the butcher's when she was working, and saying to people, "I'm having a party tonight. Do you think I could just go up . . . ?"' says May Wright. 'Everyone was saying, "Of course, Ann. Go ahead," and when she got to the top of the queue she asked for two ounces of boiled ham.'

'She was a great lady, a gregarious happy lady,' says Tom. 'She was always singing around the house. She was entertainer of the year. I think that's where John got it from. We had a terrific time.'

Tom makes it sound as though they did. At the bottom of Links Street was an ash pitch where the boys played football till the light went. If they had to stay inside, the game continued in the hall, to the detriment of the wallpaper. Under the leadership of Eddie, together with the lad from the flat above, they also had a stealing team. 'We weren't stealing to order or anything like that,' says Tom hastily, in case he gives the impression that their boyhood resembled something out of *Oliver Twist*. 'We'd steal things that weren't even worth stealing. Eddie would give the word – Ookamuckatalla – and that was us to go and steal. John and I went into a chemist once and we got this big bottle of Milk of Magnesia, I don't know what that was for. We'd gone off and come back with a big bottle of this stuff that was no use to anybody.'

As the oldest and largest, Eddie was the dominant sibling. 'He could get anything out of my mum because he'd ask for anything,' says Tom. John, meanwhile, was Auntie Maggie's favourite – she bought him his first pair of football boots, and wanted to adopt him. He was also, admits Tom, his mother's favourite – 'because he was so little. I can remember Mum talking to the Aunties about him, and so I went across to them and kept putting my football boots with studs hammered into the soles up into their faces so they'd pay me some attention.'

The kindness of the Aunties helped the family cope with the hardship of being fatherless. They were the ones who stepped in when a fire in the Links Street flat destroyed all the children's Christmas presents, which had been wrapped up and left in an alcove behind a curtain. When, inevitably, the boys crept in to have a look, the curtain flapped against the gas lamp and caught alight.

The boys were billeted with the Aunties while the place was under repair. 'If you ever felt that people should be saints, Maggie and Cathy were,' says Tom. 'We would appear at Maggie's house, the four of us. Uncle Tam, who would have had a hard day on the railway, would be sitting down having his meal. Auntie Maggie would say to him, "Hook it." And he would just get up and leave his dinner as it was and we would sit down to it. It was just incredible.'

The penalty was that every Sunday morning the family had to go to the Fishermen's Mission, where with all the other children they would have to stand in front of the choir and sing a hymn to the congregation unaccompanied, which made John feel acutely uncomfortable. He was already revealing a shyness and lack of confidence that would dog him till well into his twenties. It was the same later on, when he became engaged. Sandra remembers them being invited to take to the floor on their own at a dinner dance – 'He just started pouring with sweat because everyone's attention was on him,' she says. 'It was so weird when you consider he played football in front of 60,000 people every week.'

When it comes to telling the story of that football career, one way of beginning it would be at the ash pitch at the bottom of Links Street or even the hall of the Links Street flat where, well into his teens, John would practise his ball skills after dark. Or you could start at Fisherrow Primary, where the big cinder pitch backed onto the local abattoir and matches were played to an accompaniment of the squeals of doomed pigs. 'He was a brilliant lad,' says Jim Livingstone, who went all the way through school with him. 'We were one of the few who won the local Schools' Cup more than once, because John was in the team. All the guys knew how he was going to end up, because he could stand for hours keeping up an orange or tennis ball, years before Beckham did the same trick. He was always either inside-right or inside-left. I was centre-half and I'd be standing there thinking what to do and he'd be round me – he was so quiet the other team couldn't see what he was doing. You'd just see the ball come floating over like a wee bee. He was a good penalty taker, too – very cool.'

Yet you have to look very hard for him in their old team photo, where John is a slight, unremarkable presence among the bigger, more swaggeringly confident lads. 'He never changed much, really,' says Jim. 'He was always light-built and slim. But he was wiry, and quick, which was good because people could knock him over just like that.'

John was no more robust by the time he went on to grammar school, where the three teams were overseen by a woodwork teacher called Mr McGillivray. 'They were known as McGillivray's Boys,' says John's teenage pal Bobby Wilson who was to become his cousin by marriage, 'and from them came a lot of England and Scotland First Division players – Jock Reid, Frank Duncan, Dougie Moran, Grant Malcolm, Bert Slater, Jock Wallace. McGillivray had a leather strap, which he called Mickey Mouse. Anyone who misbehaved would be invited to "Come and meet Mickey Mouse". Everybody got the strap except John. It wasn't only that he was quiet. He would have too much concern for other people's feelings.'

And his progress? In a ghosted article for a 1962 issue of *Charles Buchan's Football Monthly*, John spoke of being played at outside-left, stuck out on the wing because it was judged to be the safest place: 'I remember people saying . . . "He's a nice wee player, but too small."' Praise, perhaps, but not very encouraging.

Of John's other recollections about his schooldays, he makes one tantalising allusion in an interview to the fact that he was 'mocked'. Apart from that, there's nothing to go on. Then again, talk to anyone about school life in the late forties and early fifties and they'll confirm that bullying was standard behaviour, that if you were small and weak-looking you were almost certain to have a hard time, and that had you suggested an anti-bullying policy to teachers who were often bullies themselves, they would have looked at you as if you had suggested something outlandish like giving lobsters the vote. So let's speculate about how John might have dealt with being 'mocked' and how it might have impacted not just on his personality but on the way he played football.

First, being able to run fast and far away from your tormentors is a fantastic avoidance strategy.

Second, if you can make people laugh you've got a sure-fire way of defusing hostility.

Third, it helps if you keep yourself below the radar. 'Any male who is slight of frame instinctively avoids drawing attention to himself, from the playground up,' says the sportswriter Brian James. 'You need to be very strong and confident to make yourself seen, because you don't want anyone bigger to come and nick the ball off you or rough you up. You learn to make a virtue of your invisibility. Your greatest wish is to be able to disappear through a wall.'

Just like a ghost, in fact.

★　★　★

When night starts to fall over Musselburgh and the narrow side streets are empty of traffic and beyond them the Firth slowly becomes a silent black void, it's an easy thing to imagine Links Street sixty years back. In your mind's ear you hear the shouts of the boys playing football while they wring the last drops of light out of the sky. Here's John now, fighting with Tom in the hall, their cheeks red from delivered slaps. Here are John and Tom, running from the shopkeeper after some heart-lurching thrilling escapade of pointless petty theft. Here's Eddie, commanding them to steal bird's eggs from the trees. Here is John again, roaming as far as Edinburgh, tennis ball at his feet.

What was it like for him, growing up in deprivation in that post-war era? Did he look beyond Musselburgh to Arthur's Seat and the North Sea and dream of a brave new world? How did being father-less affect him and his siblings? Did it make them closer as a unit, say, or hesitant to let go emotionally?

'The three boys were very close,' says Janette. 'I put that down to them not having a father. And I think we all learnt to hide our feelings. I've always found it hard to . . .' She pauses, searching for the right phrase. '. . . go forward to somebody. It was just something about us as a family – just the way you coped, right or wrong. We never talked about our father. I never in my life kissed my mother. She never kissed any of us. I think it was her having to be mother and father.'

'But when we got women, she wasnae happy,' says Eddie. 'She had brought us up.'

'She had three sons and never went to the weddings of any of them,' Janette concurs. 'I suppose it was that she didn't like handing them over to another woman.'

Nevertheless, what strikes you is how normal his surviving siblings are, and how normal everyone says John was, as well as how generous-spirited and likeable. Between them, Ann and the Aunties did a great job, you think.

And then you start to think, too, about what made John into the person he was. You hazard a guess that he got his verve and sense of mischief from his mother, and his physique and gentle nature from his father. You speculate that he seems to have been the typical middle child – keeping his head down, getting on with life. As he played on those seemingly endless summer nights on the ash pitch, with his friends and brothers and, when they'd all gone home, on his own, perhaps he already knew, too, that for him 'life' would involve the one thing at which he was transcendentally good. And maybe that knowledge was what gave this gentle, quiet boy his willpower and steel.

As it turned out, he was going to need as much of that as he could lay his hands on.

Going south to Middlesbrough are R Thomson (left-back) and White (inside-left) of Bonnyrigg. The loss of left-back Thomson would not be too severely felt but should White step up his place would be difficult to fill. The former Musselburgh Union player has become a favourite with the Rose supporters.

Dalkeith Advertiser, 1955, 25 August 1957

5

More Famous Than Sean Connery

An early-summer morning in 1956. On the racecourse and golf links on the outskirts of Musselburgh, the grass shudders in the breeze from the North Sea. Chains of white cloud hang overhead and warmth is beginning to seep into the day.

A teenage boy moves along with such apparent lack of effort you can't see how quickly he covers the ground. Somewhat bizarrely, he is wearing his joiner's apron over his trousers; it's multipocketed, with a foot rule strapped to the side. Over the top is his old jacket, the pockets baggy with nails and screws. On his feet are big work boots, with metal toes. The bag slung over his shoulder contains his work tools and lunch – a jam sandwich and a caddy with tea leaves, sugar and milk already in it; the hot water will be added later.

The boy smiles with private enjoyment as he reels in the figure in front, a panting dot in overalls that grows larger till it reveals itself to be his younger brother. John and Tom have joinery apprenticeships, and run the two miles to work every day. 'John used to stand at Mrs Foreman's pub and give me four hundred yards start,' says Tom. 'And I'm off and every day the little bastard would pass me at the same place, on a bridge across the River Esk at the bottom of Shorthope Street. It was only about sixty yards wide and he didn't pass me at the far side of the bridge, he'd pass me every day as I was striding onto it. And as he went past he would say, "Keep going, son." I always tried to get there before him and I never did. At least if I'd got a bit further onto the bridge I would have seen some progress, but nothing. He could have passed me earlier but it was always at the same place. He'd pat me on the shoulder and then just pitter away and off.'

After work, John and Tom run home again. With Eddie, also an apprentice joiner, they go racing up the stone steps to the Aunties' house. In the front room, Maggie and Cathy will already have filled an aluminium bath with boiling water from the kettle. 'The three of us would wash in that and whoever got in last, which would invariably be myself, would get in dirty water but you'd still be able to be washing yourself,' says Tom. 'We used to have black vests and the reason we got black vests rather than white was so we wouldn't look as dirty.'

Before long, John will be seen on the pitch at the end of Links Street. Even though he's in full-time work he trains harder than everyone else. The summer evenings are long and he'll be kicking a ball out there till midnight after the rest have gone home, a pallid boy so thin he's almost transparent, gliding over the rough cinders. As the summer wears on and the new season starts, there will be the luxury of grass in the form of Junior matches with Bonnyrigg Rose. Watching him will be the usual anonymous bunch of characters in raincoats and trilbies, the scouts who'll go back to deliver their verdicts, and once again he'll be hoping a big club will pick him up.

It's proving a long wait.

There are at least half a dozen clubs in England and Scotland who must have spent the years 1959 to 1964 kicking themselves that they didn't take a punt on a teenage John White. Instead, they followed the lead of Tommy Walker at Hearts, who had him watched and then rejected him with the verdict: 'He'll never make it. Too fine.'

John's football after Schools level went along the traditional route in the search for recognition. He played Under-19s for Musselburgh Union, alongside Eddie till the latter signed for Falkirk, and later on in the same team as Tom. Though still underdeveloped compared to the other boys in his age group, he had grown a few inches and during a brief spell at Prestonpans YMCA (where before him Alfie Conn, part of Hearts' Terrible Trio of Conn, Wardhaugh and Bauld, had played youth football) he moved to inside-forward whereas previously he'd been stuck out of harm's way on the wing. From there, aged eighteen, he signed for Bonnyrigg Rose, a Junior club based in a mining village eight miles south of Edinburgh.

Go to Bonnyrigg now and you'll find it's part of the rapidly gentrifying sprawl beyond Edinburgh. Its history, though, runs parallel to other such places where the clubs are all that remain of the mines – outfits like Newtongrange Star, Arniston Rangers and Dalkeith Thistle. Bonnyrigg Rose, founded in 1881, has one unique claim to fame: they are the only Junior team to have won their league in three centuries: 1897, ten times in the twentieth century, and once so far in the twenty-first, in 2010. 'There's not another Junior team can say that,' says the club's snowy-haired historian, former player Nat Fisher.

The club moved in the 1920s from their original site to the one they now occupy two hundred yards from the crossroads known as Bonnyrigg Toll. The land was gifted by the Dundas family, hence its name – New Dundas Park – and the club raised the funds to buy it outright in the 1950s. In John's time it was notorious for its sloping pitch; there was a joke going the rounds that all Bonnyrigg forwards had one long leg and one short. It's always been a social as well as a football club, and the lobby between two of its function rooms features a display devoted to its most famous sons.

There's Pat Stanton who was there in the early 1960s – he went on to play for Hibs and Celtic, and to captain Scotland. There's James Mackay – 'Inside-right at Bonnyrigg, hard as nails, scored a hat-trick on his debut and kicked everyone in sight,' according to Nat – who emigrated to Australia, for whom he played in the 1974 World Cup. And then there's Sean Connery, who came to them early on in the 1950s from Fet-Lor Amateurs, a club set up for deprived

Edinburgh children by the two local public schools, Loretto and Fettes. 'He was a big handsome guy. I think he was working as a funeral parlour polisher at the time and he can't have been working for much more than thirty-six shillings a week, but he had a corduroy jacket which I would have killed for. Top-notch.'

By the sound of it, Connery was right to decide on something other than playing right-winger as his day job. 'He wasn't the toughest of players and we'd go to West Lothian, to places like Armadale and Whitburn, and I remember the opposition defenders kicking him up and down.' And it's John's name, of course, that has been given to the newest of Bonnyrigg Rose's function lounges. 'John White's more famous in Bonnyrigg than Sean Connery,' says Nat.

Nat was doing his national service when John signed but was there for John's first appearance. 'I was on leave. Bonnyrigg were a man short so I went down and was getting ready when I looked round and saw the back of this blond head. I thought it was a laddie who was at school with me so I said hello, and the person who turned round was John.'

The match, in midweek against Newtongrange in August 1955, was John's first game and he was the scorer in a 1–1 draw. 'It was his style,' enthuses Nat. 'Ninety-five per cent of people who go to football don't know anything about it. If you *knew*, you liked. He just glided about. He didn't run. His feet were off the ground, as if he had an air cushion. I can still see some of those goals yet. It was wonderful, how he did it.'

There's a team photo of the time which shows John lined up in a motley group of men of all ages and sizes, in the red-and-white four-inch barrel-hooped strip in which the club still plays. Alongside the lumpy part-timers and middle-aged men, John, with his thick, tow-coloured hair neatly combed and his socks immaculately pulled up, is the only one who looks like a kid. Confusingly, Junior football wasn't only for the young.

'A lot of them, in John's time, were guys who were older than John and who were never going to senior teams,' says Nat. 'You'd get chaps of forty-seven and seventeen-year-olds who'd come in for a couple of years till a senior team spotted them.' It was a career trajectory already taken by other local boys made good. Dave Mackay, for instance, had been a Junior with Newtongrange Star – 'I played against him and he was a right dirty B!' says Nat – before leading the Hearts revival which would win them the Scottish Cup for the first time in fifty years.

It's hard to think of a comparable set-up in England. Players earned five shillings a week, having received a signing-on fee of seven pounds ten shillings. 'They signed you in the close season so you could use the money to go on your holidays,' says Nat. 'You could get a week at Butlins for eight pounds.'

John seems not to have been a club regular during that first season; he was sent back to Musselburgh Union for at least some of it while he filled out. 'He was about five feet seven or eight,' says Nat Fisher, 'but he was . . .' He holds his hands barely a foot apart to emphasise John's slimness. The impression is of a shy teenager who was late maturing physically and who was dominated by his rambunctious, joke-cracking older brother, who paid him to clean his boots and ordered him to carry his bag. 'John used to go to the Mall café in Musselburgh to play records,' recalls Nan, now Eddie's wife but then his girlfriend. 'Eddie would send him to keep me company while he was at the bookies.' 'He was shy all right, but if he knew the company he was fine,' says his cousin Margaret Wilson. 'At my twenty-first he took his shoes off and played keepy-uppy. Then he had a sherry and sat down on a kitchen stool to drink it. Someone said something funny and he rocked forward and fell off. He couldn't stop laughing. He giggled and giggled. To my knowledge he'd just had the one.'

Word seemed to be getting around about John's promise. At one stage during that season he was approached by Jack – known as Johnny – Love, an Edinburgh Scot who from September 1955 was player-manager of Walsall. John refers to it in an interview he gave in 1963 to *Charles Buchan's Football Monthly*:

> Johnny turned up at my home at a time when I was actually training in the lobby.
>
> 'Is your brother in?' he asked.
>
> That tells you how small I was. The Walsall manager mistook me for a younger brother!
>
> Once that little misunderstanding had been put right he made me a really good offer. But the prospect, coming out of the blue like that, scared me a bit. My mother was out and I told him I could do nothing until I had consulted her. I was told I would hear again a few weeks later.

In fact, possibly unnerved by John's boyish appearance and his insistence on asking his mother's permission – did the manager fear he had been the victim of some kind of wind-up? – Love never contacted him again.

Another manager who failed to spot an unpolished diamond was Middlesbrough's Bob Dennison. John travelled south to Ayresome Park – then Middlesbrough's ground – for a trial in the reserves with a Bonnyrigg team-mate, Alan Stenhouse, who later signed for Motherwell.

> Again I scored. Mr Dennison seemed pleased with me, but again I was told I was very small.
>
> I left Ayresome Park with instructions to do plenty of walking and skipping, and get a good quota of sleep . . .

And once again, that was the last John was to hear of the matter. Intriguingly, Dennison brought a 21-year-old Brian Clough into Middlesbrough's first team that year. You can't help wondering what could have been achieved with John supplying him from midfield.

But given that Alex Young, who had played in the same school team as him, had already made his debut for Hearts, it's hardly surprising that after these disappointments John trained as if he had something to prove. 'He was an awful guy for taking cod liver oil mixed with sherry and eggs,' says Eddie. 'He'd run round the racecourse. He was dedicated to training. I used to jump in the stand and hide till they came round for the fifth lap.'

In Tom's opinion, he overdid it sometimes. 'Once when John and I were playing for Musselburgh Union we were out on the training pitch together. I knew that John had a trial for Motherwell the next day but I could honestly say he had the most sweat on him of anyone on the pitch. At the age I am now, I'd have said, "John, take it easy, you're playing for Motherwell tomorrow." But he couldn't take it easy. Maybe when he did have a trial he's left a little bit of energy on the pitch from the night before. Because we didn't have a dad who would have said, "You're not playing tonight, you've got a trial tomorrow." But John couldn't do it any other way. That was just him.'

In fact, Tom's recollection of the Motherwell trial is slightly misleading. John, who played for their reserves against Queen of the South and scored the first goal in their 2–1 victory, was offered a job on the ground staff by Bobby Ancell, the manager. It was, though, hardly a dream deal. At the time, Motherwell ran only two teams and John couldn't be guaranteed a game every week. Added to that, he would only have been earning two pounds a week and would have been worse off than he was as a joiner, his wage bulked out by his five shillings a week from Bonnyrigg Rose. He needed the money, having undertaken to provide for his mother. Eddie was more interested in supporting his bookie. John turned the offer down.

October 1956. The air has got sharper, the pitches claggier. John has returned to Bonnyrigg Rose and this season he's big enough to make it count. In the *Dalkeith Advertiser*, he's referred to as '. . . an inside-forward of exceptional promise [as] was demonstrated at Penicuik on Saturday where left-half Young lobbed a free kick into Penicuik's goal. White, seeing that the goal was well-guarded, cutely headed the ball over the head of the Penicuik defence into the net.'

Senior clubs continue to keep a close eye on him. One such is Alloa, which has recently been referred to by Jim Rodger of the *Daily Record* as 'Scotland's most improved B Division side'. The sharpening focus on Alloa is down to their manager Jerry Kerr, who in his second season for the club is demonstrating a flair for working the transfer market. Intent on building a new side he has, according to the *Daily Record*, 'granted Jim Barclay, their left-winger, who was previously with Falkirk and Brechin City, a free transfer'. On Tuesday, 11 September, Jim Rodger reports that 'Alloa hope to have a junior on trial at inside-left against Montrose at Recreation Park'; Monday 1 October: 'Note the name – Ian Reid. He is the Celtic player temporarily transferred to Alloa, and I forecast you'll be hearing a lot more about him before the season is out'; Friday 12 October; 'Davie Ferguson, 24-year-old left winger of Alloa was transferred last night to Coventry City. Jerry Kerr told me: "We are sorry to transfer Davie but the small club must sell to exist. Last season I had to transfer my goalkeeper, Willie Nimmo, to Leeds United."'

Finally, on Friday 16 November, comes the news that 'Alloa will play a junior trialist at inside-left against Hamilton at Recreation Park.'

There's a song by Kevin Rudolf called 'I Made It' which may be a pretty standard hymn to bling and Bentleys but which conveys exactly that feeling which John must have had when Alloa took him on. It's the feeling of a young man from nowhere triumphing over the doubters and getting what he's yearned for at last.

When you think about the struggle John had to be offered terms, it's hard to believe the League clubs could be so timorous. More fool them, you think. And fifty-five years later, standing in the driveway to Bonnyrigg Rose Social Club, the main street concealed by a wall and the car park, you wish you'd seen his last joyous run over that sloping pitch as he launches himself towards the fame and glory that for so long have occupied his most private dreams.

ALLOA SIGNING

Alloa manager Jerry Kerr last night signed 18-year-old John White, inside-forward of Bonnyrigg Rose. White, an apprentice joiner, played a successful trial on Saturday against Hamilton Acas.

The Wasps' manager had to move fast as Stenhousemuir had also offered the player terms.

Jim Rodger, Daily Record, 19 November 1956

6

Are You Watching, Rangers?

'I can remember John right enough,' says George Ormiston. 'A quiet soul, he was. There wasn't much of him. Nowadays, you see the teams limbering up before the start. Then, boys just sat around the dressing room, except John. John was always doing his exercises. Knees up and all sorts of things.'

George is president of Alloa Athletic Football Club. Gentlemanly in manner, he continues in his eighties to visit Recreation Park most days, having been a supporter since childhood and, following in the footsteps of his father Bob, a director since 1957. During the 1956–7 season when John was there, he was club treasurer. As such, he paid John's five-shilling fare from Musselburgh to Recreation Park – 'His journey,' says George reminiscently, 'would have taken him over the Kincardine Bridge.'

What John would have come to was a pleasant town in Clackmannanshire, which had the distinction of being host to at least nine major breweries. All but one of them have gone now, but Alloa remains a craggily charming place of stone bridges and old-fashioned streets lined with kirks and solicitors' chambers and banks.

Its football club was founded in 1878 and it became a League member in 1921. A brief rummage through the archives produced by club historian and programme editor John Glencross tells you the following: highest ever league position – sixth in the Scottish First Division 1982–3; record attendance – 13,000 v Dunfermline 22 February 1939, Scottish Cup third-round replay (Alloa won); best performance in Scottish Cup – quarter-finals 1938–9, 1960–1, 1988–9;

most capped player – Jock Hepburn, 1 cap (Scotland v Wales 1891); honours – Third Division champions, 1997–8; B&Q Fair Play League trophy winners 1989–90.

You get the message. Alloa is no rival to Celtic and Rangers, nor Hibs and Hearts for that matter. Both Glasgow and Edinburgh are little more than an hour away by train now the branch line from Stirling to Alloa has reopened. As with most small-town outfits, survival depends on its appeal as a community club; its core support is less than a thousand, even though this 2009/10 season is the one in which it finishes runner-up in the Scottish Second Division.

In the boardroom, there's a team picture featuring the nineteen-year-old John with his forelock of fair hair and that lovely wide smile, wearing the striking black-and-gold hooped strip that gave the club its nickname, the Wasps. A sign of the constraints under which the club exists is evident in more recent photos. These days the strip is all gold with black collar and cuffs. It's cheaper; the hoops that John played in would have to be specially manufactured.

That's not the only thing that John would find different. George lists some of the changes. The old timber stand has been replaced by a modern one. There's an all-weather pitch. 'The directors' lounge was a small room,' he adds. 'There was no upstairs then. After the game it was a communal bath. We had bigger attendances, fifteen hundred to two thousand.'

In the late 1970s, the club could finally afford to install floodlights. In John's era, kick-off time had to move backwards from three o'clock by successive quarter-hours as autumn gave way to winter. Behind the stand was a bus station because that was the way fans travelled to the ground. Hardly anyone drove. Now the bus station has gone. Most of the space it took up is occupied by small business buildings, fringed by cars.

One thing doesn't alter. The backdrop to the stadium, the snow-capped Ochil Hills, is much as John would have seen it more than half a century ago. Nearby is Alva, the village that gives its name to the famous Alva Games and its landscape to a sporting event of considerable fame and antiquity, the British Hill Race Championship. It takes place on the second Saturday in July, when fell runners come from far and wide to take part in the endurance race.

It's not too much of a stretch of the imagination to visualise John, the obsessive trainer and natural-born distance runner, speeding up and down those hills the way he ran to work and back. Frustratingly, imagination is all you can use when it comes to John's early career. In the immortal words of the football chant, 'There's only one David Beckham/Wayne Rooney/(insert name of choice).' There is, indisputably, only one John White. But think of that John White, and what comes to mind is the finished article, the quicksilver, elusive Ghost of White Hart Lane. What we lack is any visual evidence of John as a work in progress.

Think of today's giants as they were in their teens – Beckham spindly-legged and boyishly appealing, Rooney half thug, half boy genius. And that's the point – we are able to think of them because their early gaucheries and glories are all on film. Thus we have instant access to Beckham making his Champions League debut at nineteen, scoring for Manchester United in a 4–0 defeat of Galatasaray. We can marvel again at Rooney's match-winning goal against Arsenal, five days before his seventeenth birthday. We can tut once again at callow lapses of temperament and feel that prickle of excitement at raw talent. With John, it's hard enough to find the footage of him in his prime. And even if you do manage to track some down, the very style of the player means that he's hard to spot as he flits across the screen between all the upthrust legs and mud-encrusted torsos.

Yet the player George Ormiston talks of so affectionately – 'He was my hero' – is easily identified as the player who within three years would be an essential component of Tottenham's success. 'It was a different style from nowadays, but John always stood out. He was always in a position to get a pass. He moved around the field.' In support of this is an undated cutting from the *Alloa Advertiser*, headed 'DEFENCES ON TOP AT THE REC': 'White has any amount of craft, yet is without the selfishness which too often goes along with clever ball play.'

Some things would already have come easily to him through those long practice games on the ash pitch in Musselburgh, and the indoor wallpaper-destroying sessions in the hall at Links Street – the superlative control that gave him the ability to take the ball from any angle with both feet, the long and short passes that made his distribution so accurate. Other things he was probably born with – the intuitive positional sense and fantastic timing come to mind.

Perhaps we can assume, though, that it was in Alloa that John first learnt to capitalise on his natural ability to run for extended periods – that exceptional energy that would mean totting up five miles per match would be nothing to him. Perhaps it was then that he realised the best way to create space was by covering a lot of ground and finding positions.

Perhaps here, too, was where he began to grow in self-belief. This was someone who in his teens had been told he shouldn't hope to make it as a footballer; someone who had already been turned down by a handful of clubs; who was considered too insubstantial to be played in the position where he excelled. Yet now national papers were describing him as a future star.

John made his first appearance on 17 November 1956. He wore the number 10 shirt, playing in what was known in those pre 4–4–2 days as inside-left, against Hamilton Academicals, as George Ormiston recorded all those years ago on a page in the accounts ledger: '10, Junior Triallist (NOT REG'D)'. His debut had been previewed in the *Daily Record*, where Jim Rodger, under the header 'NEW WING' wrote: 'Alloa manager Jerry Kerr is fielding a new left-wing – John White (Bonnyrigg Rose) and Jim Wilson (Leicester City) at Forfar on Saturday.' A week later, another page in the accounts ledger shows the line-up for the away game against Forfar. This time it reads: '10, J. White'.

Soon after, Jasper 'Jerry' Kerr put John in the number 8 shirt –
inside-right, an attacking midfielder – and coached him in how to
wear it well. The man who moulded John White was a ruddy-faced
West Lothian Scot, one of the last of the waistcoat-and-trilby
managers, before tracksuits became the norm. George Ormiston
succinctly remembers him thus: 'A pipe in his mouth. Well built.
Played for Alloa. Came to us from managing Berwick Rangers.' The
Scottish commentator Archie Macpherson – himself a legend –
remarked that he had 'the reflective appearance of a Maigret mentally
sifting through the facts'. More than that, said Macpherson, Kerr
addressed his craft with the same 'pragmatic cockiness and innova-
tive daring' that has always been a trait of the best Scottish managers.

Kerr is remembered primarily for what he achieved at Dundee
United. He went there from Alloa in 1959 and took it from being
the second club in the city to the first. He became known as having
a knack of finding good young players. His hobby horse was that
the bigger the club, the worse the talent-spotting. At Dundee United,
he was one of the first managers to see the possibilities of trawling
the Scandinavian countries for able players at a bargain price. He
was, in short, exactly the sort of man prepared to have a punt on
an undersized lad whose career had thus far been manacled to juvenile football and a day job as a joiner.

In the early part of his spell with Alloa, John opted to carry on
with his joinery apprenticeship. It turned out to be a good decision.
His signing-on fee was £20, and he was paid £4 a week with a bonus
of £1 for a win and ten shillings for a draw. Since Alloa were lying
third in the Second Division table when he went there, he figured
he might well be collecting quite a few bonuses, so he told his mother
he'd give her the £4 a week wages and keep the bonus money for
himself. Then the club, who had spent most of November in top
position, started a losing run. During the second half of the season,
the sum total of John's bonus money was thirty shillings.

A trawl through the records of that first, partial season shows that

John made twenty-five League appearances and scored six goals. At that stage he was still wearing the number 10 shirt, but the club records show that during the 1957–8 season he was playing on the right at number 8. That season he made thirty-six League appearances and scored nineteen goals. Added to that were four appearances and two goals in the League Cup, and a single appearance in the Scottish Cup.

There was, of course, no way Alloa were going to hang on to John in perpetuity. Once he had demonstrated that he could survive the Scottish Second Division, notoriously hard and packed with older guys prepared to kick, his tremendous potential drew the scouts of big-time clubs once more. Alloa survived by being a selling club – over the years other promising finds like Dennis Gillespie, Tommy Hutchison and Neil Martin were to follow John out. John attracted attention all the way through – George remembers scouts being there 'week after week, some from big English clubs'. Charlton Athletic, who had just been relegated from the old English First Division, were fairly constant suitors and Alloa were willing to sell but Charlton weren't prepared to pay the asking price of £3,000.

Nor was another, bigger club closer to home. 'Jimmy Smith was a legendary striker for Rangers in the thirties, a centre-forward in those dear dead days,' says the *Sunday Times* football writer Rodger Baillie. 'He became the Rangers trainer, then the chief scout – a very powerful, tall, muscular guy who epitomised the Rangers template; Rangers have traditionally gone for physique to an extent. That said, Willie Henderson [their internationally capped right-winger] was a diminutive five foot five but like Jimmy Johnstone [Celtic's right-winger, also a Scotland international] he was a little ball of a man. By Scottish standards, John wasn't a small man, but he was frail-looking, and Rangers had one of those already, Ian MacMillan, an inside-forward known as the Wee Prime Minister. Thirteen times Jimmy Smith watched him and thirteen times Jimmy Smith decided not to recommend they bid for him. Anyway, the more successful John became, the more Rangers decision not to sign him was held as a black mark against both the club and Jimmy Smith.'

After Rangers backed off, Hibs seemed to be making all the running. Then an offer came from Falkirk – 'out of the blue' according to George. A bidding war followed, both clubs making a final offer of £3,300. Falkirk sealed the deal when one of their directors, a licensed grocer called James Doak, threw in a crate of whisky.

John's last game for Alloa was against St Johnstone on 27 September 1958. He moved to Falkirk in October, taking with him the one medal he had picked up while at Alloa, for winning the Stirlingshire Cup. Maybe he hoped he could achieve considerably bigger things than that with Falkirk. Maybe he even dreamed that Rangers would come for him after all.

He wasn't to know that four hundred miles away events were taking place which would land him with a different destiny entirely.

SPURS LACKED A GENERAL

Tottenham Hotspur 1, Chelsea 1

Spurs needed someone to 'general' them. Skipper John Ryden, steady enough at centre-half . . . appeared the strong, silent man when the odd piece of advice might have steadied over-anxious forwards and brought them some semblance of order. Danny Blanchflower could have done it, but in the role of just another player he didn't sparkle in his normal manner.

Harold Mayes, Empire News, 25 August 1957

7

The Captain

Summer 1958. Lots of Hertfordshire is still pretty rural, a county of small towns and dreamy villages bedded down in arable fields. The place is largely bare of cars. You could take to the middle of most roads with impunity. On the sleepy lanes that thread around Cheshunt, some two dozen people are doing just that – a group of footballers on a pre-season training run.

The Northern Irishman leading them has the slim shoulders and lean limbs of the marathon runner. Compared to those following him, he is getting on in years but some inner demon drives him to stay ahead of the pack. He runs in an idiosyncratic way, stiff-legged, almost crouching. His 32-year-old knees let him know they don't like this hard surface. Get closer and you see how his fair hair clings sweatily to his damp forehead, how his cheeks are red with effort. Even in this state, though, he's a handsome man with a look of the young Jimmy Stewart about him – a long, generous-mouthed face, with alert, eloquent eyes under thick, dark brows.

The chances are he will be first back to the Tottenham Hotspur training ground. The players who follow him into the clubhouse will change and lark about, then drift off for a round of golf, or get the bus to the bookies, or go to the pub and while away the afternoon playing snooker. By then, the man will be long gone. He'll disappear, casually but expensively dressed, in his Sunbeam Rapier to Bloomsbury, refuse the offer of drinks (he's teetotal) and sign a contract with a publisher for his first book; or to Fleet Street for a meeting with his agent (an unheard of thing for a footballer to have) and new editor. Since his days at Aston Villa, he has combined football with journalism, lately on the *London Evening News*. Now his work will be appearing nationally.

Later on, he – Danny Blanchflower – will probably put together his column. He's not long away from being summoned before the Spurs directors, who will demand to see his copy before publication. His response will be that if they care to pay him more than the *Daily Mail* do then that will be fine, otherwise they will have to buy the paper like everyone else.

Read Danny's journalism now and it is elegantly expressed, mildly opinionated and ... well, pretty anodyne, really. Back then, the simple fact of a footballer, thick and crude as his breed is reputed to be, having not just the temerity but the literacy to express his own point of view in the national press was as peculiar as a talking bear.

In person, Danny is notoriously loquacious. 'On one occasion Aston Villa had just beaten Tottenham in the Cup,' recalls the journalist Brian James, 'and after speaking to Joe Mercer [manager of Manchester City] I rang White Hart Lane to interview Danny. He talked for fifteen minutes while I made feverish notes. I went to write what he'd said into my piece and I literally could not get more than one sentence out of it, which was, basically, "If Joe Mercer thought it worked, it worked." Wrapped up in fifteen minutes of Blanchflower-ese.' 'Some years later I got hooked up with CBS when they were trying to start the North American League,' says the former *Daily Mirror* journalist Ken Jones. 'They wanted a co-commentator to provide colour and analysis. I recommended Danny and they arranged to meet him for lunch at the Savoy. "What's this fellow like?" they asked. I said, "Well, you'll get to say hello and two hours later you'll get to say goodbye, and not much in between."' Danny may not be a drinker himself but, says Terry Dyson, 'He'd turn people to drink, I'd think, with all his chatter. But lovely fella. Brilliant for our team.'

As Danny puts together his column, the fallout from last season will still be on his mind. Spurs have some fabulous players – the balletic chain-smoking Tommy Harmer, the rocket-shooting Bobby Smith, Blanchflower himself. In February they signed Cliff Jones, who is destined to become the best winger in Europe – some would say in the world. But if Danny analyses the 1957–8 season (and he's someone who can bring to the game detached thinking along with romantic passion), the first thing that leaps out at him is the inconsistency:

24 August 1957, a 1–1 draw with Chelsea
28 August 1957, Portsmouth 5, Spurs 1
31 August 1957, Newcastle United 3, Spurs 1 ('Spurs never in the hunt', pronounces one of the papers)
4 September 1957, Spurs 3, Portsmouth 5, with Portsmouth (they seem to be Tottenham's nemesis) 3 up in the first fifteen minutes

It's not wholly dire; on 7 September they manage their first win of the season, 3–1 over Burnley at White Hart Lane. No one's entirely bowled over, though. 'This is better, Spurs,' states Alan Hoby in the *Sunday Express*, 'but still not good enough ... Why do I say this when the winning margin in Tottenham's favour could, if the ball had run a little more kindly, have been 6–1, not 3–1? Because I remembered the cultured and classic football that Danny Blanchflower and his co-stars played last season. I also remembered that, despite the monotonous success of Manchester United, Spurs, at their best, were the most attractive bunch of ball professors in the game.'

And so the season goes erratically on:

11 September 1957, Birmingham 0, Spurs 0; Spurs sixteenth in the table
14 September 1957, Preston North End 3, Spurs 1

18 September 1957, Spurs 7, Birmingham 1

21 September 1957, Spurs 4, Sheffield Wednesday 2 ('4 goal spree but Spurs not out of the woods yet')

28 September 1957, Manchester City 5, Spurs 1

2 October 1957, Wolves 4, Spurs 0

5 October 1957, Spurs 3, Nottingham Forest 4 ('Spurs defence collapsed'; 'Spurs let 2–0 lead slip')

A turning point of sorts is reached in the second week of October when they beat Arsenal 3–1 at White Hart Lane to headlines of 'BLANCHFLOWER BLOTS OUT GUNNERS', 'DANNY BOY'S BEST EVER', 'THE MASTER TACTICIAN OF TOTTENHAM'S CONVINCING WIN', 'BLANCHFLOWER INSPIRES SPURS'.

Danny may have spent the rest of the season being inspirational – by general consensus he has played the best football of his life, lifting Spurs to finish third in the table – but after their disastrous start they were never contenders for the big prizes. In his column, he may decide to play devil's advocate. Do Spurs really want not just to survive in the First Division but win honours at whatever cost? Or should they carry on playing with a flourish, so that even defeat is turned into a memorable occasion?

Meanwhile, there's the issue which has concerned everyone since the end of the 1955–6 season – the fact that he's not Tottenham captain any more. As one reporter commented after the October defeat of Arsenal: 'This is the best game I've seen Danny play. He isn't Spurs skipper, and I can't understand why on earth he isn't, but if ever a man played a captain's game, Danny did.'

But to explain why he isn't requires not just a column; it's essential to go back into prehistory. Or at least to 1954, when Danny made the fateful decision to join Tottenham Hotspur.

Danny was brought to Tottenham by Arthur Rowe, architect of the brilliant and expectation-busting push-and-run side who went from the middle of the Second Division at the close of the forties to win the First Division championship in 1950–1. This was one of the great teams of history, featuring two men who in due course became colossi of the English game – Alf Ramsey and Bill Nicholson.

It's inevitable, though, that the team aged and slowed. By Christmas 1954, they had fifteen points from twenty games and relegation was a real prospect. Rowe saw Danny as the player he wanted at the heart of a new Spurs. He is quoted in Dave Bowler's magnificent book *Danny Blanchflower: A Biography of a Visionary* as saying he would 'never forget, as we stood sizing each other up, as people do when meeting for the first time, the way [Danny] looked at me out of those big, sparkling Irish eyes. I instinctively thought, here is a good guy . . . He made other people play. He protected the players behind and supported those in front. I wanted him as captain.'

In December 1954 Rowe duly got him, from Aston Villa, at a price. £30,000 sounds a piddling amount in terms of transfer fees these days. In fact, it was the highest sum ever paid for what was then called an attacking wing half – a deep-lying playmaker who wore the number 4 shirt. Then again, with his artistry, imagination and independent thinking, Danny was one of the boldest, most original figures in the British game. He possessed a football brain that was unique and utterly remarkable. He would take a ball deep in his own half, look up and in a microsecond compute every possible permutation of man, ball and movement before launching a forward pass so sweetly accurate it could land on a bottle cap.

'Danny was a one-off, a visionary and a perfectionist,' says Laurie Pignon, who reported the game for the *Daily Sketch* during the 1950s. 'Football was an art to him – almost like painting pictures. He had a wonderful pass – he could see the forwards so well. The things he did on the field were inspirational.'

The former *Daily Mirror* journalist Ken Jones, cousin of Cliff, recalls, 'There was no physical presence about Danny whatsoever. Though he was strong in a tackle, he didn't look as though he could have won a ball in a raffle. But he was a cerebral player, always a thought ahead, and he kept things in his mind to use later on. He would do things that other people wouldn't attempt. The kind that would persuade others that anything was possible.'

'He'd take a ball forward and you'd think, "Someone's going to tackle him, surely,"' says the *Guardian* sportswriter David Lacey. 'He'd take the ball past players and you didn't quite see how he did it. He'd drop a shoulder. He was one of those guys who had a picture of the game in his mind, like Johann Cruyff in the Dutch World Cup team of 1974. A good captain. Rhinus Michels, the Holland manager, used to say, "I don't need a coach, I've got one on the pitch," and it was the same thing with Danny.'

Just how seriously he took his role as captain can be deduced from what Linda Baker, wife of the full-back Peter, says: 'When Danny signed, he took Peter to the Grenville, the poshest restaurant in Enfield, to find out how Tottenham was run because Peter had been there the longest.'

With Danny in the side, Spurs lost only one of their next eleven games and won seven of them including a 7–2 hammering of Sheffield Wednesday. The younger players looked up to him. 'It was because he showed us how to make the most of ourselves,' says Mel Hopkins, the Wales international who played his first game at seventeen for Spurs with the push-and-run side. 'We were a family club and he was like Grandad, sitting on the bench looking down on everything.'

'He was a lovely, intelligent man,' enthuses another Wales international, Terry Medwin, who joined Spurs in 1956. 'He had lovely ways with him. He was so nice and so pleasant. He could read things. Not just football but life in general.'

If the team loved and admired him, so Danny felt the same for Arthur Rowe, who was his mentor and role model. Sad to say, the two men had only a brief time working together before Rowe, already mentally worn down by the pressures of management, became completely crushed after Spurs lost a fifth-round FA Cup tie against

York City of the Third Division (North) and subsequently sank back towards the relegation zone. At the end of that season, suffering from acute depression, he resigned.

His replacement was the assistant manager, Jimmy Anderson, a one-club man on the cusp of retirement – he'd started at White Hart Lane as boot boy in 1908. Anderson's philosophy of football, designed to save the club from relegation and rebuild it, was forgivably work-manlike. He was not, in the words of the author Julian Holland, 'one of the great thinkers of the game'. Anything in the way of planning and innovation he left to the new first-team coach Bill Nicholson, a much younger man who not long back had been a defender on the push-and-run side. But by all accounts Anderson was a genial man, who was Tottenham through and through. As far as Danny Blanch-flower was concerned, though, he had one obvious flaw – he wasn't Arthur Rowe.

Their first skirmish was over Danny's decision to send the defender Maurice Norman up into the forward line in a FA Cup semi-final against Manchester City when Spurs were chasing a 1–0 deficit. Using Maurice as a giant roving frightener was a strategy that had worked well in the past but not this time. A furious Anderson felt he had lost face in front of the directors by Danny having made changes to the formation without his say-so. Over the rest of the season, the relationship deteriorated further, with Danny insisting that as captain he should have a say in what went on on the pitch. Anderson, jealous of his authority, refused to allow it.

Once the team were safe from relegation, Danny stood down as captain and Harry Clarke took over. The stand-off was such that when Harry Clarke was left out of the team there was no question of Danny resuming the role, which went to Tony Marchi instead. When Tony moved to the Italian club Lanerossi and Anderson needed to find his third new captain in just over a year, he asked Danny to return. Rebuffed, he appointed the centre-back John Ryden instead. That George Robb, Bobby Smith and Tommy Harmer also performed the role at one time or another gives the whole affair a sense of farce.

Yet it's important to treat Jimmy Anderson with generosity. In his three seasons as manager, Spurs reached the semi-final of the FA Cup and were second and third in the championship. Deconstruct the team that will go on to win the Double and you realise that it was under his watch that its core had been put together. He brought in Maurice Norman and Bobby Smith. He signed Terry Medwin and Cliff Jones, brought on Peter Baker and Ron Henry through the reserves, took on Terry Dyson as a professional when he came out of the army, and revived the career of Tommy Harmer as Danny's midfield general. Tony Marchi sums him up with fairness: 'Jimmy Anderson didn't really know a lot about football but he was very good at knowing where the good players were.' Years into the future Danny will pronounce on the issue himself: 'Jimmy was a great scout, but there's a vast difference between spotting good players and being able to handle them.'

In the end, it was Anderson's limitations as a man manager that did for him. Or maybe that should simply be his limitations as a manager of one specific man, Danny Blanchflower. He was up against a rival who had the players' loyalty, a gifted tactician both on and off the pitch, a man whose celebrity extended beyond sport. Long term, there could only be one winner.

Look now at the back pages of newspapers from those long-ago days and what strikes you is the juxtaposition of reports as the 1957–8 season comes to an end. Set into the *Evening Standard*'s report of the final match of the season (Spurs' 2–1 win over Blackpool with goals by Terry Medwin and Bobby Smith) is a brief paragraph headed:

ANDERSON – 50 years today.
Jimmy Anderson, the Spurs manager, was today presented with a silver tea set by the directors of the club. The presentation marked 50 years service with Spurs. He started on the ground staff.

Next to that, another item reads:

DANNY WINS PLAYER OF THE YEAR VOTE
Danny Blanchflower, Spurs right-half and Ireland's skipper, has
been elected 'Footballer of the Year' for 1957–58 by the Football Writers' Association . . . Danny has had one of his greatest
seasons.

The contrast couldn't be more obvious between the man at the
top of his game and the man on the way out. Within weeks of the
start of the 1958–9 season, Anderson will have gone. A leader such
as Danny Blanchflower needs someone even stronger to lead *him* and
Anderson's departure clears the way for just that person.

This man will show himself to be someone who recognises Danny's
qualities without feeling threatened by them. He'll have the shrewd-
ness and nerve to let Danny be the boss on the field and an emotional
intelligence when it comes to dealing with men that will allow Danny
to bow to his judgement. He will be someone who doesn't just know
where the good players are but is aware which ones he needs to form
into a sweet-running team. More than that, he will be the one who
realises that Danny's specific qualities and needs as a player demand
that John White be brought to White Hart Lane.

Supreme Spurs smashed to a fantastic 10–4 win over Everton at White Hart Lane yesterday – and manager Jimmy Anderson wasn't there to see the greatest victory in the history of this free-spending club. Anderson retired yesterday after 50 years with Spurs, with whom he has done every job from groundsman to manager. Billy Nicholson, his assistant – who refused the Sheffield Wednesday job a month before the season started out of loyalty to Spurs – takes over. Director Sidney Wale said after the match at Tottenham: 'Mr Anderson, who is almost 65, has retired, at his own request, because of ill-health – and that's the genuine reason.'

Sunday Express, 12 October 1958

8

A Serious Man

White Hart Lane, October 1958. The almost supplicatory gesture of the Everton goalie, knees buckling, hands in the air, gives the first clue that a football massacre of massive proportions is going on. There are hollow-cheeked, sweat-streaked figures around the goalmouth, defenders staring with expressions of beaten surprise at the trajectory of the ball.

Poised in mid-air, Bobby Smith seems as overwhelming and deadly as a Flying Fortress. It's his third goal, Tottenham's seventh. There are three more to come. The roll call of Spurs goals at the end reads like closing credits: Alfie Stokes (2), Bobby Smith (4), George Robb, Terry Medwin, Tommy Harmer, John Ryden. The 10–4 result equals an ancient record; the only other top-flight match to produce fourteen goals was sixty-six years back, in 1892, when 12–2 was the final score at Aston Villa v Accrington Stanley. Jimmy Harris scores a hat-trick for Everton and it barely gets a mention.

When the players walk off after the final whistle to be met by the waiting figure of Bill Nicholson, there is a famous exchange of dialogue. 'We don't do this every week, you know,' Tommy Harmer tells him. 'It can only get worse,' Danny Blanchflower adds.

Later, sitting in the oak-panelled office vacated by Jimmy Anderson, Bill considers the future. His plan is to win the championship, but with a team that is near the bottom of the table – just eleven points from twelve games – it's more urgent that they avoid relegation. Tottenham's bad start to the season was what cost Anderson the job, and Bill is working without the safety net of a contract; if he's good enough they'll keep him and if he isn't they'll sack him.

Bill Nicholson is the kind of manager who half a century or so on from that day in 1958 simply doesn't exist any more. The life he will lead would be unrecognisable to today's managers. It's impossible to visualise him wearing Armani or driving a Mercedes. The thought of Gareth Bale dropping round to mow Harry Redknapp's lawn as Ron Henry did Bill's is beyond comprehension.

He will arrive at the ground at nine every day and be the last to leave it at seven. He's going to take responsibility for everything in the club from the first team to the tea lady. He'll be so wrapped up in his task that when his daughter gets married he'll shed tears because he never noticed her grow up. On the other hand, in a career that will eventually have him hailed as one of the great managers of English football, a master of team-building who will create the club side of the century, there won't be a light bulb that needs replacing at White Hart Lane that Bill doesn't know about.

Bill is a genuine and honest man, but having observed many managers in the course of his career, there is one thing he knows already. It's a job that involves ordering people about and making decisions that affect their livelihoods, and the nice guys don't go very far. Bill is not going to make the mistake of being nice and the first test of his authority is right here in front of him.

NO GO, DANNY

Blanchflower wants a move – Spurs 'can't afford it'

Danny Blanchflower, 33 on 10 February is unlikely to get the birthday present he wants most – a move to a new club. Spurs, who paid Aston Villa £30,000 for Danny in December 1954, announced yesterday that the star who has won a record 36 international caps for Northern Ireland, has asked for a transfer. And manager Billy Nicholson told me last night: 'We really cannot afford to let a player of his calibre go. I shall put Blanch-

flower's request to the board when they meet in two weeks'
time. I cannot advise them to accept it.'

Ken Jones, *Daily Mirror*, 30 January 1959

What happened was this. A 4–3 win over Leicester followed the
crushing of Everton in October, but after that Spurs notched up just
one win in eleven games. For most of the next three months they
were in the lowest third of the table. A lot of the trouble stemmed
from Danny's impulse to go forward in attack when the ball was
played into the box rather than marking someone and doing his defensive job.

In January 1959 Bill left him out of a home game against Blackburn Rovers, replacing him with the young, aggressive defender Bill
Dodge. Since Danny at the time was more or less the Spurs story it
was like writing God out of Genesis, but without him, Spurs won
four successive games. In public, Danny acknowledged that Bill had
been right. But Danny was not a man who took kindly to playing
in the B team, let alone at number 10, a role he hadn't played since
his days at Barnsley, his first League club, and least of all within
days of his thirty-third birthday. He might only have a season or so
in the top flight left in him and he wanted to be in it every week.
He asked for a transfer which Bill turned down; in spite of the first-
team revival the club was still in danger of relegation and he would
need Danny if they ran into injury trouble.

Within six weeks, Danny was back in the first team. Bill also
recognised there was something else he needed from Danny – his
inspirational authority as captain. After all, he'd achieved what he
had set out to do, which was to make Danny see things his way. He
reinstated Danny at the beginning of March; that day the team drew
1–1 with Wolves, the League leaders.

After that the results began to speak for themselves: 7 March,
Spurs 6, Leicester 0; 14 March, Leeds 3, Spurs 1; 21 March, Spurs 3,
Manchester City 1. In the later words of Danny, the party had started.

And in the even later words of Bill: 'There was no acrimony. He was one player you could have a rational discussion with and still remain friends.'

'Since Danny went, I've never been able to talk as well to anyone about the team. I miss that sometimes.' Bill Nicholson, quoted in *The Glory Game*, by Hunter Davies.

Bill makes it sound uncomplicated, but in fact that friendship – Bill, the man who gave the side values and leadership, and Danny, his captain, who took over on the field of play – has always been one of the wonders of football. People who talk of Danny use words such as 'visionary', 'whimsical', 'iconoclast', 'eloquent', 'philosophical'. Ask those who knew him to describe Bill, on the other hand, and you get a completely different picture.

The default adjective has always been 'dour'. Here's Eddie Baily, his former teammate and later bag carrier at Spurs: 'A typical Yorkshireman – not exactly cavalier in his ways.' Here's Ken Jones, the *Daily Mirror* football writer: 'Grumpy sod. Never satisfied. There'd be no words of praise.' And here's Mel Hopkins, who made his debut at seventeen in Bill's final season as a player in the push-and-run side: 'Bill was football, football, football. It was his life. He'd have lived in the ground if he could have. You'd pass him in the corridor: "Nice day, Bill." Bill: "Is it?" He'd been a really hard player and he was the same as a manager. It took a lot to excite him. The game was played and that was it till the next one.'

'You could never tell by looking at him if he'd won or lost,' agrees Les Allen. 'You'd think you'd had a good game and then he'd tell you that you played badly. But he was fair. He did it to everybody, to his credit. And there was nothing big time about him.'

That's about right. While Danny's second marriage was already in difficulties, with wife number three on the horizon, Bill had been married since he was twenty-three, pragmatically to the girl who lived three doors away from his digs and was his first and only date.

Bill's life in 1958 when he took over from Jimmy Anderson had not changed conspicuously by 1974 when he stood down. He lived in the same house, a throw-in from White Hart Lane; while Danny drove a Sunbeam Rapier, a top-end two-door hardtop coupé with fins and twin carbs, Bill's wheels of choice in the 1950s were bolted to the chassis of a Morris Eight Series E, production of which stopped in 1948.

'There was a strange relationship between Danny and Bill Nick,' says Ken Jones. 'They didn't belong in the same room. But Danny had great respect for Bill Nick and vice versa.'

'Coming back on the train from a northern match once, I was talking to Danny when Bill joined us,' says the former *Daily Mail* sportswriter Brian James. 'The conversation immediately became stilted. It was because you were always speaking at one level with Danny and then with Bill you had to engage other parts of your brain. There were two quite separate discussions going on. He was a serious man and not easy to get to know. You wouldn't call him hostile but he was very self-contained. He had areas in which he was interested, and beyond that, nothing. If you got talking to him about any subject other than football he'd say, "Oh yes?" with polite interest and then quickly change the subject, as if he didn't want to go down that road with you.

'But because he and Danny were so different, they appreciated that part coming in from the other which they were not capable of giving. Bill appreciated there was a dimension of football – belief, joy, enthusiasm – that he wasn't good at, so he went along with it when Danny was doing his messianic visionary bit. And while Danny was never slow to give an opinion I never heard him diminish Bill by so much as a word or sentence.'

'The players thought Bill was wonderful,' says Sandra Hart. 'John had total respect for him. Whatever Bill said, went. But he was socially inept. What did you talk about? It could only be football, couldn't it? When John and I got engaged, we held a party. Everyone was having a great time. Then Bill walked in and the atmosphere plummeted.'

'Bill was always a very good coach,' says Tony Marchi. 'As a personality, hmm. You've got me now. Very serious, I'd say. Could have a laugh but very serious in his football. Don't get me wrong. Not intimidating, not at all. He was just so serious, that was all.'

Seriousness is not perhaps a surprising mindset for someone who grew up in poverty in Scarborough as one of nine children. He won a scholarship to grammar school but left at sixteen to work in a laundry. His father, a hansom-cab driver, died of bowel cancer the year Bill joined Spurs as an apprentice. He played his first match for them in the Midweek League against West Ham as a teenager and went on to be a defender in Arthur Rowe's side. Like many of his generation, he looked the same at twenty as he did at forty; about five foot eight, with a muscular, solid build, a forehead like a ridge-cut crisp and crinkly fair hair parted in the middle. He was, says David Lacey, 'a typical solid English midfield player, a very calm guy, cautious and not easily ruffled'.

In the army he had been a drill sergeant, and the style never quite left him. 'You never argued back,' says Terry Dyson. 'You respected him. He had everything organised. He did everything by the book. He was straight down the line.'

'He brought in a military discipline,' says Cliff Jones. 'That's how he was. He didn't waste words.'

'He wasn't a teacup-thrower,' says Brian James, 'but his style reminded you of Nobby Stiles's comment about Matt Busby: "When Matt called you in it wasn't to hand out the sweeties." Most of the players would have thought the same with Bill.'

Bill was not without a sense of humour – David Lacey recalls him as having 'a sort of barking laugh' – but top of his dislikes was sloppiness. 'Small carelessnesses got to him,' says Brian. 'I was once in the Tottenham car park talking to him after a game and he went on for about twenty minutes, exasperatedly demonstrating how *not* to take a throw-in. "You're taking a throw-in. There's a man there – throw it to him. Not three yards away from him." He'd go on about things like a player standing two yards out of place.'

'If anybody stepped out of line, we were pulled up,' confirms Cliff. 'You'd hear those dreaded words from Cecil Poynton, the trainer: "Bill wants to see you down the office." Once I got a couple of goals against Fulham and Bill said, "Well done, Jonesy." He never gave great words of encouragement, so I said, "Aye aye, Bill, steady on," and he said, "A pat on the back is only two feet away from a kick up the arse and I give plenty of them."'

But the man who was to replace the Double-winning striker Les Allen with Jimmy Greaves in November 1961 with the comment 'A football manager can't afford sentiment', and who expressed glee at upsetting the people of Edinburgh when he bought Dave Mackay to partner Danny in midfield – 'It must have hurt them to lose such a good player. That made me feel good' – could sometimes reveal a streak of bluff kindness. 'Maurice Norman was a good lad and a gentle giant,' says Cliff. 'He was the only one Bill wouldn't have a go at. Bill would put an arm round him instead and say, "You just need to get a little bit closer to that centre-forward, Maurice," because if Bill had kicked him up the arse, he'd have started crying.'

'As a player Bill Nick was a plain wing half-back but when it came to coaching it was another matter,' says Ken Jones. 'Underneath the harsh exterior beat the heart of a football romantic and he put his imprint on that team.'

OUR NEW PLAYER

As you all know, on Monday last, the 'deadline date' for the registration of transfers in the Football League, we signed David Mackay, half-back, from the Heart of Midlothian Club in Edinburgh, and supporters will join us in giving him a hearty welcome to our ranks. David, a former Schoolboy International, joined Hearts back in 1952 and in recent years he has established quite a reputation as one of the outstanding half-backs in Scotland. His first Cap came in 1957 against Spain, and he played for Scotland in the World Cup series in Sweden last summer. To date this season he has been Captain of the Scottish team in the International Tournament against Wales and Ireland.

Tottenham Hotspur Football and Athletic Club
Official Programme, 21 March 1959

Spurs manager Billy Nicholson stunned Scottish soccer a few hours before last season's transfer deadline when he lashed out £30,000 for Dave Mackay, Hearts skipper and wing half.

It was a top secret, out of the blue deal . . .

Ken Jones, *Daily Mirror*, 26 September 1959

Perhaps the best way to get a handle on Bill is to read his autobiography, *Glory Glory: My Life With Spurs*. Published in 1984, it was inevitably produced with the help of a ghostwriter, but the journalist Harry Harris has done a lovely job in capturing Bill's voice – honest, direct and uncomplicated. You get a real sense of the perfectionist who was at his happiest on the training ground, who spoke of his despair during a match he'd recently witnessed: 'None of the players wanted to control the ball and make an accurate pass. Every kick was a long one, transferring responsibility as far away as possible . . . It was not a pleasure to watch'; of the passionate lover of great football who when his side won the 1961 FA Cup and thus his heart's desire, the Double, was so acutely disappointed by the way they played that all he could do was inveigh against them as they trooped off the pitch; of the shrewd assessor of personality whose barking laugh can be heard as he delivers his opinion of his old team-mate and rival Alf Ramsey: 'He was eager to acquire knowledge . . . He wasn't the type to share it.' Here, too, is a man who spoke of his players with simple affection: 'They were whole-hearted enthusiasts

... nice people who wanted their colleagues to be as successful as they were.'

What really comes over, though, is Bill's enjoyment of the chase. In 1984, from a distance of twenty-five years, the huntsman in him spoke with relish of how he put his Double side together: the patient surveillance and covert phone calls; the long train rides to nab his quarry; the soup-roast-and-steamed-pudding lunches in railway hotels with the manager whom he had just relieved of a prized footballer while other managers were still getting their coats on prior to setting out. If one of them rang him up to enquire about one of his own, his response would always be: 'I'm on the lookout for new players myself. Got any available?'

'I'm not sure he had great vision,' says Brian James. 'That was Danny's role. Bill was a man who recognised the tiny components that combined would make a team of world-beaters. He was like a mechanic looking at a fine engine, and knowing which cogs needed oiling and which parts needed adjusting or replacing.'

The signing of Dave Mackay is a case in point. When he took over from Jimmy Anderson, Bill had a list of possibles already prepared. The young Hearts captain had been at the top of it since Bill had seen him snuff out the threat of Johnny Haynes in an England v Scotland Under-23 international at Ibrox Park. As the 1958–9 season entered its final phase, Bill was tipped off that Hearts needed money to finance a new stand, but he had to act quickly. Had Matt Busby got wind of Dave's availability the whole future of Spurs might have been different. Bill caught the night train to Edinburgh and concluded the deal within twenty-four hours.

Dave always played full on even at a practice match or a five-a-side in the gym, and is described by Cliff Jones as 'the type of player we were missing, someone competitive and with great energy, someone who drove the team on'. But that hardly begins to put across the essence of the man. Dave Mackay combined massive skill with the pain threshold of an armoured tank. Even people who weren't born when he was a player carry around a mental image of him thanks to that photo of him hoisting Billy Bremner into the air by the shirt after a seriously bad tackle, while Bremner's face registers sheer terror: 'Sorry, Dave!' There's that other photo, too, taken when he broke his leg at Old Trafford, sitting up on the stretcher and pushing people away; even in agony he refuses to roll over and submit. In a game where someone only needs to have lasted two seasons at a club to be embraced as a legend, Dave is the real, solid granite article.

For Terry Medwin, he was 'a wicked man. God – captain of Hearts at only twenty. He didn't want to lose anything. Danny was great but Dave was special.' 'He wanted to win at all costs,' agrees Mel Hopkins. 'He'd bring his own granny to the ground if it meant winning. Soon as the match finished, he'd go back to being nice, kind Dave.' 'Solid, tough and a winner,' sums up Terry Dyson. 'I never beat him at anything. I was playing him at snooker once and he smashed a cue because he was so desperate to win. Which he did.'

'Danny was the inspiration,' says Brian James, 'but when players did something you would catch them glance quickly, looking for Dave's approbation. They wouldn't want that glare of his.' 'He was,' says the former pro golfer Jim McAlister, his fellow Scot, 'a *fierce* competitor.' But perhaps the best line ever about Dave was written by Julian Holland in *Spurs – The Double*: 'Dave Mackay, the left-half, is a small man which is as bad a way of describing him as possible.'

In spite of an injury that prevented him taking part in every game that remained, Dave brought enough to the team to make sure they avoided getting relegated that first season. There was the triumph, too, of his instant rapport with Danny. Dave put in all the hard grafting, fetching and carrying; he obliterated threats from opponents; he freed Danny to set up the next attack. He was, said Bill later, 'a mighty player . . . If he had served in a war, he would have been the first man into action. He would have won the Victoria Cross.'

But that didn't mean Bill was satisfied. Danny's combination of agile brain and ageing legs increasingly pressed for a specific type of link man between him and the forward line. Ideally it would be someone intuitive, responsive and unselfish, who could pass supremely well, short or long, off either foot; who could provide goals as well as assists; who had the physical power to range over every single fleck of pitch.

Did this paragon exist?

Maybe, in Scotland, he did.

It's nice to picture Bill riding on the East Coast line, with a gleam in his eye, quietly making his plans for glory and maybe feeling that little jolt of anticipation as he crosses the border one more time. His destination is Falkirk and his quarry is the signing who is going to make it all happen.

Turning to changes in the Club personnel, it will be recalled that Mr Anderson retired in October last from the position of Manager owing to reasons of health, having completed 50 years' service with the Club in varying capacities, a truly wonderful record. We are pleased to say that his health is now very much improved, and we all wish him many happy years of retirement. His successor in the managerial chair was Mr Nicholson, who first came to us as a young player from Scarborough back in 1937. His outstanding services to us on the playing field are too fresh in memory to need repeating. On giving up his playing career in 1956 he was appointed Assistant Manager, and he has held many appointments with English representative teams. All supporters will join us in wishing him a happy and successful career in his new sphere.

Tottenham Hotspur Football and Athletic Club Season 1959–1960 Official Handbook

Foreword by Fred J. Bearman, Chairman

9

The Tribe
Rob, 2007

The first of October, and the glow from the floodlights is setting fire to the evening sky as 36,000 people thread their way around the ground and through the turnstiles. It's the night Spurs celebrates its 125th anniversary and the match is against Aston Villa; you can't get a fixture much more redolent of the Double side's history than that.

With twenty minutes to go before kick-off, you can sense a little bit of a difference in our mood. Not everyone at the last home game was completely enthusiastic about the prospect of tonight. We've started the season disappointingly. The rumours swirling around the stands are about Martin Jol and his job – will he be manager much longer and who will be his replacement? There is, it follows, a degree of cynicism about this evening's ceremonial, with jokes about Tottenham doing their cheapskate little rocket from a milk bottle on the halfway line. Now we're here, though, we're aware there's a buzz. They've given out silk flags, 36,000 of them. OK, with everyone waving them it's a bit like being in North Korea, but it's actually stunning to see.

I'm in my usual seat, the one I've had for ten years at the Park Lane lower end. Block 34, right behind the goal, level with the penalty spot. My little patch of Tottenham. I'm with the usual people. There is a very small ripple of seats around you where there are people who you're willing to interact with – your immediate neighbours to the front and to the side. There are eight of us in this little tribe within a tribe. It's a weird relationship with a group of guys who you see at intervals of varying frequency. You might get together three times in ten days then not at all for three weeks. We're now at the stage where we do that shaking hands thing that blokes do. We know each other's Christian name but not surname or job, unless that information is provided incidentally. The rest of the relationship consists of ten minutes' conversation before the start: 'What's the team?' 'Why has he picked so-and-so?' You have these little conversations during a game. 'Do you think they should substitute somebody?' 'What the hell's going on?' It's a very nice, blokey relationship. You find it just enough. Then, thankfully, the whistle interrupts.

Not long before, I'd been experiencing a feeling that wasn't far removed from beginning to fall out of love. It wasn't so much a reflection on the 2007–8 side as on us – the supporters – and our own raised expectations. Hoping for a fifth-place finish when we were low down in the table. Talking about still being capable of pushing for a UEFA Cup place when we'd lost 3–1 at home to Arsenal. Story of that match: Gareth Bale gave us the lead, Emmanuel Adebayor equalised, Cesc Fabregas gave Arsenal the lead and then Adebayor got another in stoppage time. At times like these, someone will say: 'Come on, it'll get better.' Then someone else will say: 'How long have we been saying that now?'

In the past, part of the joy of being a Spurs fan had always been that even if we lost there would be something that was fantastic. David Ginola was in a crap side but you'd go and watch Ginola. But that Saturday we lost to Arsenal I'd got home feeling completely resigned. It was a bit like discovering your god's not God. I walked in the house and said to the girls, 'Look, if you want to go and support someone else, you can.'

The point is, though, they can't. Being Spurs is in their DNA, the same as it is in mine. When I look back on my childhood, there was only one moment when I wavered, when Frank McLintock, captain of the Double-winning Arsenal side of 1970–1, lived near to us in Winchmore Hill. There's a photo in existence of me wearing the red shirt he gave me. I've also got a signed photo of the Arsenal Double-winning squad.

My affair with Arsenal lasted just one summer, and briefly made me cry. My excuse is that I was six years old and very impressionable. It was what politicians refer to as 'a moment of madness' when they're found out by the tabloids. Later, the Arsenal manager Bertie Mee asked me: 'Do you play football yourself? Well, if you're interested, come along and train with us.' For a start, I couldn't believe an adult had asked me such a daft question. In any case, my dalliance with Arsenal was long over and I rebuffed him. Spurs and I have lasted many summers, even though they have made me cry more times than I care to recall.

This evening begins with a presentation of legends. It makes you puff up your chest a bit and for me it's quite special. First Dave Mackay, Cliff Jones and Steve Perryman take their bows. Then they bring the cups out, and there's not many clubs where that can happen. Once it gets dark at White Hart Lane, a lot of shadows appear and this procession almost seems like ritual – the summoning of spirits, communicating with the ancestors, with our own version of a tribal dance. I like to imagine it's what you'd do before you went into battle.

The face of an old man appears on the big screen, wearing its familiar expression – a sort of benevolent pugnacity. Everyone knows his name and what his job was. We join in a minute's applause for Bill Nicholson – 36,000 people concentrating their . . . what is the emotion? Admiration? Gratitude? Appreciation? It seems more intense than that. It's for the man who came to be known as Mr Tottenham Hotspur. It's not that foolish feeling where you say you love someone just because he's scored against Arsenal. It's a special blokes-only thing – an expression of love for another male. Where else in today's society would you get that happening?

The team are in a commemorative 125-year anniversary kit. Blue and white, halved like Blackburn's. They play fantastically well for twenty minutes. Dimitar Berbatov scores.

You think, That's it, it's on its way.

Someone says, 'Here we go.'

Someone else says, 'How many times have we said that?'

Then suddenly it happens. We're 2–1 down.

Then, almost predictably, Paul Robinson, our keeper, throws a ball into his own goal and we're 3–1 down.

Astonishingly – astonishing, that is, to anyone who does not support Spurs – I think, We can still do this. It is not blind optimism. I know this club.

I am thinking the same thing at 4–1 down. Even as the Villa fans have started singing: 'Happy birthday to you, happy birthday dear Tottenham.' Even as people are leaving the ground, which – as ever – amazes me. This is Spurs. Anything can happen.

And it does.

Tottenham 2 (Chimbonda, 69) Aston Villa 4.

Tottenham 3 (Keane, [pen] 82) Aston Villa 4.

Close to the end of what seems like every Spurs game in memory, we are no longer losing. When Younis Kaboul scores the equaliser in injury time, it's brilliant, euphoric theatre. I came out thinking: Chelsea – unbeaten at home for three and a half years. Arsenal – the untouchable bores, too scared to lose. But I don't think there can be many clubs where you can see a 4–4 draw full of the good, the bad and the ugly. For pure entertainment over the years, Spurs has no rival. And Bill was the cause of that. Which is why we – this collective of fans – put so much store by him. He built the club.

This thought is followed by another.

If Bill hadn't signed my dad, I wouldn't be standing here now.

When manager Jerry Kerr signed John for Alloa many said: 'He won't do.'

His displays for the Wasps soon had the scouts on his trail. But again the same cry was heard: 'He won't do.'

But I'll always remember being with Falkirk scout Jimmy Allan at a Morton v Alloa game. His mind was made up . . . Falkirk should buy White.

Jim Rodger, *Scottish Daily Record*, October 1959

10

Good Times, Bad Times

There isn't much left of Falkirk. That's to say, hardly anything remains of the ground where John played between the Octobers of 1958 and 1959. Brockville Park was demolished in 2004; now a Morrisons superstore stands there. Similar fates have befallen many other grounds that formed the stage set for John's life – Burnden Park, Ayresome Park, Filbert Street, Roker Park, Maine Road, just to give a few examples. The high-street locations and warm and homely wooden stands of the pre-Taylor Report era have given way to out-of-town new builds, and Falkirk now play at a shinily handsome stadium, east of the town towards Grangemouth.

'The last year Falkirk played at Brockville Park was 2003,' says Michael White, the club's historian and a Bairns fan since boyhood. (In case you're wondering, there are a lot of Whites in this part of Scotland; Michael isn't a relation.) 'When they sold to Morrisons people were buying everything. I've got one of their stand seats. A friend of mine bought some of their crash barriers. He keeps them in the garden and sometimes we go and lean on them for old times' sake.'

The road bridge over the railway line still exists. Two hundred yards from the old stadium, it's the one John crossed with all the other Edinburgh-based players after they arrived at Falkirk Grahamston station on match days. The locomotives that used to rattle under it belching steam are part of Falkirk folklore. 'One game a train steamed past and the whole pitch was covered in the stuff,' says Michael. 'There was a goal scored and the goalkeeper hadn't moved.'

Cross the supermarket car park, though, and it's impossible to imagine that you're walking over what was once a football pitch complete with teams and goalposts and a roaring crowd – and, for football nostalgics, probably kindest not to. But there, in 1958, somewhere between what's now a frozen-food aisle and the central trolley park, John had the sweet satisfaction of scoring the fourth goal in a 5–5 draw with Rangers, the club that had so determinedly repudiated him while he was playing for Alloa. The *Daily Record* confirmed that 'The root of the trouble lay in the complete inability of the barrel-chested Telfer to quell the ever-mobile White ... Shrewdly varying his tactics, White moving from wing to wing repeatedly lured Telfer out of position with the result that at times Rangers' defence appeared completely paralysed.'

Things were going well for John. He'd made his first appearance in a Falkirk shirt on 11 October 1958 at Parkhead in a 4–3 Falkirk win over Celtic, when he lived up to his habit of scoring on his debut. Now that he was playing in the top division, he was also on the brink of international selection; a season earlier, as a player with Second Division Alloa, there was no way he would have been considered for Scotland's World Cup team that had travelled to Sweden that summer.

It was a good time for all the White boys. What the papers referred to as 'Musselburgh's two footballing brothers' were destined to become three. Eddie was already at Falkirk when John arrived, and had made his First Division debut at centre-forward. Now Tom, who had followed John through Musselburgh Union, was about to see his own professional career launch with Raith Rovers.

'We were out with John's friend Jimmy Knox,' says Tom of the moment he turned professional, 'and Jimmy Knox had a little Renault Giordino sports car and in the back of this Renault was Vince Halperin centre-half for Hibs, and he was about six foot six. We decided we'd go to my mum's house. Well, I'm in the back of this little car drinking pop and I decided, I'm not getting out. So when I look up at the kitchen window, Mum's waving. "No, I'm not coming, can't be bothered," I say to her. Next thing, Jimmy comes to the window: "Come up." "No, piss off." Next thing John comes to the window: "Bert Herdman's in here wanting to sign you."

'Bert Herdman was the manager of the Rovers. There's no way in hell I'm going to get out because John was such a piss-taker, and if I'd got out they would all have gone, "Ah haaaaa!" I just couldn't get out of the car. I just could not get out of the car because I felt no, no, no, he's taking the piss out of me. So I stayed there and the next thing is, this man comes down the steps and says: "Bert Herdman here." And I say: "Yeah, yeah, pull my other one." But I look closer and he's got a bowler hat on and everything, proper dressed. It's him, it's Bert Herdman, saying: "I want you to sign for Raith Rovers."

'So I went in and I signed. All of a sudden there was three of us professional footballers, which wasn't bad, three of us from a little household making it, you know. But here's the daft thing, when John signed for Falkirk he got a £20 signing-on fee. And he gave it straight to my mum. So when I signed for Raith Rovers and I got a £20 signing-on fee, I reluctantly gave it straight to my mum too. I didn't want to give it, I would have kept it, but because John had done it I'd got to do it!'

The Falkirk side John joined featured some outstanding players. Eddie, who had signed a year earlier, had competition getting in a first team that featured the likes of Alex Parker, Bert Slater, Dougie Moran and John McCole. The brothers' first two games together were the last two League games of the season. By then Falkirk were having a desperate struggle to stay in the top tier. So were Dunfermline. Inevitably, everything came down to the last match, with Falkirk at home to Raith Rovers and Dunfermline away to Partick Thistle. If Falkirk won they would stay up. Any other result and Dunfermline would send them down.

Geographically, the teams of Falkirk and Raith are barely fifteen miles apart, and the local rivalry added an extra edge. There were no laptops and mobiles to speed communications, so to meet the printing deadline of early editions reporters had to dispatch chunks of the action as it took place. When Raith went 1 up after twelve minutes, you can practically hear the exasperation that seeps out from the dry old cutting from the *Falkirk Herald*: 'The futility of playing John White at centre was again shown. The inadequacy of Eddie White as a controller of the ball was even more marked at inside forward and all over the attack lacked drive.'

The Sod's Law of running reports dictated what happened next. Eddie scored the equaliser. It was 1–1 at half-time.

'In those days you relied on a guy coming round well into the second half with a piece of paper with the half-time scores,' says Michael White. 'This guy had a severe limp. The friend I was with lashed out threepence [for the phone] and we found out it was Partick Thistle nil, Dunfermline 7. By this time there were shouts of "Fix!" But if Falkirk were to beat Raith, they would stay up. Raith went 2–1 up instead. Then Falkirk were awarded a penalty at the railway end and when no one else wanted the job John came forward to take it. Now, the Raith goalkeeper Charlie Drummond lived in Falkirk and worked in the docks at Grangemouth so it's Charlie Drummond, Raith goalkeeper but Falkirk boy, standing there pointing surreptitiously to the right for where John was to send it. Charlie was quite prepared to be beaten. And John runs up and thumps it over the top and that was the nail in the coffin.'

In fact, Eddie got a slow-motion equaliser four minutes from time. It was too late to make a difference and, anyway, immaterial – the final score at Firhill was Partick Thistle 1, Dunfermline 10.

'They all trooped off,' says Michael. 'There were a lot of tears because some of the players realised they'd have to move on if they wanted to develop their careers, and I think all of us were aware we wouldn't see much more of John and Bert and the better players.'

MUST OUR NEW STAR RISK HIS CAP CAREER?

My appeal to Falkirk – transfer White for ONE year

John White ... John White ... John White ... that was the
name I heard over and over again as I walked out of Hampden
after Scotland's triumph over Germany. One hundred thousand
people had been convinced they were seeing the birth of a great
international star.

Yet the sad truth is that White – with a career hardly begun
– is face to face with a threat of complete football obscurity.
For I have to say that it is my complete conviction that one
more year with his present club, Falkirk, may well end all
White's hopes of a Scotland future.

The simple facts are that White is 22 years of age; that he
is completing his military service; and that he now belongs to
a club which has just been relegated to the Second Division ...

Scottish Sunday Express, May 1959

One reason John wanted to move on in order to stay in the First
Division is that another part of his football life had really taken off.
Just after the end of that season the curtain went up on his international career, with a brilliant debut in a friendly against West
Germany at Hampden. Another player who got his first cap that day
was Ian St John, who was then with Motherwell, a similarly sized
club to Falkirk at the time.

Neither had been included in the original line-up. The selection
committee who in those days ran the team had picked Bobby Collins
as inside-right and Andy Kerr as centre-forward. After Kerr was
injured, Ian was drafted in. Then Denis Law, at the time playing for
Huddersfield, dropped out so the team was reshuffled and John
brought in at number 8.

All five goals in Scotland's 3–2 victory came in the first half. 'It
was a very young Scotland side captained by Bobby Evans of Celtic,'
recalls Ian St John. 'I remember there being a massive crowd, 100,000

plus for a midweek friendly, and John scored within the first few minutes of the match. You could see he was a fantastic player, just wonderful.'

The *Daily Record*'s chief football columnist, Waverley (W. G. Gallacher), agreed, commenting: 'White was a bonny player, always a trier and ever on the move. Sometimes he found the tackling a bit too strong for him but as long as he had the space he was a grand inside-forward, quick thinking and producing the right ideas.' In the *Scottish Sunday Express*, sports editor Harry Andrew wrote: 'It is only a few months since he came out of the Second Division. He is still mixing the Army with his soccer. He faltered and faded in Wednesday's second half. He needs full time effort and training . . . He could put Scotland right-back in the international hunt [and] might even help us to the Championship of the World.'

If you look at the year John spent with Falkirk, you realise that it was an extraordinarily eventful period – the first time he'd sampled top-flight football, lived away from home and been acclaimed as the Messiah of the international side. In terms of suddenly having to grow up, though, equally far-reaching but more painful experience was waiting for him in the army. What happened during his time in Berwick inevitably cast a shadow over what should have been a care-free life.

John had been given his call-up papers a month before he signed for Falkirk. For the next two years he would be Lance Corporal White J. of the King's Own Scottish Borderers in Berwick.

Most men now in their mid-seventies and older will have indelible memories of national service. It was imposed between 1947 and the early 1960s to enlarge the armed forces. By the time John was called up it entailed a two-year spell posted to join regiments at home or abroad – Germany and Austria at the time were occupied.

There was no risk, though, of John having to leave the country. Sportsmen of any type received preferential treatment. 'On my first day,' recalls the sportswriter Ronald Atkin, 'we're all lined up and

Ann White holds her son, John, outside their Links Street home in Musselburgh, Scotland in 1937

Absent fathers: John's own dad (*centre*, pictured with friends), died when John was young, leaving his wife Ann to look after the four children alone

Picking a pocket or two: Edwin White (*right*), would ask his two brothers, John (*left*) and Tom, to steal petty items as youngsters

John White
(*crouching at front*),
Eddie White
(*standing left*)
and their friends

McGillivray's Boys. John White (*front row, left*) and Bill Hunter (*front row, centre*)

John (*front left*), aged fourteen, as a trainee joiner

Bigger than Sean Connery: John (*front row, second from right*) was a huge success for Bonnyrigg Rose, a junior side that once featured a pre–James Bond Connery

Going pro: Alloa signed an eighteen-year-old John White (*front row, third from left*) as inside forward in 1956

The White stuff: All three of the White boys, John (*left*), Tommy (*middle*) and Edwin (*right*) would go on to play football professionally

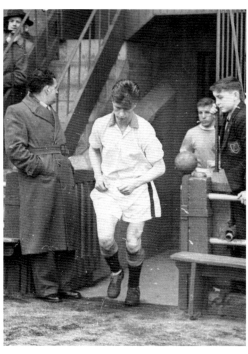

Moving up: John joined
the Scottish First Division
side Falkirk in 1958

John's first taste of national
service was as a PT instructor
in the army…

… but he soon moved on to national service of a different kind, scoring on his Scotland debut against West Germany in May 1959

John White with Denis Law (*right*) and the rest of the Scotland team (*below*)

John in a Northern Ireland shirt, pictured shortly after the match between Scotland and Northern Ireland where Danny Blanchflower allegedly first spotted John's talent

one of the sadistic drill sergeants says, "Which one of you is Sewell?" and Danny Sewell, who's a very promising boxer as well as the brother of the actor George, puts up his hand. He's told, "Step forward." He's marched off and while we go through several weeks of hell drill training we never see him again because he's made an assistant PT instructor living a life of luxury pausing only to box for the R.A.F. It's a way of keeping the bloke at the base by making a permanent post for him there – the sportsmen kept up their careers courtesy of Her Majesty's government.'

'I was stationed in Catterick,' says the journalist Brian James. 'I played in the Northern Command Cup Final. Most of the other players had got some professional background. We were deeply envious of people like the England batsman Brian Close who was always off playing cricket, and Jimmy Shurben, off playing football for Sunderland. Our regimental quartermaster sergeant was centre-half for York City and he was quite famous.'

'So John was made a PT instructor,' says Tom White. 'By the time I was called up the public had got tired of footballers living the life of Riley in the army and I was one of the last servicemen posted out to Aden, so basically that was fourteen to fifteen months of my professional career knocked on the head, but in John's time it was a cushy number. John hardly did any parades, he'd just be playing football and running – he came second in the national cross-country championships.

'He used to train the lads on the beaches and they did exactly what he told them, and one day he made them run into the sea. Got the whole squad lined up in a straight line and said: "Right, go." They just kept running into the sea and he's running the other way, taking the mickey out of them.'

A nineteen-year-old Rodger Baillie first encountered John when he was playing for the British Army in a friendly at Greenock Morton. 'I was sent to cover the game for the *Daily Record*. Greenock was notorious for bad weather and as I was speaking to John afterwards the rain was coming down. John said, "How are you getting back to town?" so I told him I was going to walk to the train station. "I'll get you a lift in the team bus," he said. What a kind gesture. A nineteen-year-old rookie. He could have just left me. So many players wouldn't have given a toss.'

As Tom puts it, though, 'There was a part in John's life that he wasn't happy about. I remember him one night leaving our house to go back to the barracks and telling me on the way out, "I'm in trouble." He'd got caught out with this girl. It was somebody who used to go out with a few of the boys, and he hadn't had many girlfriends and he was quite naive. It was a worrying time for him. He was a good man, John, and he wanted to do the right thing.' According to Tom, John offered to marry the girl but the colonel in charge of the barracks – more aware, no doubt, of the contribution such a marriage would make to the sum of human misery – refused him permission, telling him instead that the best thing he could do for everyone involved was to pay maintenance for the baby son who arrived in due course.

'I sort of accepted it had happened,' says Sandra. 'It was all in Berwick, before I was on the scene. To them, John's family, it was a shock-horror thing, but I wasn't even curious about her. It's hard to put yourself back in those times. Nowadays, I'd think, "Was he had?" But once we were married I paid the maintenance money, bought the postal order and sent it off in a registered envelope. In those days you couldn't set up a direct debit, and I did it because if I'd left it to John he would have forgotten it.' Sandra stopped making the payments when John was killed. 'I never heard that she contacted anybody.'

It is, as Sandra says, hard to put yourself back into the mindset of that era. It's always the knee-jerk reaction to blame the girl, but far from being a man-trap or gold-digger, was she perhaps unlucky and just as foolish or naive as him? With so few facts to go on, it's difficult to make a judgement and it feels uncomfortable prying even this far into so very private a matter. It is, though, part of the story of John as a young man, and it also reminds you that in the late fifties in Scotland, as in the rest of the UK, to have fathered a child 'out of wedlock' was as scandalous then as it would be unremarkable now. John White's paternity suit inevitably became the subject of gossip among journalists, and throughout the rest of his life a reputation clung to him that was perhaps spectacularly wide of the mark.

ARSENAL KEEN ON WHITE, *Scottish Daily Mail*
LIVERPOOL JOIN THE QUEUE FOR JOHN WHITE, *Scottish Daily Express*

When the 1959–60 season began, Falkirk wore a denuded look. Relegation to the Second Division had emptied it of most of its stars. The international full back Alex Parker had moved to Everton along with Eddie O'Hara. John McCole went to Bradford City, and Liverpool signed the keeper Bert Slater in exchange for Tommy Younger, who became player-manager when Reg Smith left to take over Millwall.

Younger arrived with twenty-four Scottish caps and a burgeoning weight problem; he'd been inactive due to a bad back. 'And he got fatter and fatter. He just went like this,' says Michael White, arms wide. 'They used thirteen goalkeepers that season, including, allegedly, one who had one eye.'

Relegation hadn't harmed John's reputation. The papers were all referring to him as 'Scotland's brightest prospect' and speculating whether Falkirk would ever sell him: 'Supporters blame the club for being relegated because last season they sold three stars.' That particular report featured two rather hopeful final sentences: 'And White himself might not agree to any move. Unlike [Bert] Slater, he has not said he did not fancy Second Division football.'

'John realised that being in the Second Division wasn't going to help his prospects. says Rodger Baillie. 'So early autumn Falkirk were feeling the draught from relegation and agreed to accept offers.'

This far on in time, it's impossible to confirm with any precision just when Bill travelled from London to Falkirk to see for himself the player who by now the whole of football was talking about. The stand where he sat is, like everything else, long gone. What you can gather, though, is that he went there towards the end of September just *before* John was officially put up for transfer. In his autobiography he notes succinctly: 'I had had good reports about him and went to watch him in a League match. He didn't make a single bad pass.'

Just how Bill was tipped off about John is a story in itself.

SPURS ROCKED BY BIG GAME CALLS

Tottenham Hotspur, unbeaten First Division leaders, face a vital match next month, knowing that at least three stars will miss each game.

Bill Brown, goalkeeper, and Dave Mackay, wing half, were chosen yesterday to play for Scotland against Ireland on October 3. Their other first team wing half, Danny Blanchflower, will be wanted by Ireland.

The international clashes with Spurs' home game against Burnley, another team challenging for the Championship.

Brown and Mackay are two of the five Anglo Scots chosen to play against Ireland.

Team: Brown (Spurs), Caldow (Rangers), Hewie (Charlton), Mackay (Spurs), Evans (Celtic, captain), McCann (Motherwell), Leggatt (Fulham), White (Falkirk), St John (Motherwell), Law (Huddersfield), Mulhall (Aberdeen).

Daily Telegraph, 22 September 1959

11

London Calling

Y ou can begin the story of John's transfer to Spurs in a number of places. There's the car park at White Hart Lane where Bill met Danny and Dave as they arrived back from Belfast the day after Scotland beat Northern Ireland. The legend goes that Bill asked: 'What's this fellow White like?' and Danny and Dave both recommended him so highly that Bill decided to buy John then and there. It's a nice yarn, though disappointingly it didn't actually happen quite like that.

Somewhere else you could begin is a few hundred miles further north in Falkirk, where the manager Tommy Younger put John up for sale at the end of September 1959. Over the next few days Everton, Liverpool, Arsenal, Burnley and Newcastle all made interested noises; Chelsea and Leicester made offers. Tommy Younger liked the sound of the one from Leicester, whose smart young manager Matt Gillies already had a reputation for being a shrewd judge of raw talent (he was responsible for furthering the careers of Frank McLintock and Gordon Banks).

Leicester put the same money on the table as Chelsea – £13,000 – but with the added inducement of a player. Gillies and his chief scout went to Falkirk to seal the deal, which went so far down the line that the press even knew which of the Leicester squad were up for grabs. 'It was generally accepted it would either be a right-winger, Tommy McDonald – who was eventually signed by Jock Stein at Dunfermline – or a guy called Jimmy Walsh (ex-Celtic) who wanted home at the time,' says the journalist Rodger Baillie. 'Tottenham came in the next day.'

In fact, the story of how John came to join Tottenham really begins much further back and a while before Bill Nicholson became Spurs manager. Bill was still just the coach at White Hart Lane when Walter Winterbottom, England manager at the time, thought highly enough of him to put him in charge of the national Under-23 team. It was in the course of those duties that Bill struck up a friendship with a football writer covering some of the matches, the *Daily Record*'s Jim Rodger.

'Jim Rodger,' says Baillie, 'was an ex-miner and probably Bill Nicholson's best friend on this earth, which bearing in mind Bill's social skills was a difficult task. He was a wee fat man who would talk to anyone from Harold Wilson to the office cleaner – when Wilson paid a prime ministerial visit to Scotland once there was a welcoming party to greet him at Glasgow Central Station, and ignoring the massed ranks and proffered handshakes, he said: "And how are you, Jim?" And that's not apocryphal. He had an enormous armoury of contacts and the friendship between him and Bill was one of the closest in football.'

At the *Daily Record*, Jim's job was to be the journalist who covered transfers and his past as a miner meant he was especially revered by Alex Ferguson. It was in the days before agents and Jim would do the deals and tap the players. 'When Alex Ferguson went from Dunfermline to Rangers Jim was the one who tapped Fergie,' says Baillie. When Bill Nicholson was looking for that holy grail for all managers, a goal-keeper who can dominate his penalty area in the way that Peter Schmeichel did later for Manchester United, it was Jim who fixed up the transfer of Bill Brown from Dundee. He was also responsible for getting Ian Ure to Arsenal and Ian St John to Liverpool and had a hand in Denis Law's move from Manchester City to Torino.

In terms of lifestyle, Jim didn't exactly large it. He lived with his wife Cathy in a prefab in Shotts, in the heart of what was originally the Lanarkshire coalfields. Bill stayed with them whenever he went to Scotland. 'When Spurs drew Rangers in the European Cup

Winners' Cup and Bill came up to look at Rangers, he brought the entire allocation of tickets destined for Rangers to distribute to their fans,' says Baillie. 'So in that little prefab were thousands of tickets for White Hart Lane, because Bill trusted Jim completely and knew they wouldn't go astray.

'Jim trudged into the newspaper office every day on the train – he never drove a car. He never took money, either. His pay-off wasn't any percentage of the deal but the exclusive stories he got out of it for himself and the *Daily Record*. He covered youth teams a lot, so he'd hand an autograph book round the team bus. They'd write down their names, addresses and phone numbers. Of youth teams, four or five would make it and he'd have their number while the rest of us were scrambling.

'He was an incredible wee man. Lord Beaverbrook would say there's no better thing in newspaper than *news* and that's true. I wouldn't say he had a way with words but by God he could beat us all to stories.'

If you look through a season's worth of *Daily Records* between 1957 and 1958, Jim Rodger's 'Transfer News' makes constructive reading. What stands out is the consistency with which he reports the goings-on at Alloa. It was Jim who had assiduously tracked John's progress there, a pretty safe assumption too that he was behind John's transfer to Falkirk. As for his best pal Bill down in London, there can't have been many better turns you could do a friend than make sure he buys John White.

The team John was coming to had opened the new season by beating Newcastle 5–1 at St James's Park – the afternoon featured a Cliff Jones hat-trick. Even so, they still had to field accusations that they lacked mental strength. No one could have accused Cliff Jones of faint-heartedness and Bobby Smith was highly willing to get stuck in, but others in the forward line weren't always so. The longest-standing problem was at inside-left, where neither contender had been able to stake a permanent claim to the shirt.

When Dave Dunmore made his first appearance, he had been hailed as a potential world-beater. He had all the qualities – speed, size, grace and a cracking right-foot shot – but according to Julian Holland in *Spurs – The Double*: 'on too many days he was a strangely ineffectual player ... unlucky in his control of the ball, lacking in the brazen confidence that makes a great player'. The problem with Johnny Brooks was more straightforward. 'Johnny said himself, he just didn't have the desire,' says Les Allen. 'I was brought up in a family of nine, and you have to fight because things don't come easy. John White would have felt the same. We were both from tough backgrounds. You do find this. When you appreciate that things could be so much better, you go and get it.'

'For all the surfeit of skill, Spurs often die at the heart of battle. The heart seems to leave them,' wrote Alan Hoby in the *Sunday Express* on 30 August 1959. You can guess what happened next – they beat West Bromwich Albion 2–1 away. On 3 September, under the headline FIGHTING SPURS IN WIN SHOCK, Ken Jones in the *Daily Mirror* praised '45 minutes of fighting football that mocked the "no spirit" label hung on this £180,000 line up ... As long as they can combine their super soccer with this sort of grim determination, they will take some stopping this season.'

Ken had it right. By 13 September, following a 5–1 crushing of Manchester United – it was the match in which Dave Mackay scored his first goal for Tottenham – the papers were calling them Super Spurs. They were at the top of Division One, ahead of Wolves and Burnley, and a week later the reputation of Dave Mackay as a hybrid between a miracle worker and a steamroller was enhanced at home to Preston. The result – 5–1, with goals from Bobby Smith, Dave Mackay, Cliff Jones (2) and Dave Dunmore – was accompanied by reports of Preston players 'moaning as they tottered – bruised, dazed or limping – away from White Hart Lane'. A concussed Tom Finney ended up in hospital after a pile-up of heads, and for the last fifteen minutes Preston were down to nine men after their inside forward

Gil Lambers fractured an ankle when he clashed boots with Peter Baker.

Suddenly Spurs were meriting a different kind of headline: BRUISER BOBBY BATTERS WEST HAM; OFF-FORM SPURS GET TOUGH. It was in this area that Bill Nicholson had his reservations about John.

'John looked on the light side to Bill Nick,' says Ken Jones. 'He'd had problems with Tommy Harmer being skinny; he didn't want another one. So Bill rang John's commanding officer in Berwick and asked if he was physically up to it. 'Lacks stamina?' the guy said. 'He's only just finished second in the army cross-country.'

The *Scottish Daily Express* reported that Bill promptly made Tommy Younger an offer of £20,000 over the phone. Younger accepted on the spot and then called John's barracks. He needed John to sign the transfer forms but it turned out John was on guard duty.

It was the first John knew of the move, and to get leave to travel to London he paid another soldier £3 to stand in for him. Then he got a ride to Musselburgh, changed into his civvies while his mum fed him tea and sandwiches, and set off to meet Tommy Younger to catch the night train at Glasgow Central. He didn't even know which London club had come in for him until Younger enlightened him.

Some twelve hours later, sleep-deprived, creased and rather daunted, John was a Tottenham player. He was already beginning to wonder what he'd taken on. Later he told Sandra he couldn't believe how many houses there were when he arrived at King's Cross. He was overwhelmed. 'You can imagine him coming down from Scotland,' says Sandra, 'from a totally different background. They were poor. He was just a Musselburgh boy, naive. Apart from his trial at Middlesbrough, he'd only been to England once, to Scarborough, on holiday with a friend. His mum had bought him a new raincoat. His jumper had holes in it so he wouldn't take the mac off.'

Jim Rodger duly got the scoop. His byline appears in the *Daily Record*, 9 October 1959, under the headline: SPURS BUY WHITE FOR £20,000. Such a sum sounds meaninglessly old-fashioned now, almost as antiquated as talking about farthings and groats. It's hard to say what an equivalent figure would be these days — not only do you have to adjust it in line with inflation but also you have to allow for the massive increase in value now put on footballers thanks to television money. You can only guess. The Croatian midfield playmaker Luka Modric, twenty-two years old at the time and a player whose insubstantial build gave rise to similar doubts, cost Tottenham £16.5 million in summer 2008. What is certain is that for Falkirk, it was a massive return on the £3,000 they'd paid Alloa. For Spurs, of course, the money would be immaterial. John would turn out to be priceless.

TRANSFER SHOCK — SPURS LAND £20,000 WHITE
But he misses 'game of season'
After ten hours of transfer turmoil yesterday, Spurs signed John White, Falkirk inside forward, for £20,000 . . . John White, who cannot turn out for Spurs until he has played for the Scottish League on Wednesday, will watch his new club in their top-of-the-table tussle with Wolves today.

A spot of farcical officialdom had intervened. 'It was some quaint rule,' says Rodger Baillie, 'that if you'd been selected to play for a match you couldn't be transferred out of Scotland till the game was played. And John couldn't play for Spurs that weekend because he was already due to be playing for the Scottish League against the Irish League.' For the record, the Scottish League won 7–1 and John scored.

Meanwhile, Bill's timing had been nifty, to say the least. On the day John was arriving in London with Tommy Younger, the Wolves manager Stan Cullis was urgently phoning Falkirk. Wolves had belatedly joined the chase, but Cullis wanted to see John play before deciding how much to bid.

Wolves had been the overwhelmingly successful club in English football for most of the fifties. Stan Cullis had been their dominating central defender in the 1930s, and twenty years on, in 1954, he'd won the League championship with them for the first time. Over the next few years he came to be known as the Master of Molineux. The team's long-ball game had towered over English football for most of the decade.

Which made it all the sweeter when Spurs crushed Wolves 5–1. Bobby Smith scored four of the goals; all the photos of the match show defenders in a sort of ballet of desperation around this giant among English strikers.

Tottenham's record now stood as unbeaten after twelve games; they were top of the table. For John, watching them from the stands of one of the most famous clubs in the world, a 22-year-old player from a Scottish Second Division club, it must have been revelatory. You picture him, with his square army haircut, wearing his Mussel-burgh boy's suit, absorbing the brilliant play and the massive tiers packed with fans – nearly 60,000 people were at that game – in an England whose drab, post-war existence was about to explode into the exuberance and glamour of the sixties; you think of him learning that the balance of power in English football was shifting again, and experiencing the daunting but intoxicating knowledge that he was going to be part of it.

JOHN WHITE DID NOT FAIL

Slow start but found his touch

After being subjected to two bewildering high-pressure weeks of what the publicity profession calls 'the build-up', John White, whose only crime had been that he plays football better than most, made his first appearance before the Tottenham public on Saturday.

It was difficult in the early stages of their introduction to determine who was the more disillusioned. Pale, slightly-built and of anonymous appearance, White looked as ill-at-ease as a Pioneer Corps private suddenly posted to Sandhurst. The crowd, apparently anticipating another dynamic caber-and-claymore character of the Dave Mackay calibre, remained dishearteningly silent.

Ian Wooldridge, *Daily Mail*, 24 October 1959

12

Desire

King's Cross, a wintry Friday evening in 1959. A slim, pallid lad joins the line of people streaming along the platform after getting off the Glasgow train. If anyone paid him any heed at all, they'd note the kitbag slung over his shoulder, the neat turnout and the way his thick fair hair is tamed by the giveaway short back and sides, and probably conclude that he's a soldier on weekend leave.

He is; a special one with a forty-eight-hour pass to play for Spurs. No one runs up with an autograph book, though. Last year, back in Musselburgh, he was someone – John White of Falkirk and Scotland. Here in London no one even guesses he's a footballer and he's too modest and diffident to draw attention to himself.

He disappears into the noisy, cluttered darkness to catch a bus to a B&B in north London, anxiously checking he's on the right route. He's been making this journey for two months now and the city still seems like a foreign country. He's too edgy and unhappy to take in the sights and sounds and not there long enough to find out what they are. In any case, there are more important things to think about.

What position is he going to play in tomorrow? Will he get a game at all?

There have been a lot of wonderful books written about the Double and the players who achieved it: by Julian Holland, Ken Ferris and Dave Bowler; by Danny Blanchflower himself (*The Double and Before*). None, though, make more than scant reference to John's first season at Spurs. While Dave barged in and made an immediate impact on everybody, the details of John's life beyond the pitch in autumn and winter 1959 are sparse. 'He was just a slim lad who didn't say a lot,' says Terry Dyson. Even Cliff Jones, who was John's best mate, is vague: 'He was just there.'

Unusually, Cliff is wrong. The reason no one remembers much about John's early weeks at Tottenham is simple – for most of the time he *wasn't* there. The move from Scotland should have been the fulfilment of a dream; in fact, John was a lost soul, coping with weekly multi-mile round trips and unable to train or socialise with the rest of the team. Instead, on Sundays, he would trudge back to King's Cross for the afternoon train to Scotland where he would turn himself back into Lance Corporal White J., PT instructor.

In his autobiography, Bill Nicholson records: 'When [John] arrived he said, "I'm not good enough to play with these players." He had a bad inferiority complex.' John confided as much in an interview he gave in 1963 to the *Scottish Daily Express*: 'For months the little-boy-lost feeling persisted. As a National Service man I joined the rest of the boys only on a weekend pass from the K.O.S.B. barracks at Berwick. Spurs played me out of position on the wing. The Army game had slowed me down. Nobody had heard of John White. The kids with autograph books weren't interested. At away games I felt like a hamper boy.'

Nor can John have drawn confidence from his introduction to White Hart Lane. Spurs were the money club of their day. Rearing up like a mountain range behind intimidating iron gates, the stadium had a new gym and covered practice court next to the main entrance. Row upon row of luxury cars were parked out front. He had been accustomed to turning out weekly in front of four-figure crowds at Recreation Park and then Brockville. White Hart Lane, in contrast, was a cauldron – three tiers of 60,000 passionate, articulate, demanding fans who did not simply want victory but expected it on specific terms: don't just win, win well. It must have seemed, from where John was riding in on the bus, like going from the local fleapit to La Scala.

In the dressing room, his teammates would have looked glamorous and stylish, like the Hollywood Rat Pack. They wore made-to-measure suits (John was not yet to know that they were provided without charge by a tailor fan in the East End). He must have thought Danny Blanchflower, with his newspaper work and his air of learning and seniority, belonged to another species. Dave Mackay was much closer to John in age and a fellow Scot, but with his shades and maroon Jaguar and confident strut he would have seemed years older in self-belief and experience; John couldn't even drive. Lonely, insecure and mute with shyness, it's astonishing that he managed to achieve anything at all.

The press assumed that John had been signed as a replacement for Tommy Harmer at inside-right. If that had been Bill Nicholson's plan, it now looked as if he was having second thoughts. As 1959 drew to a close, Tommy Harmer was still very much there. Inside-left, then, in the number 10 shirt? That was where John had played on his debut – Saturday 17 October, away to Sheffield Wednesday at Hillsborough. Cliff Jones and Terry Medwin were playing for Wales that day and a weakened Spurs lost 2–1 – in doing so, terminating an unbeaten run of twelve games – but John scored Tottenham's only goal.

Even so, if he'd been hoping for praise for the good judgement he showed when after a mere twenty-two minutes of English football he came in at the right time to meet a ball from Tommy Harmer, it didn't come. Applause from Bill, he was discovering, occurred marginally more frequently than airborne pigs.

A week later came John's first home game. As if to emphasise the priorities in football in those days, the lead item in the Spurs–Forest programme was a lengthy article about the club chairman, Fred J. Bearman – it was his fiftieth year as a director. A snippet followed. 'OUR NEW PLAYER: Supporters will join us in giving a hearty welcome to our new player, John White, who was transferred to us from the Falkirk Club on October 8th . . .' The welcome was not, in fact, that hearty, either then or in the following weeks. Among the White Hart Lane faithful, the consensus was that John, still playing on the left, was largely invisible and worth nothing like the money Spurs had paid for him. When winter set in and the London fog made the eyes smart, and the tackling got wilder, and the pitches were of a condition that a hippo would deem too soggy to wallow in, he and Tommy Harmer, both attacking midfielders, both as brawny as twigs, were struggling.

7 November 1959: SHOCK DEFEAT FOR SPURS
Spurs 0, Bolton Wanderers 2
Spurs attack was now disorganised. Individuals were carrying the ball too much, and unable to beat the strong-tackling, close-covering Bolton defence.
15 November 1959: LUTON MUD WIPES SHINE OFF SPURS
Luton 1, Tottenham 0

John would not have needed to read beyond the headline to guess what was coming next: '. . . basically their trouble seemed to stem from the fact that Tommy Harmer and John White, two delicate ball players, were bogged down . . . On this performance the crowd may wonder why the £20,000 was spent to oust such a forceful player as Dave Dunmore.'

Accusations of gutlessness in Spurs' attack persisted. A 1–1 draw with Fulham at Craven Cottage on 12 December was deemed by Alan Hoby of the *Sunday Express* as having 'as much goal power as a powder puff. Harmer, White and Smith were out of the game for long periods. Right winger Medwin goes on being out of form. The only real forward was the unstoppable Jones . . .'

December must have had John reaching a nadir of insecurity. Midway through the month Les Allen was signed from Chelsea in a direct swap with Johnny Brooks who, before John's arrival, had played at number 10. Les duly took over the left midfield spot and instead of breaking up Danny Blanchflower's alliance with Tommy Harmer, Bill gave John the number 7 shirt.

On 19 December, Spurs greeted Newcastle at White Hart Lane with a forward line of White, Harmer, Smith, Allen and Jones. That day, Spurs won 4–0 to go top of the table. Though John's goal in the sixty-fifth minute was acclaimed as snipe-quick and 'beautiful', it was Tottenham's 'tiny, tormenting inside-right Tommy Harmer', his rival for the number 8 shirt, who was acclaimed as the 'hero of Super Spurs'. With Harmer and Blanchflower hitting peak form together, there seemed no way that John would be playing his natural game as an attacking midfielder any time soon. The thought can't have passed him by that he had come full circle – stuck out on the wing, out of harm's way, just as he had been at school.

Of course, if he'd looked later on through old match reports of that period the first thing he'd have realised was how *well* he did. That first appearance at White Hart Lane, says it all: 21 October, Spurs 2, Nottingham Forest 1; 'John White . . . showed that he is the best Scottish forward to hit London since the great Alex James started his brilliant career with Arsenal thirty years ago,' said the *Daily Express*, hailing him as 'A great Scot for Spurs'. The Forest manager, Billy Walker, praised his accuracy: 'He didn't put our lads in possession once – and that takes a lot of doing.' The chipped pass he made for Bobby Smith's second goal was perfect. 'When that boy passes – he passes!' said Bobby.

There was more. 1 November: Manchester City 1, Spurs 2; 'inside-left John White was just red hot. He burned his way through the City defence with searing football.' 29 November: Blackpool 2, Spurs 3; 'It was White who really showed Spurs the way to turn clever approach work into goals.' 6 December: Spurs 2, Blackburn 1; 'the attention given by Blackburn to White was a tribute to the almost academic artistry and imagination of this most promising young

Scot.' 19 December: Spurs 4, Newcastle 0; 'Playing on the right wing [John White] demonstrated a foot skill and artistry which, joined to his superb positional sense, stamp him as a great footballer in the making.'

With hindsight, it seems odd that John can have felt so unsure of himself, only when you're in the middle of a rough patch you tend not to think that rationally. After a dozen games out of position, he must have wondered whether he had a future with Spurs. His legs would have felt heavy because the training he did in the army was geared only to good general fitness. The disappointment of the crowd weighed on him. So did the transfer fee. Bill Nicholson, as Les Allen has said, was 'a very dour, hard man' to whom it would have been impossible to confide his troubles. And unlike Les, whose father had been at his side from Bill's first approach, John had no dad to reassure him and lend him confidence.

Instead, he was on his own in a city where, according to Dave Mackay, Scottish accents were rarely encountered, and Isobel, Dave's wife, was reduced to tears because she couldn't make herself understood. And when you're lost and downhearted and far from home and you feel small and insignificant, spirits and self-belief plummet. It's the sort of mindset in which you don't take in the words of praise, only the boss's criticism and the barrackings of the crowd.

John's disconnection and quiet despair could have carried on indefinitely. Instead, as the new year got under way, fate stepped in. It took the form of an invitation to Sunday lunch with Harry Evans, Tottenham's assistant manager, and his family. This kind and sympathetic gesture, which was repeated intermittently over the rest of the season and was to have far-reaching consequences, gave John his first real anchor in London.

And more than that, John, despite appearances, was tough and resilient. Stubborn, too – he had refused to give up on his football ambitions in the face of a string of rejections as a youngster. All his life so far he'd just kept going because that was the maxim he'd learnt as a child back in Musselburgh: after the blow comes, you've just got to get up and get on with it. Wasn't it what he'd said to his kid brother Tom – 'Keep going!' – when he'd patted him on the shoulder and passed him every day at the same spot as they ran to work?

But it wasn't simply fatalistic stoicism that drove him forward. Desire is not something that can be taught. It is as innate as red hair and musicality and long legs and beauty, and it shows itself in many discrete ways. There is the sort of incandescent enthusiasm that was peculiar to Terry Dyson; Cliff Jones's almost knee-jerk bravery; Bobby Smith's brash, bruising swagger; there is the deep competitiveness mediated by calm cerebration – that was Danny Blanchflower's way. As for Dave Mackay, he wanted to win so fiercely that he pushed his body very close to destruction and turned Tottenham's fortunes round as a result.

John was a quiet, self-effacing personality. But, as Les Allen has pointed out, he had managed even so to fight his way out of hardship. He had prodigious ability; the conundrum was that so did others, but they hadn't made it. What separated this likeable, considerate, decent man, so ordinary in many ways, from the others who were his match in talent? He stood apart from them because when the chips were down he had the merciless, unyielding, steely core of desire, the resolute determination to go on when weaker souls were prepared to admit defeat.

Put simply, he wanted it more.

It's hard to identify the exact turning point, but if you look through the old match reports from the middle of that season, one day stands out: 27 February 1960. Spurs were leading the championship table by a point when they took on Blackburn Rovers at Ewood Park. Blackburn Rovers 1, Spurs 4. Bobby, Dave, Les and Cliff were the scorers. John, who made three of the goals, was acknowledged to be man of the match. He was no longer simply a promising young player. That day he imposed himself on the game.

Blanchflower, Mackay, White. The press were already speculating that here was a world-beating midfield in the making and that Spurs now had a team capable of doing the Double. In the words of one reporter at Ewood Park: 'The championship winning look beamed from the face of every player.'

Except maybe one, who wouldn't have been human if he hadn't had mixed feelings about it all.

SPURS WON'T LET TOMMY GO

Tommy Harmer, Spurs' ball-juggling inside forward, will not be leaving White Hart Lane. His dramatic 'out of the blue' transfer request that shook thousands of Spurs fans over the weekend will come up before the directors on Tuesday. And I understand that he will be told 'Sorry you can't go. You are too good a player to lose.'

After a surprise recall to the attack against Everton, Harmer told me: 'My request has been put in writing. Now it's up to the club what happens next. I have asked for a move because I can see no future for me in the present set-up.'

Ken Jones, Daily Mirror, 23 November 1959

13

The Battle for Number 8

Bloody Spurs. Typical. Now they're not going to win the championship they're unbeatable.

Saturday 23 April 1960 at Molineux is not a day or place to be a Wolves supporter. 1–3 doesn't begin to convey the extent of the crushing. The game belongs to Tottenham. Three goals, by Bobby Smith, Dave Mackay and Cliff Jones, are all made by the sustained, stunning approach work of two men in midfield. The press bash away at typewriters: 'Blanchflower in dazzling form . . . little Scottish inside-right John White who had a superb match . . .'

Brought in from the periphery of the wing, John has had one of those master-of-the-universe games, contributing everything that is good about the team attack. Now he's got the chance to show what he's capable of, what he's made for: he can deliver the movement and passes that set up goals for others; he can score goals himself; he can create and finish; he gives Spurs something that no other side possesses.

For the past six weeks the side has looked drained, frazzled by the persistent tension of battling for the championship and finally conceding defeat. The League title can only go to Wolves or Burnley now. As often happens, once players have been released from their fear of failure, all the tiredness and tension has gone. That's not been the only difference about Spurs today, though.

One significant player is missing.

* * *

Somewhere in the Pathé news archives is a black-and-white clip, so old it practically has whiskers, of a skinny little footballer with a massive hairdo that seems too heavy for his body. When you look at his shorts – baggy and huge over spindly legs, the effect is of a tent with a couple of ropes trailing outside – you're inclined to ask if he was wearing them for a bet.

The player is Tommy Harmer, the match long forgotten. None of the famous names he played with and against – Danny Blanchflower, Stanley Matthews, Johnny Haynes, Billy Wright – are in evidence. Because he's alone on the pitch and the clip rolls in slow motion, the effect is closer to a ballet performance than a display by a top-level footballer: graceful, sinewy, controlled of movement. His feet are as sensitive as fingertips but their grip on the ball is almost prehensile in its strength. To generations who have grown up on exhibitions of brainlessly running domestic players who can't trap a ball first time, it's a masterclass.

Tommy was a crabbed, nervous, scrawny East Ender who never weighed much more than nine stone. To the journalist Brian Glanville, he was 'like a tiny, mobile signal box, guiding and switching the play . . . he would juggle with the ball, elude [defenders], and send his team on the attack with a perfectly judged pass'. In an interview of the period, the *Sunday Express*'s Alan Hoby described him: 'Harmer the Charmer . . . a cartoonist's joy . . . hollow-cheeked with legs like bent matchsticks, he moves at a dawdling jog-trot.'

He started work at fifteen in the dispatch office of a local printers for 15s 8d a week. Two and sixpence of this went on his weekly subscription to the Printing, Bookbinding and Paper Workers' Union, and he once stated in an interview that he had kept up his membership, even after signing for Spurs. 'It is what they call an "out-of-trade" card but it entitles me to go back to my old job as a folding machine and guillotine operator, whenever I need it. And that's what I'll do when it's all over.' The tone of caution and gloom was classic Tommy.

Maybe that wasn't surprising. His playing career was blighted by being out of sync. He was, says Cliff Jones, 'a very astute football man who was unfortunate in his time with Tottenham. He couldn't get into the push-and-run side because he came in too late to be a regular. Then along came the Double side and he couldn't get a look-in there. When they had the really great sides he just didn't fit in to them. But he was the best ball player I'd ever seen.'

Tommy's quirks – their legend has outlived him – included a unique way of taking penalty kicks. He would run up to the ball sideways on, turn and screw it back across the goalkeeper. The trick shots that were part of his armoury were those more familiar to a tennis player: backspins, swerves, dinks and benders, huge blistering passes down the middle, raking cross-field balls to the wing. According to Brian Glanville: 'He and the fluent, flamboyant Blanchflower could scarcely have been more different characters, but on the field they balanced one another perfectly – each a technically accomplished, highly intelligent footballer, given to holding the ball before making shrewd use of it.'

'He had to have a cigarette before a game,' says Cliff. 'No smoking in the dressing room of course. So he'd go into the toilet, thinking no one knew. If he didn't have one, he was a complete wreck.'

Tommy's long-standing partnership at the heart of the team with Danny peaked in 1958. 'Harmer with his ineffable accuracy and his mesmerizing control of the ball . . . led his forwards with such flair that Spurs became runners-up in the Championship,' writes Julian Holland in *Spurs – The Double*. By the 1959–60 season, though, he was approaching his thirty-second birthday – old in footballer years. In mid-November, when the Russian club Moscow Torpedo came to White Hart Lane for a friendly, John was picked for the role of inside-right in Tommy's place. He scored the last of Spurs' goals in their 3–2 win.

Tommy promptly put in a transfer request, claiming he was

'unsettled'. The directors turned him down. Bill, who didn't want to break up Tommy's partnership with Danny if he could avoid it, tried John at inside-left and then outside Tommy on the right, although it meant his talents were under-deployed. Most of the rest of that season was about Bill trying to get round the problem that while both John and Tommy were skinny men you couldn't fit both inside a number 8 shirt.

NO STOPPING TOMMY AS HE MAKES FOUR
Spurs 4, Newcastle United 0
In ankle deep slush [Harmer] had Newcastle dizzy with his body swerves and close control. He made all 4 goals that sent Spurs back to the top of the First Division.
Ken Jones, Daily Mirror, 24 December 1959

For footballers who played in it, winter 1960 is always going to be remembered for its gruesome weather. 'Even if you had one of the best pitches in the country they were never repaired,' says the journalist Ronald Atkin. 'They finished up as a great brown bare expanse. You slopped through the mud. There was no under-soil heating, no pitch coverings, not even basic ones. You just went out and played on it, marking out the lines in red if it snowed. Or they swept the pitch where the lines were. Winters were more wintry. It snowed more. But they played on that sort of crap.'

'Fifteen pieces of leather sewn together, all joins and laces – when you headed the ball that winter you knew what you were heading,' says Les Allen, who in those conditions scored five goals in a fourth-round FA Cup replay against Crewe Alexandra at the start of that February (Spurs won 13–2 – it's said they eased up at half-time when the score stood at 10–1). Tommy Harmer scored one of the goals. In fact, in that six-week quagmire there was hardly a Spurs victory in which he didn't play significant part. During January they beat

Arsenal at White Hart Lane (MAGNIFICENT HARMER DAZZLES ARSENAL, according to the *Sunday Express*), then Manchester United when players were 'caked head to toe in slimy black mud'.

It was around that time that talk began of the Double. Danny was acknowledged as the driving force; Tommy, it was said, was the player who was making it happen. 'One man, above all the others, is the unorthodox juggling genius behind Tottenham Hotspur's glorious run of success,' wrote Alan Hoby in the *Sunday Express* of 24 January after the win over Manchester United. Spurs were 'the present First Division kings . . . playing with their usual skill on a pitch like thick brown porridge'. In the *Evening Standard*, interviewed by the Arsenal centre-half turned journalist Bernard Joy, Bill spoke with an unusual lack of caution: 'I think we've got a good chance of doing the Double this season.' According to Danny, 'The players are very confident that we can do it. Things are running right and teams who usually do well against us, like Newcastle at White Hart Lane and Birmingham at St Andrews, were beaten this time.' Even Tommy displayed optimism: 'It looks as though we might win something.'

Such ambitions were quickly dashed. Injured, Tommy sat out the 3–1 defeat by Blackburn in the FA Cup fifth round. 'Spurs miss that Harmer magic,' said the *Sunday Express*. 'On a semi-swamp of a pitch, they simply collapsed against this ruthless, razor-tackling Blackburn.'

That was the Double out of the window, and in the League they entered one of those weird, yo-yo phases. John was absent with the army at the start of March when they lost 2–1 away to Burnley, their closest rival along with Wolves. Back for Saturday 5 March, he scored in the 4–1 defeat of Sheffield Wednesday at White Hart Lane (Cliff Jones got a hat-trick); 'the delightful White, slowing the game to his pace at will'; 'only fitting that the fourth goal should be shot by White' – the *Sunday Express* again. They drew 1–1 at home to Luton, the bottom club. Wolves caught them up. Everton beat them at Goodison. Of the three fixtures over the Easter holiday weekend, they beat Chelsea at Stamford Bridge on Good Friday, lost to Manchester City at Maine Road on Saturday, and faced Chelsea again – at home – on Easter Monday. Chelsea won, with one wonderful goal; it was scored by a teenage Jimmy Greaves. Even the Spurs fans roared their acclamation.

In the end, the title race went to the wire. Wolves were top, with all their games played. Burnley, with a game in hand, had to beat Manchester City. They did. The FA Cup, however, went to Wolves. Somewhere between the end of March and May, Bill had started playing John at inside-right in Tommy's place. It's too late to ask him why, but the guess is that if he couldn't win the League with Danny and Tommy, it was worth trying to win it with Danny and John. At White Hart Lane, the last game of Tottenham's season finished Spurs 4, Blackpool 1. John, wearing the number 8 shirt, scored the first of the goals.

If Tommy was the nearly man, the 1959–60 team was the nearly side – one good enough, though, for David Lacey to nominate it in 2009 in the *Guardian* as one of his Six Beautiful Teams of the Last Fifty Years. The others were Real Madrid (1959–60), Real Zaragoza (1965–6), West Ham (1966–7), the Brazil World Cup-winning team of 1970 and the Ruud Gullit-era Milan of 1988–9, which shows how good they were.

Why that side and not the Double team? 'I thought it was better,' says David. 'I watched them against West Brom and my first impression was that this was something new. English football had been dominated by Wolves – the breathless, long-ball game, played very well. Really this was a development of Arthur Rowe's push-and-run but it wasn't typically English football. It was more profound – subtle and thoughtful. There were two seminal matches. Spurs beat Wolves 5–1 at White Hart Lane, and the following spring went to Molineux, beat them 3–1 and they were even more dominant. That was one of the games that told you power in the game was shifting.'

In *Spurs – The Double*, Julian Holland writes that John was 'not as accurate as Harmer, and often not so shrewd in making the telling pass. But he has a mobility that Harmer never possessed. Harmer with the ball was a menace to a defence such as post-war football has seldom known. But Harmer without the ball was too often a passenger in a side ... [White] is able to lose his marker at will. Furthermore, he has a wider vision of the game than Harmer ever had.'

'John's great asset was always going to be his mobility,' says Cliff. 'He was that little bit extra. It really kicked off once he was playing inside-right. The great thing about him was that when you picked up the ball there'd be at least one man to pass to. Bill could see that was going to be his big strength – that he was always available.'

That July, just before the start of the Double season, Tommy made his last first-team appearance. It's at the pre-season photo call. John isn't in the picture – he was still in Berwick, a month away from being demobbed. But when the season began it was John wearing number 8 and running the forward line. That October, after 222 appearances and 51 goals, Tommy was sold to Watford.

Why, then, is he included here, a man who never made the Double side, never won medals, never played for England? Primarily because only a player as exceptional as John could have dislodged Tommy Harmer from that side. But it's also important to pay tribute to a man who is an ineradicable part of Tottenham's history.

Compare the two of them now and Tommy seems to belong to a bygone age in a way John doesn't. Though their career trajectories intersected for a season half a century ago John is simply – well, modern. You could see him playing in any top-class side today because his sort of game – the ability to get something going from anywhere on the pitch, the assists and the goals, his genius for off-the-ball play, the flexibility to initiate an attack or contribute to someone else's – is the game played by Andres Iniesta, Cesc Fabregas and all the other great playmakers of the game in the twenty-first century.

'Nobody in the world is more imitative than the professional foot-baller,' says Brian James. 'John, I suspect, would have been a prime example of the quiet copier. He would have had a very sharp appreciation of what another player was good at. Stick him alongside Iniesta and he'd have seen things in Iniesta's game and he would have loved it. He would have thought, wow, and he would have had the basic skills to do it too.'

Tommy, on the other hand, seems part of an era that is becoming as far away from us as arquebuses and spinning wheels: the days of wizards of the dribble and mud-clogged boots, of ball-juggling inside forwards, of players encased neck-high in January mud and of floodlights as brilliant as planets in black city skies. And here's Tommy now, picking his way over the cold wintry quagmires, controlling a sodden bundle of leather and stitches as if it was as delicate as a chrysanthemum.

'Harmer was a truly great player,' writes Julian Holland. 'His tragedy was that his gifts were never fully suited to the type of play current at Tottenham. Under Rowe he was too subtle and too static. Under Anderson he was denied colleagues quick and responsive enough to turn his genius into Championship-winning football. Under Nicholson he lacked the mobility that the new manager looked for. Nor could he supply the rapid improvisational touches that Nicholson knew were necessary to overcome planned, coherent defences in 1961.'

When Tommy Harmer is spoken of these days — and he still is — he is usually tagged as an unlucky player, the one who missed the party, like the guy who got dropped from the Beatles just before they got famous.

Remembering him like that would be a pity. It's a bit corny to say that though he was small, he was a giant, but for the generation who saw what he could do, there's no better word.

WHITE IS THE STAR OF 6–2 VICTORY
Tottenham 6, Aston Villa 2
So brilliant Spurs create a record start to their season by gaining their tenth successive win. In front of a 61,356 crowd they were irresistible against Aston Villa here today and they added a killing venom to their usual poise and skill . . . The forwards, who were generaled by man-of-the-match John White, were five white-shirted sprites darting in and out of Villa's heavy-footed defenders . . .

Bernard Joy, *London Evening Standard*, 24 September 1960

14

A Real Nice Fella

Tottenham v Aston Villa is the kind of game Spurs supporters wish could go on forever – a goal spree in the early-autumn sunshine, four up after half an hour, the feeling they're never going to lose again. Two Villa defenders freeze in surprise as John – where did he spring up from? – poises, perfectly balanced, and knocks home the opener, only six minutes in, with his left foot. It's his first goal at White Hart Lane this season.

John's second comes soon after, from a swapping of passes with Terry Dyson. Minutes later, Dave Mackay thwacks a thirty-yarder into the goalie's body and Bobby Smith whips round to tap in goal number three over the corpse. Only twenty-six minutes gone, and more is to come. Within a few minutes, John lobs the ball over the head of the Villa right-back, doubles round him and slides a pass to Terry Dyson for goal four. The second half features a Les Allen goal from what one paper calls 'another gorgeous Dyson–White move'. Dave Mackay gets Spurs' sixth in the closing minutes.

The victory over Villa is their tenth win in a row – a League record and a trailer for the fantastic things to come. Villa's two goals barely rate a mention. Nor, come to that, do most of the other Spurs players. Every reporter is too busy raving about John: 'the wonderful White'; 'this supreme ball-artist'. Tottenham are 'inspired by the delicate artistry of their Scottish inside-forward John White'. In the *Sunday Express*, it's 'White, that cunning genius'. The *London Evening News* calls him 'immaculate'. 'The expert intervention of John White,' says the *Daily Express*, 'was the very poetry of soccer.'

Just over a year from his arrival at Spurs, John is a transformed man. You could, as Terry Medwin asserts, ascribe it to 'settling down. For people like us, coming down from small clubs in Wales or Scotland, it was a big thing to come to London – a different way of life. I'd see the change in him in his second season as a change in confidence. Becoming a real part of the team.'

But in a way, Terry's summary simply begs another question. What or who was responsible for giving him that injection of confidence? The answer has to be that for the first time in ages John had stability in his life. Not only did he now have a permanent London base but someone at his shoulder to support and encourage him.

Father figures in movies come in all shapes and sizes and incarnations, from Gregory Peck as the lawyer Atticus Finch, stalwart and decent, in *To Kill a Mockingbird*, to John Candy as Irv Blitzer, the rumpled, reluctant coach of the Jamaican bobsled team in *Cool Runnings*, and Splinter, the rat in *Teenage Mutant Ninja Turtles*, who trains the turtles in ninjitsu. All of these, of course, are inventions of a screenwriter's imagination; the father figure is a stock archetype of storytelling and if you listed every example in film and literature this chapter would be ten feet long. And even then you would probably never come up with Harry Evans.

How John ended up living with Harry and Alma Evans and their daughter Sandra – and what it led to – is a lovely story that would probably never come about now. It begins on the 1960 August Bank Holiday weekend, when John arrived at White Hart Lane having just been demobbed from the army. No one seems to have been expecting him and the club wasn't even able to arrange a bed for the night – all the landladies Spurs used were away on holiday. So Harry, who happened to walk through the reception area at the moment of crisis, offered to put him up in the spare bedroom. 'It was meant to be for a couple of nights,' says Sandra, 'but we never got rid of him.'

Harry, of course, had already taken pity on John the season before, inviting him over for Sunday lunch before John had to travel back to his barracks in Berwick. For John it was a soul-strengthening glimpse of home life, with cheerful, easy-going Harry chatting about football, and Alma making a fuss of him by serving what she fondly believed was his top meal, steak and kidney pie. 'The first time my mum made it she thought he really enjoyed it because his plate was clear,' says Sandra. 'It turned out later he'd put it on the fire when she went to wash up, but for ages she thought it was his favourite and always cooked it when he came round.'

Tubby, dark-haired and warm-hearted, Harry was the archetypal back-room man, an ex-player whose jocular boast was, 'I kept Alf Ramsey out of the Southampton side, you know.' When John signed for Spurs, he hadn't long been there himself. The 1959–60 season's *Official Handbook*, a publication as glitzy as a packet of J-cloths, hailed his appointment as assistant manager towards the end of the 1958–9 season. At the time, Tony Marchi had only just returned to Tottenham after two years in Italy. 'When Bill took over he never had an assistant manager really,' explains Tony. 'Then one day before a match I was in the car park when Bill beckoned me over. He was with a man and a woman and a girl in her teens, and he said, "I want you to meet Harry Evans."'

He was, says Tony, 'about five feet eight tall and very jovial. You had this big Spurs side yet nothing was ever mentioned about Harry, and yet he helped Bill such a lot. He did the office work so Bill could do the coaching and training that was his love. He was a nice man to know.'

'Harry was happy,' concurs Linda Baker, Peter's wife. 'Always seemed happy, anyway. Got things done quietly, no fuss and bother. He was a good foil for Bill because Harry could be diplomatic. Harry could smooth things.'

'Yeah,' says Terry Dyson. 'Harry, he was perfect for Bill. Brilliant. They just had a rapport. It's easy to talk about people when they're gone but he was a real nice fella.'

Just how useful Harry could be was proved by his contribution after Spurs' close-season trip to Moscow in 1959. 'One night during the Moscow trip we were told we were going to the Bolshoi Ballet,' says Cliff. 'Oh, Jesus Christ, we all thought. But it was an amazing experience. You could see the effort and fitness of these dancers, the power they had – explosive, from the abs. Harry discovered that the dancers did weight training in a big way and after we got back to London he got a famous weightlifter called Bill Watson to come in and do strength work with us as part of our training.'

One year on, seeing a rather waiflike John in the foyer at White Hart Lane must have struck a chord with Harry. He knew more than most what it was like not to have a home to go to. Born at the Lying-In Hospital on York Road, Battersea, in April 1919, he was orphaned at two in the Spanish flu epidemic; one of his sisters died too. His other sister, Grace, who was ten years older than him, was sent to an orphanage and Harry was taken in by his Aunt Fan, who wasn't kind to him at all. Harry's dad had been a roadsweeper and baby Harry had a Post Office book. 'My mum always reckoned that was why Fan took him in,' says Sandra, adding that later, 'he had to take Aunt Fan's grandchildren to the park, and they were given bottles of cold tea and bread and margarine which had to last all day. He didn't hear from his sister. He never had anything for Christmas or birthday except once when he got a football which he took outside and kicked through a window. He ran away from home a couple of times. He was frightened of Fan, even as an adult.'

He and Alma were both sixteen when they met. They married during the war; Alma's house had been bombed and Alma had nothing special to wear, but her sister Emily managed to cobble together a wedding breakfast. 'When they came back from the church, my dad said, "Got to go now because Aunt Fan's making dinner,"' says Sandra. 'Later on, she used to make Harry a Christmas pud every year. He used to put them in the boot of the car and they'd stay there for three or four years, like ballast. One year she gave him a framed photo of his mum and dad. He tore the back off to see if there was any money in it – there wasn't. The photo went in the back of the shed.'

Before the war, Harry had been clerk to a wine and spirit merchant while playing football as an amateur for Sutton. In 1939, he got his call-up papers and joined the RAF, where they made him a PT instructor and kept him at Farnborough, one of two adjacent garrison towns – the other is Aldershot – in Hampshire all through the war. Although his great love was sport – he'd played cricket for Surrey Schools as well – he was also a projectionist for the Army Kinematic Corps and a drummer with Micky Kennedy's Dance Band, which played gigs at the local dance hall. Sadly, though that building remains, it's now the empty shell of the Carpet and Bed Shack, which closed in 2007.

After the war, Harry stuck around in Hampshire, first as a player on Southampton's books, then – after a brief spell at Exeter – returning to join Aldershot, playing what would now be classed as a holding role in midfield. During the war, when a lot of top-class footballers were based there, they'd had a fantastic team that had included Frank Swift in goal, Joe Mercer, Stan Cullis and Wilf Dixon, with – for a couple of seasons – Tommy Lawton up front (he scored sixty-six goals in forty-four games). By the time Harry got there, though, they were back to their pre-war state of bumping around in the old Third Division (South).

Peritonitis, a serious and painful abdominal infection requiring surgery, brought about the end of Harry's playing days when he was relatively young. He stayed on at Aldershot, studying at night to get coaching, physiotherapy and secretarial qualifications – at one stage or another he was the club's coach, trainer, manager and secretary. 'Mum and I used to make up the wage packets – we were a bit like MPs' wives,' says Sandra. 'After home games, when all the directors had left, Mum, Dad and I used to go to the town hall with the gate money. The mace-bearer, Ted – he was the mayor's chauffeur too – used to let us in and we'd count the money, put it into bags and put it in the safe.' One director sticks in her mind fifty years on, the pudgy-faced one who owned a sports shop in the town and who once said to Harry when the opposing team ran out onto the pitch, 'One of their players is a bit small, isn't he?' 'That's because he's the mascot,' said Harry.

As seems to happen to all managers – eventually Harry was sacked. He applied to Spurs, hopefully, for the job of assistant manager and Bill, who could tell a good egg when he saw one, took him on.

While all this was happening, Sandra was in the middle of studying for her A levels and she had only just turned eighteen when John moved in. This was no case, though, of a star-struck teenager meeting an idol.

'I never even thought about it when Dad brought John home,' says Sandra. 'I'd been brought up around footballers. It was just normal. In a small town like Aldershot, everyone knew who Dad was. Other people might have thought, Ooh, fancy meeting all these famous players, but they were just friends of my mum and dad.'

John, though, was to become something more. It's too much of a reach to call Harry the father John never had, and to call the Evanses his surrogate family would be a slur on Ann and the Aunties, but without Harry John's first full season at Spurs would have been a lot different and that much harder.

'It was a friendship – they were mates,' says Sandra. 'But Harry definitely took John under his wing and John modelled himself on him. Like John always washed up and wiped because he'd seen Harry do it.' She can't help laughing. 'John once mentioned it in passing to Danny Blanchflower and Danny said he didn't have anything to do with that side of things – he wouldn't. "He bloody would if he lived in this house," said Alma.'

But it wasn't only that Harry provided the kind, manly support that John needed to thrive in the cauldron. It didn't take long after his arrival at Berkeley Gardens for John and Sandra to fall in love. If he'd ever at any stage nursed regrets about leaving Scotland for London, he had none now.

QUICKSILVER WHITE HAS A WONDER MATCH
Wolves 0, Tottenham 4

Spurs sweep on gloriously. In another dazzling display of regal elegance and artistry they preserved their 100% record by grinding Wolves into the damp Molineux grass. The jam-packed 53,000 crowd saw the football team of the season as these magical masters from Tottenham strutted and strolled their way to their eleventh consecutive victory . . .

There was Irish right-half Danny Blanchflower, at his impeccable best, directing the one-way traffic. There was Scottish inside-right John White, flitting irrepressibly here, there and everywhere. He is pale, he is frail, this White – that is, by the normal he-man standards of modern soccer. But not only has he the uncanny brilliance of the Continentals; in his quicksilver ability to flit unnoticed into the open space he reminds me of Wilf Mannion.

Alan Hoby, *Sunday Express*, 1 October 1960

15

Ghost Appearance

It's officially autumn. The sun gets paler, the pitches grow soggier and Tottenham's record run bucks a trend.

LOOK HOW THEY FLOCK TO SPURS is the Saturday-morning headline in the *Daily Express* sports pages of 1 October 1960, over an announcement of a slump in attendances. They are more than a million and a quarter down throughout the league compared to the first five weeks of the previous season. Tottenham, in contrast, are a club worth leaving the house for. 'Spurs, in their record-setting run of 10 wins in a row, have never played to fewer than 40,000 on their own ground and are the biggest crowd-pullers at every ground they visit.' At Arsenal, they register a gate of 60,088, over 25,000 more than watched Newcastle, the closest contenders as a draw.

Another massive turnout is recorded at Wolves's ground, Molineux. October's big game is the first fixture of the month, on the first day of the month. Dave Mackay is absent, lying 'weak and wan in bed with food poisoning'. Tony Marchi, who has his first top-flight game of the season in Dave's place, is adjudged to have played so well in a holding midfield position that 'the great Dave Mackay was scarcely missed'. The goals come from Cliff Jones, Danny Blanchflower, Les Allen and Terry Dyson.

It's John, though, who receives the bulk of praise in the papers for this 4–0 defeat of their long-term rivals, outdoing even Danny in column inches: 'Watch this White. He is only 23 and he is going to be one of the great ones'; 'Wolves were skilfully taken apart by three master surgeons called Blanchflower, Marchi and White'; 'a glorious bit of football by White, who pulled down a difficult pass from Smith and beat Flowers on a sixpence before sending a neat lob which Allen pushed home'; 'as on other occasions this season, Blanch-flower and White nearly always stood out' ; 'White wrong-footed the entire Wolves defence'.

In Monday's *Daily Telegraph*, where it's suggested that 'Spurs would be an ideal Great Britain XI', Tottenham are said to have squashed all doubts about their ability to follow through. As the glamour club of their era, they are described as an expensively assembled side of 'English, Welsh, Scottish and Irish stars . . . welded into a team eager to challenge the world . . . a ready-made answer to the moaners who see no future in our style of presenting the game at international level. The season is not quite two months old, but already Spurs are favourites for the Cup and the League, the dual target Wolves narrowly missed last season.'

It's obvious by now that bringing John in as a link man between Danny and the forward line is paying off spectacularly. 'Danny was terrific on the ball,' notes Les Allen later, 'but he was getting on in years. That's where John was worth millions. He had such a coverage of the field. You'd see him one way and then he's the other end of the field. I've never seen anyone who could cover the ground so quickly – all over the field, not just on the right. And a lot of ability and skill. Just when you think he's back in defence sorting it out – "Bloody hell, it was John crossing that ball!" He was so far up on the list of assists. He made it easy for you. All you had to do was the finishing. That's the big thing – when there's a player who can pick you out and make it easy for you. He could ping 'em in. So accurate. He did it all the time. He was a good team man.'

Terry Dyson puts it more succinctly. 'John, yeah, he was quiet. He didn't shout. He just turned up in these positions.'

TRAUTMANN STOPS THE SPURS. White Hart Lane, 10 October, a midweek game. The unbeaten run of wins comes to an end with a

1–1 draw against Manchester City, reportedly almost wholly down to Bert Trautmann, 'the greatest goalkeeper in Britain on the miracles performed last night'. Spurs are still undefeated, though. A second sequence builds up, of games without defeat. The City Ground, 15 October: Nottingham Forest are sploshed 4–0. Seven minutes from kick-off, John scores the opening goal; Les Allen spots him 'unmarked in the middle' and it's 'a study in cool artistry' as John 'chipped the ball as neatly over [the goalie's] head into the net as if he had used a niblick'.

Spurs carry on winning, even if the 3–2 victory at home to Cardiff on 22 October is pretty underwhelming and 'ultimately only a disputed penalty got them through'. There's no mention of John – he obviously had a disappointing game along with everyone else – but the following week he's on the score sheet again. St James's Park, 29 October: Newcastle United 3, Spurs 4. 'John White snapped up a loose ball, moved into the penalty area at stupendous speed and smashed the ball into the net.'

Then there is the Bonfire Night game against Fulham at White Hart Lane, where Spurs go into half-time 2–0 up through Les Allen and Cliff Jones. Then, in the last fifteen minutes, it's an onslaught. More goals come, from Cliff, then John, then Les again. The 5–1 win offers more proof – so says the *Evening Standard* – of the rapport established by John and Danny: 'Their strongest point was the ability of Blanchflower and White to divert the frontal point of attack on to Fulham's weak points.' John is 'Scotland's flitting . . . inside-right, a dazzling schemer'. Other positive comments hark back to Spurs' old weakness: 'Danny Blanchflower and his men have developed the power in defence and attack to combat the worst of the weather and the mental toughness to withstand the strain of the big occasion.'

Finally Spurs have a bad day at Hillsborough, where the unbeaten run ends in a 2–1 defeat by Sheffield Wednesday. It's 12 November and their seventeenth game of the season. Significantly, John fails to get the forward line buzzing: 'the rhythm had gone out of the attack and little was seen of White, who is usually the inspiration of the forwards'.

But Spurs have had too good a start to worry very much about that. At St Andrews the following Saturday, 'Scotland's John White started Spurs' victory with a classical goal, and Terry Dyson (2), Cliff Jones (2) and Bobby Smith added to Spurs' glory.' Birmingham City are 'dazzled by the brilliance of Tottenham Hotspur' and Spurs are 'inspired by their Young White Magic'. A Birmingham defence is 'shot to pieces by Spurs kaleidoscopic attack, persuaded forward by White's quiet artistry and the cavorting Jones'. 6–0 is the result.

There's grumbling from the crowd at the Hawthorns, where a disputed first-half goal helps Spurs on the way to a 3–1 win over West Bromwich Albion on 26 November. The goal is the outcome of John's back heel through the legs of a West Brom defender to Bobby Smith. It's claimed that he was standing 'at least three yards offside' but the goal is given. John's cross sets Bobby up for another.

On 3 December, it's pretty wild in both penalty areas at White Hart Lane as last season's champions Burnley hold Spurs to a 4–4 draw. The game, which takes place in dire weather on a boggy pitch, is hailed as 'the match of the century', 'a red-blooded masterpiece' and 'an epic that lifts British football to new heights'. Tottenham are 4–1 up after forty-seven minutes but 4–4 after seventy-five. Reports, though, highlight 'the faultless brilliance of White on the right'. Three of Tottenham's goals are scored in fifteen minutes of the first half, in a series of moves which 'came with a ferocity and a suddenness which shattered Burnley . . . The man who sparked off the spell was inside-right John White. He refused to panic when Burnley had his colleagues reeling with beautiful football in the opening 15 minutes. By continuing to play methodically he steadied the other forwards.'

Deepdale, 10 December. 'PRESTON UNLUCKY TO LOSE' is the headline when Spurs play a side that is already in the relegation zone. The Preston goalie Fred Else is beaten only once 'when John

White pounced on a half-clearance to shoot through a ruck of players after 16 minutes'.

A week later, Tottenham go to Goodison. December starts for them with a 3–1 win over Everton, who are closest to them in the title race. 'LEADERS SUBDUE MIGHTY EVERTON' is one headline as, with what is now a standard piece of action, 'White . . . slipped elusively into the open space, collected Jones's neat chip forward and beat the advancing Dunlop'. By now, there are ten points between Spurs and their pursuers – a gulf which would be impressive in current terms, let alone in 1960 when the system offered two points for a win, not three – and Spurs are being predicted to win the League by a record margin.

SPURS CHASE THE RECORDS

Phew! Spurs go sizzling on at the top of Division One. Four points and five goals were stuffed in their Christmas stocking . . .

Daily Express, 17 December 1970

The Christmas holiday brings symmetry in the form of home and away games against West Ham, with only Christmas Day in between. John scores the first – a diving header – in the 2–0 win at White Hart Lane ('in front White, as elusive as ever, flitted cleverly into the open spaces, the West Ham defenders, like a posse in a Western, constantly arriving either late or in the wrong place').

In the return fixture at Upton Park, where West Ham are beaten 3–0, he scores the second 'nine minutes from the end, running unmarked onto Smith's flick from the left'. And then comes Tottenham's final goal. John once again initiates the move which gives Terry Dyson the opportunity to play a one-two with Bobby Smith.

The *Daily Telegraph*'s end-of-year round-up comes to the conclusion that 'Consistency is the keynote of every department of the prospective champions' make up. Notably in attack where all the regular forwards have reached double figures. Smith . . . has scored 18, Allen 13, White 11, Jones and Dyson 10 each.' The opinion is stood up well in Tottenham's final game of 1960. White Hart Lane, 31 December, and it's Spurs 5, Blackburn Rovers 0. The goals are provided by Les Allen (2), Bobby Smith (2) and Danny Blanchflower, with Les's second 'a tailor-made effort by White'. Everything, though, takes second place to the grit of Tony Marchi, filling in for the injured Dave Mackay. When he jumps for a header in the opening minutes, he ricks his back and can't move without pain. 'Everyone thought Marchi had a poor game,' comments Bill afterwards. 'If they had only known what he was up against they would have realised it was one of his greatest.'

As you read through all the match reports fifty years on, you get the strongest impression possible of how John did it. He was 'unmarked in the middle', he 'flits unnoticed' into positions, he had 'the genius of appearing at the most unsuspected but most productive points of action'. From the descriptive point of view, some of it makes florid reading: 'the delicate dynamite of the Pimpernel player John White'; 'Space-man White – this Scot always manoeuvres in the open spaces', but that doesn't mean that sometimes you would prefer these old-school sports journalists were lost for words. Entertaining readers, conveying the drama of a match and encapsulating the essence of a player or a team in a limited amount of time, without benefit of laptop or mobile, was a challenge. What's more, it's thanks to all this fancy imagery and alliteration that you can infer John's playing style was something so new that it inspired even the most world-weary observers to poetry.

And then, of course, curiosity sets in. When did John's nickname begin to appear? Who first thought of calling him 'the Pale Ghost of White Hart Lane'? Go back again through the match reports of that double season and you find the theme begins to pick up – he's a 'wraith' and a 'phantom', he's 'frail-looking' – by the end of

October, but it takes a bit longer actually to find the game in which the Ghost first walked.

The answer is eventually – and only partly – provided by an ancient clipping from the fifth-round Cup tie against Aston Villa on 18 February 1960: 'And with John White, the Wandering Ghost, in far better form than last week . . .'

Frustratingly, the cutting has no byline; nor is there any indication of the paper in which it appeared, though from the look of the typeface and layout the report ran in the *Sunday Express*. The only other sighting is similarly without date and provenance, but presumably comes from a preview of that match. John is described as 'A Scottish international whose ability to flit into the open spaces has earned him the title, "The Ghost of White-hart [sic] Lane"'.

Perhaps it isn't surprising that – like a lot else to do with John – its origin is vague and elusive. Perhaps only John would have a nickname that arose without fanfare, with the name of whoever coined it lost in the mists of time. As Terry Dyson says of John himself, 'It just turned up.'

THE TOAST TO EACH OTHER CELEBRATES THEIR ENGAGEMENT
The happy couple are 23-year-old Tottenham and Scotland footballer John White and Sandra Evans, 19-year-old daughter of Tottenham's assistant manager.

John met Sandra at Tottenham home games and when he moved from his Musselburgh home to London last year, Mr Evans offered to put him up until he could find digs. He has been there since.

'But I have only been going steady with Sandra for about four months,' he said. 'We have not made any wedding plans yet.'

Slim, honey-blonde Sandra is a research worker for a Canadian public records office in London.

Evening News, March 1961

16

First Sight
Rob, 2010

I first saw my dad as a moving object on a sunny Saturday in May 1973 – the kind of day which, in the 1970s, was paradise for the football fan. Cup Final day was the only one in the calendar that got devoted entirely to the game. *On both channels.*

I can see myself now: getting up early, hastily putting on my boots and football kit, racing downstairs to the living room. If the curtains were closed and the atmosphere fugged by a combination of strong perfume and cigarette smoke that meant Alma, my nan Evans, was already in there, staking out her territory. She smoked all the time – if you went in the bathroom after her it was like being in a sauna sponsored by Benson & Hedges.

I never saw Mum sit and watch a game; it was as though the football part of her life was over. But my nan Evans was a great watcher of football on TV. Sunday afternoons would feature her sitting there kicking an imaginary ball and shouting at *The Big Match*, getting really worked up over something that didn't actually matter much to her in the general scheme of things, like the Swansea City game they always had to throw in for Welsh viewers. It was bizarre, really, to see her so animated because she was quite a glamorous, movie-starish woman in other ways – the Ava Gardner type, sexy and imperious.

So anyway, Cup Final day. Coverage in the seventies would start at 10 a.m. and you'd leap back and forward between the sofa and the control button switching between BBC and ITV. ITV led with *It's A Cup Final Knockout*. Then you'd get *Cup Final Swap Shop*; *Cup Final A Question of Sport*; *How They Got to Wembley*; *Meet the Players' Wives*.

From midday, *Grandstand* and *World of Sport* kicked in: The Teams Leave Their Hotel; Elton Welsby Doing Interviews on the Team Bus. There would be flashbacks to previous Cup Finals, and that was when I first saw my dad as a moving object in a clip of the 1961 final – Leicester v Spurs.

It didn't go on for long. He just darted forward and delivered a cross. But I felt an instant connection. You can always recognise your own type and here was the blueprint. Actually to see physical evidence, even though it was in black and white, felt fabulously, heart-poundingly exciting and moving. You don't think these things consciously at nine years old but here was that tangible, irrefutable evidence – not just that he was a great player but that I was part of him and he was part of me.

Much later on we got a video player and when someone gave me the video of that final I watched it over and over again, comparing our common mannerisms and movements. I had the same arms. Edwin and Tom were great bull-like men with massive thighs, but Dad and I were wiry and fine-boned. I studied the way he ran. It wasn't a strange running style but it wasn't the normal free-flowing gait either. He covered the ground in short quick steps, upright and light-footed; he reminded me of a Highland dancer. And, as you would do, I promptly ran along the shopping parade in Winchmore Hill watching my reflection all the way. I ran like him too.

These days I probably spend far too much time looking at old clips of Spurs on YouTube. Every time I do, I feel the same as I did when I first discovered the cardboard box of treasures. Firstly, that these players – my dad and his team-mates – are real football heroes; they seem to have so much time and space. Secondly, that it never takes me long to find him – I've still got the same sort of primal instinct – and that as soon as I do my concentration freezes on every detail. Thirdly, that everything around me has stopped and that I have a sense of enchantment and a huge hole in my chest at the same time.

The hollow feeling isn't the raw grief of bereavement, just sadness at the loss of knowing my dad. Yet as usual when I look at him it's magical. To see him move really brings him to life. He's celebrating with Cliff and Peter and Terry – running and smiling. Look at the way his socks are pulled up right to his knees, while Bobby's and Dave's are corrugated round their ankles – he's so smart and tidy. See how pale he looks, while Danny is red-faced with effort. Those details are what makes it so special. To see him so wonderfully and comprehensively alive is fantastic.

Maybe this is why – in spite of all rational evidence to the contrary – I still find myself asking the same questions. Is he still around in some way? Does he know I'm looking for him? I guess I think he is, and he does.

To explain why, we need to go back to the seventies again, and a strip in *Roy of The Rovers* called 'Billy's Boots'. It was about a kid who owned a pair of boots with mystical powers. They'd belonged to some old player and when Billy wore them his game would be directed by an unearthly force that naturally resulted in triumph.

From when I was about eight to my teenage years, not just when I was playing football but during all the standard adolescent dilemmas and dramas, there'd be times when I'd try and think myself into the 'Billy's Boots' mindset. It wasn't necessarily about wanting the magic touch that would bring me victory, or even simply help getting through. What it all boiled down to, really, was wanting to know that in some way my dad was still there for me.

Around the time I was fourteen, the hope that there was something more of him available than just photos and clips morphed into conviction. I was round at a friend's; we were having a seance. As you do. Six or seven or us, closing the curtains, fingers on the upturned glass. There were a lot of questions I wanted to ask but I was too scared. Maybe I just pushed the glass a bit harder as I felt it move from letter to letter to spell out a sentence . . .

H-O-W-J-A-N-E-T-T-E-I-S.

OK, it wasn't the most amazingly coherent sequence of words. But any doubts I felt were eradicated right there. Ever since, I've never been less than 100 per cent certain that the person we contacted was my father. It couldn't have been a trick. Nobody there would have known Janette's name – people haven't a clue who your aunties and uncles are. It had to be him.

Many years later, curiosity drove me to see a clairvoyant at Bloomsbury Theatre, where I spent the evening alternately paralysed with self-conscious fear that she'd say something specific to me in front of the audience and crestfallen when she didn't, because I felt absolutely certain that something was going to happen.

Something did. Something strange. At the end of the session, she said: 'I can see someone wearing wet-weather gear. Something to do with really bad weather.'

Then, I was euphoric. Bad weather! Maybe it was all a bit vague – Dad hadn't been playing golf decked out in oilskins or a sou'wester – but this had to be connected to a lightning bolt, surely!

Hmm.

Thinking it over now, it's easy to explain away. A clairvoyant is bound to get something right at some point – it's the law of averages. More than that, if you want something very badly – and I would have accepted my father reappearing as a giant skateboarding penguin if that was what it took – you'll bend any flimsy bit of material to fit your case. Even so, a small but insistent conviction is still lodged in my mind that if I discover the right password or mantra or have the right key then I'll meet him in some way.

In my more rational moods – which is most of the time, day to day – I see that I will never really know about my dad, and the man who was hero enough to be part of that fantastic team in that unrepeatable era was lost to me on 21 July 1964. But I choose to hope this will one day be disproved. And in some way, though he'll never walk into the room, I know he's there.

In the meantime, I'm left with these fantastic magical pictures of him doing what he did, and trying – still – to access some, I don't know, molecule, or little branch line in my DNA, that trace memory somehow located in a remote synapse that will put me right there – with him? as part of him? – in the Double year: scoring six minutes from kick-off against Aston Villa in September; taking Wolves apart in October; carving holes in the Sunderland defence in March; sitting in the dressing room at Wembley listening to Bill Nicholson's pre-match pep talk followed by Danny Blanchflower's rallying speech before going out to play Leicester.

And in finding it I'll get the answer to all my questions. There's so many of them I probably won't know where to begin. Though as good a starting place as any would be with that 1961 Leicester v Spurs final.

What was it like to walk out onto the Wembley pitch that day, knowing you were ninety minutes away from doing what the world thought was impossible?

How did it feel to win the Double?

11 MEN JUMP FOR JOY

A trainer weighs up his team

Cecil Poynton takes a candid look at the pride of Tottenham as they prepare for the FA Cup Final.

Inside-right John White (24): A fine ball-player who has never needed attention from Poynton on the field. Extremely quiet, studious footballer, who likes a sniff of ammonia on leaving the dressing room.

Shoot magazine, May, 1960

17

Immortality

White Hart Lane, March 1960. John shifts his shoulders and miraculously finds a sliver of air between two defenders. He takes up as much room as a swipe card.

The shot he makes skews off a Sunderland man's boot, but this prize has Tottenham's name written on it already. The ball goes straight to Les Allen's foot. Les barely has to twitch a toe to put Spurs one up.

The match is the FA Cup sixth-round replay between Spurs and Sunderland. It's four days after Sunderland – they're in the Second Division – have held Spurs to a 1–1 draw at their ground, Roker Park. Spurs, leading the First Division, have to win or they can forget about the Double.

John sends Cliff Jones away. It's a searing shot, deflected by the Sunderland goalie, only for Bobby Smith to barge and batter his way to hooking the ball back from an unfeasible angle. Two goals up in half an hour, both made by John.

Wherever it was he went, the wait is over. John has come back.

You have to rewind to the start of the year to see how important that match was for John. In the weeks leading up to it he had been well out of form for all but a couple of games. Then again, the whole side was feeling the pressure. By the start of the new year, they had twenty-five games behind them. Their record was remarkable: twenty-two wins, two draws, a solitary defeat. In the process they had scored eighty-one goals. But by the time they turned out for the FA Cup third-round tie against Charlton at the end of the first week in January, they were reduced to taking the field with a line of battered bodies. Bill Brown was out of it, Dave played with his knee bandaged up, and it was small wonder Bobby Smith had been off form – he kept going in spite of a small crater in the inflamed bone on the outside of his right knee. Cliff, meanwhile, hadn't played since getting injured in the Christmas Eve game against West Ham, when he ended up limping so badly he was taken off with twenty minutes to go, leaving Spurs with only ten men.

In fact, at this point anyone who feels misty-eyed about football in the early sixties might like to bear two things in mind. The first is that the kind of tackles they went in for then would have made Holland's brutalising of Spain in the 2010 World Cup final look slightly effete. The second is that the rules hadn't yet been relaxed to allow substitutions, so as long as an injured player was conscious and capable of some sort of movement he was kept on the pitch. 'If he was walking wounded they'd stick him out on the left wing where he might still be able to pass with his good leg or something,' says the journalist Ronald Atkin. 'It used to piss me off because I was a left-winger and they obviously thought it was the least important position.'

Terry Dyson hobbled through the Charlton match – Spurs won 3–2 – after getting clattered in the early minutes. He was lucky such a prolonged insult to his ankle didn't put him out for weeks. 'Physios never had training then,' he says now. 'They read everything out of a book. Twist an ankle, they'd get you to put it in a bucket of cold water. Or just rub it with oils or whatnot.'

John didn't get injured, but he was struggling nevertheless. It wasn't the crass and malevolent tackling, or the pressure, or the wear and tear of aquaplaning over boggy winter pitches that affected him, but an inexplicable lowering of mood and loss of form. The trick, Danny Blanchflower had told him, was to know your own capabilities; you recognised a bad day when you saw one, rode with it and took fewer chances. The problem was, there were too many bad days. Lethargy seemed to zap him every year around that time, whatever he tried; these days he'd probably be told it was seasonal affective disorder and prescribed the updated version of 'oils or whatnot'. Back then, he simply got on with it.

The last thing he – in fact, any of the side – could have wanted was a League game at Old Trafford two days after beating Charlton. It wasn't much of a surprise that Manchester United won 2–0. Cliff, who still wasn't fit, missed that match too, though he returned after three weeks out in time for the Arsenal game on the Saturday. That day Tottenham's opponents tackled – and hacked at – Cliff in a sturdy way that suggested a message had gone out to give him a hard time. Vic Railton of the *Evening News* described his treatment thus: 'The Welsh wizard . . . was brought down at least four times by heavy tackling, but came up smiling each time.' 'Cliff was incredibly quick and brave,' says Ken Jones. 'He'd not wait for crosses, he'd come in to look for the ball. Only five foot seven but he'd go crashing in.' John did have a halfway decent game against Arsenal; he made Spurs' final goal in their 4–2 win.

Spurs didn't have much trouble beating Crewe 5–1 in the FA Cup fourth-round tie that followed, but February began with a bad-tempered clash with Leicester and the 3–2 loss of their unbeaten home record. When they met Aston Villa in a League fixture, it was just a week before they were due to meet again in the fifth round of the Cup. The result that first afternoon was Aston Villa 1, Spurs 2, but John and Cliff were both judged to be guilty of 'weak play . . . way below their normal form'.

The following Saturday in the Cup tie it was a different story: Cliff scored both Tottenham goals, Villa scored nothing and John was said to be 'having a wonderful match after last week's flop', 'slipping the lunging Villa tackles like a wraith' and giving the Villa defence 'a harrowing time'. But the home game against Wolves which followed fizzled out in a 1–1 draw: 10-MEN WOLVES TAME THE SPURS.

Wolves, one of the clubs now closing in on Spurs, were down to ten men after ten minutes when their centre-back endured the Bobby

Smith Experience – taken away to get his ribs strapped after Bobby collided with him while scoring Spurs' only goal. During their winning sequence back in the autumn Spurs would never have let go of the advantage. This time, Danny Blanchflower gave away a goal within another ten minutes when he rejected a plain clearance shot in favour of a fancy pass. John, too, 'fell into the error of trying to be too clever when straightforward tactics were needed'.

The game on 1 March saw Harry Evans in charge of the side who went to Maine Road for the League match against Manchester City; Bill was at Leeds watching Sunderland, Spurs' opponents in the following Saturday's Cup tie. In another rufty-tufty game (Bobby Smith v the City goalie Steve Flett was the highlight), Spurs won with a goal by Terry Medwin, stand-in for a now flu-stricken Cliff. And then came Sunderland.

ROKER ROAR RATTLES SPURS
Sunderland 1, Spurs 1
Five minutes after half-time, a roaring inferno of sound erupted from the packed bowl of Roker Park. Sunderland, one goal down and fighting like red-and-white-striped furies, had majestic Spurs rocking right-back on their educated heels . . .

Alan Hoby, *Sunday Express*, March 1961

Like the lost opportunity against Wolves, this was exactly the sort of game that five months back would have been problem-free. Instead, after Cliff had put them into a first-half lead an eighteen-year-old number 10 called Billy McPheat announced himself with an equaliser just after the restart. Spurs were totally fazed. No one was where they had dreamed of being. If they couldn't beat Sunderland, they certainly wouldn't be able to hold everything together in the title race. Beating a Second Division team was a basic, Year One qualification. Without that, there would be no Double.

Reports in the papers were scathing: 'Blanchflower, White and

Allen, all key men, failed to find the customary accuracy of pass.' John, in particular, was singled out. He was never to recover his 'poise and accuracy' during the game; after being presented with a 'dream chance', he 'blazed wildly over the bar'; 'Tottenham's forwards could not find any rhythm, largely because White was not putting his passes right.'

Then abruptly, after that day at Roker, a corner was turned. It's impossible to identify what it was – perhaps recovery from fatigue, or the sudden awareness of the lighter days. But after weeks of struggling to find his touch, the whole picture seemed to brighten. A burst of energy propelled John forward. His mojo was working again and he could sense the patterns made by his team-mates without having to think about them consciously. His opponents found it impossible once again to keep track of his movements.

It sounds miraculous to the point of absurdity, but at the replay with Sunderland, which Spurs won 5–0, everything he did went right. The goals were from Les, Bobby, Terry (two) and Dave, but it was John (that 'flitting genius') who set them up: 'White, who with Danny Blanchflower fashioned the stream of fantasies of soccer which streamed from Spurs . . .'; 'Amid all the hubbub one man stood out – the frail-looking White at his impeccable best. The match had three decisive moments, and the first came from one of White's inimitable moves . . .' ; 'In a twinkling White unfolded two matchless individual efforts . . . Recovering instantly when beaten . . . he turned like a hare and shook the crossbar with a drive. Next, opening a gap in defence with a twist of the shoulders, he glided through and shot. The ball spun off Hurley. Allen, racing in, lashed it in.'

It would be going too far to say everything was easy from then on. Just before the Cup semi-final against Burnley, Spurs lost 3–2 at Cardiff. The press verdict was that 'Cardiff's middle line . . . was on peak form and Allen and White were blotted out'. But at Villa Park on 18 March Tottenham safely negotiated the obstacle of Burnley 3–0 (John made the third goal, for Cliff).

So Spurs were going to Wembley, and a Cup final against Leicester

City. Whether they'd be going there as League champions suddenly didn't seem such a certainty. Since the beginning of the year, they'd been averaging a point a game, and experiencing a steady erosion in their lead which, by the evening of 18 March, Sheffield Wednesday had reduced to four points. On 15 April the two sides were due to meet at White Hart Lane. By then, would that game be the decider?

On 22 March, Newcastle sauntered away winners from White Hart Lane. Three days later, Spurs drew at Fulham. It was almost a month since they had won in the League. Meanwhile, up at Hillsborough, Wednesday occupied themselves by crushing Manchester United 5–0.

If you ask the surviving members of the Double side about it now, they talk as though it was a breeze. You suspect, however, that distance has lent insouciance. The reality of the Double was that every game played was increasingly challenging, pressurised and important, and to keep winning week after week, month after month, entailed extreme self-belief, discipline and desire. The reality was that the Double was bloody hard.

It wasn't enough just to be better than everyone else. The stuff that goes on in a football team's collective subconscious is for the neurologists and shrinks to explore, but even so there's got to be, surely, some very thin yet powerful and unbreakable dividing line between detached and often narcissistic individualism and the profound, rock-hard commitment to each other and a cause that makes one group of players throw themselves into it body and soul – and, in doing so, carry with them the knowledge that even then they might fail – while another team, comparably skilful, will only take it so far, till the prospect of easing back and relaxing and no longer having to fight becomes more attractive than a prize there are no guarantees of winning.

Which was exactly what had happened to Spurs a year back. And as they pushed themselves through the spring of 1961, each of them must have gone through a similar unconscious process. Did they want the Double or not? They had lost out on it once. They didn't want to lose out again. If they gave up now, they would be known forever as the side that bottled it, brilliant but spineless. All that thinking and training and innovation would be thrown away. Everything they'd worked for since pre-season training back in July. All they'd gone through physically – exhaustion, cuts, bruises, knocks, sweat and pain.

If they failed at the last moment, it wouldn't be because they didn't have the talent. It would be because they didn't have the nerve. They could decide to commit themselves to giving everything, in spite of the aches and tiredness. Knowing that if they did it they would live in people's memories long after they had gone. Or they could give up now, take comfort in having played the best football and look back on what they'd done as a triumph of sorts – proof that even the most outstanding team in the land couldn't do it because the Double was impossible.

At Easter, they made their decision.

Immortality it had to be.

SPURS MAKE IT RECORD EASTER TREBLE.

Good Friday, White Hart Lane: Spurs 4, Chelsea 2.

Easter Saturday, White Hart Lane: Spurs 5, Preston North End 0; 'White, that slim perfectionist, is drifting secretly to the left-wing as he was in the best days of autumn.'

Easter Monday, Stamford Bridge: Chelsea 2, Spurs 3.

The following Saturday, at St Andrews, they beat Birmingham 3–2. It doesn't, on paper, look like a demolition job, but one reporter was moved to give Leicester 'a personal warning. John White has run into form at the right time. I thought he had a magnificent first half, beating men with his passing and footwork. He had a part in nearly every attack.' Sheffield Wednesday managed only a draw against Leicester that day. Even so, they were still arguably in with a chance when they arrived at White Hart Lane on 15 April for what was nominally the title decider. In 1951, the push-and-run side had lifted the League title against Wednesday and now it was game on again.

A goal down after twenty-nine minutes through Wednesday's Don Megson, tension pulled Spurs away from their fluent, fierce football, made them slightly hesitant, fractionally inaccurate. Both sides were terrifying in the tackle; Dave Mackay had his name taken – a big deal back then – and Cliff needed two stitches in his knee. But the title was clinched in two minutes of brilliant mayhem. Three minutes before half-time, Terry Dyson beat Wednesday's Peter Swan – calling him practically twice Terry's height isn't too much of an exaggeration – in the air and laid a header back to Bobby Smith. Bobby pulled it down as if he had glue on his boots, turned and volleyed it home. One minute later, Maurice Norman headed a free kick down to Les Allen, whose right foot produced the championship-sealing goal.

Half the Double was theirs. Now for the other half.

By the week of the final, Spurs had lost two of the last three League games and were said to be playing relegation-zone football. It was easy to make a case for Leicester, who'd been the first side to beat Spurs in a League game that season and who had Gordon Banks in goal. 'Leicester were a very advanced team and the Double side didn't finish the season very well,' says the journalist David Lacey. 'They were sort of limping to the finishing tape.'

But at every defining moment in the season – the crushing of Aston Villa and Wolves on the cusp of September and October, the replay against Sunderland, victory over Villa again, this time in the Cup fifth round – it had been John who made the difference. So was he, they asked themselves, going to do it again?

The day before the final, they'd gone to Wembley. 'We were just messing about on the pitch,' says Cliff, 'and John was doing an imaginary commentary in a Kenneth Wolstenholme voice. "The ball comes floating across to White on the eighteen-yard line. He rifles the ball past Banks in the Leicester City goal! And White has scored, five minutes after kick-off!"'

So what happened?

'The next day in the first ten minutes he gets a chance in almost exactly the same place,' says Cliff. 'It was the chance he was talking about. The ball comes to him. And he smacks it over the top of the bar. It sails down the tunnel somewhere. *Not* according to plan.'

In fact, the final itself was frustratingly mundane and anticlimactic. The Wembley pitch felt to them as though they were playing on cushions; it slowed them up. The fear of losing, at the very last obstacle, being the one who missed the open goal, or conceded the penalty, seemed to leach away most of the passion. But it wouldn't be right to say they played with the lack of zest that they would take to a no-mark mid-table game. They had so much adrenaline they felt choked by it. So it was as if everything conspired to stop Spurs playing their normal game.

Spurs found the Leicester defence hard to crack. Then, with nineteen minutes gone, the Leicester right-back Len Chalmers didn't see Les Allen coming into the tackle and turned; trying to block the ball, Les caught his leg. From then on, Chalmers was a passenger on the wing. Ten-man Leicester were making fewer breakaways. Nothing much was happening in either goalmouth because both defences were on top. Ron Henry, masterly in his tackling, interception and use of the ball, was Spurs' best player.

'It wasn't a very good game,' says Cliff, who had a goal disallowed a few minutes before half-time. 'Ten men always defend well. They don't usually win games but they make things much harder. Leicester usually played an open game too, but at Wembley they shut the space down a lot more and made it hard for us to play. John and Danny weren't really involved.'

The real action didn't happen till the second half: Les Allen and Terry Dyson's build-up, Terry's pass, Bobby Smith taking a quick chance. He saw Gordon Banks move one way so he changed his mind and shot the other way. Then he fell over. It was only when his pals began to thump him on the back that Bobby realised he had scored.

Spurs relaxed into something like their true selves. Leicester had had the stuffing knocked out of them. With seventy-seven minutes on the clock, Terry met a mighty centre from Bobby to head the second goal. Two minutes later, as if to symbolise Leicester's acceptance of defeat, Len Chalmers hobbled off the pitch.

And that was that, really. Final whistle. The Double done. There were no more challenges, no more vital games, only a grudging ackowledgement from Bill. 'He was so dissatisfied with them over that game,' says the journalist Ken Jones. 'He just felt they hadn't played.'

Well, Bill was Bill. Study the footage now and you see John next to Cliff as they get their medals. He looks as though he's in paradise. They all do, and it *was* paradise.

Because the Double has become a relatively commonplace achievement in modern football – it's taken for granted that any club with the financial resources to buy the world's best players and maintain a vast squad should manage it – you tend to overlook how groundbreaking it was in 1961. Clubs had been trying since Aston Villa in 1897 – in a much smaller League and considerably different circumstances – but no one could bring it off. It was like walking on the moon or building a city in the sea – an impossible dream. Only an extraordinary, exceptional group of men could have done it.

'It's a mystery really, what that team had,' says Ken Jones. 'It was a team that took chances. It was a very mature team – they respected Bill's knowledge and understanding. Bill himself was a dour wing half back player but a romantic when it came to coaching. The Double was his dream. And Danny's belief brought it to fruition.'

'The Double,' says Les Allen. 'It just flowed. It was special – I wish I'd realised at the time just how special it was. Bill Brown could throw the ball and it'd just go like that –' he traces a pair of zigzags – 'and it'd end up in the net the other end. We used to do it in training. Against the reserves. It just used to happen. Bill Nicholson would ghost through it till everyone knew what they were doing. He didn't have to build a team atmosphere, either. It was always there, and John was a big factor.'

Some found it astonishing that so slight and frail-looking a character could have played at that level at all, even more so the fact that of the six who played every game, one was John. Anyone who was surprised clearly didn't know him.

Back at the Evanses' house in Berkeley Gardens the day after the final, he spent most of the day getting stick from his family for missing a sitter. Fair enough – the Ghost hadn't really turned up. In the scheme of things, though, did it matter? Twenty-four years old, yet to reach his prime, he was part of a team which had performed magic, turned a ball game into art, created beauty in a mean and dreary world, and he knew there was much more to come. This was a player who as a teenager was told he was too small and weak to make it at the top level; who was turned aside thirteen times by Rangers, the club of his boyhood dreams; who was shy and unconfident to an almost laughable degree. And yet, when he arrived at Spurs in his early twenties, through his genius for the unexpected, his unselfishness and his energy, he transformed Tottenham's fortunes from runners-up with a reputation for bottling it to a team of immortals. Thin, pale, quiet, he was the Wandering Ghost, the self-effacing, mysterious boy who no one noticed until it was too late. Perhaps that was his most impressive piece of magic of all – taking ownership of his biggest weakness and turning it into his greatest strength.

LAST-MINUTE DRAMA ENDS A DREAM

Scotland 2, Czechoslovakia 4 (after extra time)

Brussels, Wednesday night. A nudge shattered Scotland's dream of going to Chile for the World Cup . . . with only 30 seconds of the 90 minutes to go. The score was 2–2. John White put through a perfect pass. Denis Law streaked for the ball, with the centre-half running alongside. Denis got there first. But just as he put his foot to the ball to shoot . . . the Czech nudged him. He was knocked off balance – and the ball flew over the bar.

Daily Record, 30 November 1961

18

Chile, Bye-Bye

There's a school of thought – OK, it might not be one with a massively long roll – which holds that if John hadn't made that trip to the golf course in July 1964, the Jules Rimet Trophy would have ended up in a different display cabinet in 1966. To this day, Denis Law maintains that if they'd had John White then Scotland, not England, would have been champions of the world.

Ian St John agrees, at least on the quality of the putative World Cup holders. 'Between him, Denis and myself you could not have picked a better trio,' he says. 'John had a flow about him and gave great service. He had great energy. Denis was electric and used to feed off that service and he was always looking for flicks. All three of us really complemented each other, and with Davie Wilson on the wing Scotland were always a real threat. It was a real shame we never qualified for a World Cup.'

That it was. Ian, Denis and John were part of the so-called 'golden generation' of the early sixties, a side you could describe as top dollar and it wouldn't raise eyebrows. The team of all the talents – Scotland could call on the services of Bill Brown, Alex Hamilton, Eric Caldow, Pat Crerand, Jim Baxter, Ian Ure, Dave Mackay, Willie Henderson, Alec Scott, Ian St John, Davie Wilson and Denis Law along with John – were described by Brian James as: 'Arrogant, aggressive and confident in their skill, superb in the way they faced the challenge . . . the Scots played like men.'

They also played, ultimately, in a lost cause. To Ian's mind, the problem was simple: 'We really never had a manager in those days.

The manager when we first played was briefly a guy called Andy Beattie, but the team was actually picked by committee, and the best way to find out whether you were playing was to buy the evening paper. Scotland had the players, just no one to pull them together. The SFA never realised what they had, they were amateur, naive and had no class. It was really only the spirit of the players that made representing Scotland such an honour. If they'd had a manager like Bill Shankly they would have been world-beaters.' 'Compared to what we have now, they were wonderful,' says the journalist Rodger Baillie.

John had earned his right to the 'golden generation' tag when he'd scored on his debut in the friendly against West Germany in May 1959. At the time, the *Daily Record*'s Waverley wrote: 'He is one to depend on for the future.' That might have been easier said than done. 'Anglos' – Scottish players with English clubs – often seemed to be, at varying stages of that period, unavailable or unwelcome, and John was within months of going to Tottenham. In 1959, according to Brian James in his book *England v Scotland*: 'the S.F.A. had been told that a number of Scottish First Division clubs were pressing for a complete ban on "Anglos" . . . The Scottish clubs had been far from impressed by the coincidence that their star players most frequently asked for transfers after mingling with "Anglos" – the suggestion was that, at best, Scotland's home stars were being tempted by careless talk about the money made in England, or, at worst, that the "Anglos" were being used as recruiting agents.'

'It seems a shame that many of the great players who went south went through a period where it became difficult for them to get picked for Scotland,' says Ian St John, who left Motherwell for Liverpool in 1961. 'The team was picked by a committee of selectors and at that time it sometimes made sense for them to raise the profile of players at the clubs where they were board members thereby making those players easier to transfer. Playing in England and getting picked for the Scotland side meant that you had to be doing really well as a player, and it's quite amazing that we managed to get the number of caps that we did.' Opposition also came from Scottish managers, who proceeded to thump their tubs in the sports pages. One such offered the SFA the ultimatum: 'Pick my players, or pick "Anglos" . . . I won't have them mixing with each other.' It was a sentiment that often seemed to be shared by the journalists themselves.

'In Scotland, it was always a good opt-out on a slow news day for a columnist to say Ban the Anglos,' says Rodger Baillie. He doubts, though, that John's total of twenty-two Scottish caps would have been larger if he hadn't been victim of some anti-Anglo conspiracy. That had largely fizzled out as an issue by the time he was in contention for a regular place in the international squad. Instead, opposition came from closer to home. Embroiled in the ill-fated challenge for the 1959–60 League championship, Bill Nicholson had taken Spurs away for a breather at Brighton when Scotland contacted him to ask for the services of Bill Brown, Dave Mackay and John in the May 1960 home international at Hampden. Bill refused to release them.

Later Bill recanted, telling Brian James: 'I was wrong, both from Scotland's viewpoint and our own. I became convinced . . . that insisting these players stayed with the club cost us the League title. They were upset about my decision. They didn't go about shouting the odds, but it affected them all. None of them were ever as effective in the last matches as they had been until then. I don't think they were bloody-minded, the title meant as much to them as it did to me. But they couldn't seem to shake off the effect of being disappointed over missing those caps. We would have been better to have let them go, perhaps lost that match . . . but have had them returning full of pep for the rest of the season.' That was the season Spurs finished eventually two points down on the champions, Burnley.

Even so, while the twenty-two caps John did receive might not seem a huge number for someone that good, you can look at it another way – there weren't that many up for grabs. In that era, other than the three home fixtures a year and perhaps an odd friendly, the only internationals were the World Cups. There was also the matter of timing. 'By the time John joined Falkirk, it was just after the 1958 World Cup in Sweden,' says Rodger. 'It's unlikely he would have played in that because he would have been very young when the qualifiers were being played, and hadn't even moved from Alloa. It was remarkable that he was picked even at Falkirk.'

It's unarguable, too, that come 1961 John's status in the Scotland squad was that of first pick. That was the year they were attempting to qualify for the 1962 World Cup in Chile. Drawn in UEFA Group 8, they beat the Republic of Ireland home and away in the first week of May before heading off to Bratislava to meet Czechoslokia. They lost 4–0. Hostilities resumed on 26 September in Glasgow; the result was Scotland 3, Czechoslovakia 2. In October, Czechoslovakia went on to beat the Republic of Ireland both in Dublin and in Prague. Scotland and Czechoslovakia were going to have to meet again on neutral territory in a play-off the following month.

While all that was going on, of course, there were two other matters competing for John's attention. One was the climax of the Double season and the start of the next, with Spurs going into Europe for the first time. The other concerned his personal life. He married Sandra.

By the time John moved in with Harry Evans and his family, Sandra had already met him twice, once at one of the players' post-match get-togethers in the Bell and Hare and then on one of the occasions when Harry brought him home for Sunday lunch. He didn't make a huge impression either time – 'He seemed to be very shy, not noisy like the others.'

Not that shy, it turned out. During his first week in residence at Harry's, John overheard Sandra tell Alma she was going to the cinema to see *The Birds*, and invited himself along. What happened pretty much sums John up. 'At one moment during the film he hid under the seats,' said Sandra, 'and it took a few minutes before I realised he was joking. And obviously not as quiet and shy as I thought.'

The next development isn't hugely surprising – they became an item. On dates they usually went to the cinema or hung out in the Rose and Crown on Church Street, where they'd sit in the little snug bar with a shandy or lager and lime (neither of them were drinkers). Most of the other players were married, with children; they babysat for Joan and Cliff Jones, the Browns and the Mackays. And Sandra saw a lot of great football.

'I remember the atmosphere of every match,' says Sandra. 'There was a church on the bus route we took and if we saw a wedding taking place that was a good sign. In the evening, it was magic. There was a romance about it. There was a nice atmosphere in the team. They all got on. It was a good time. Everything was going right. It's when it's all before you. Weren't we lucky?

'I don't think he ever got into the Tottenham glamour bit. He didn't take fame particularly seriously – he used to laugh if he was recognised, though he was quite pleased to be asked to sign autographs. He was shy on the surface, a bit quiet, but he had this other side where he was very funny and made you laugh. He used to whistle when he was upset. I think I was a bit of a princess, and sometimes there was some whistling. But I can't remember him ever losing his temper.'

John had already made up his mind they'd get married and that Christmas he bought her a red coat – 'You can imagine, it was the best coat in the world' – and she wore it for the Cup tie against Sunderland. 'When Bill saw me, he roared, "You shouldn't be wearing that." I had no idea he wouldn't have anything red around because it was Arsenal.'

She had gone up to Sunderland on her own on the Friday and stayed in a hotel Harry had arranged for her. 'The plan was for John and me to go on up to Musselburgh with John's cousin Bobby Wilson and Uncles Tommy and Tam who had gone down to Sunderland by car. Then after the game ended in a draw Bill was most reluctant to let us go, but very grudgingly let us on condition that we fly back early on Monday morning.'

By then they were officially engaged. They'd planned a May wedding but postponed it because of the birth of Sandra's brother Andrew in March. But they went back to Scotland that summer to meet the rest of John's family, arriving separately – Sandra, who was at work, flew up the week after John drove up in his new Ford Zodiac. 'He passed his test in two weeks and drove up the A1. He saw a couple of blokes hitching back to Catterick, said, "Do either of you drive?" got in the back and went to sleep. He could sleep anywhere – he had this immense power just to shut off. I went to meet him after a game at West Brom once, and all the others came out but not him. I asked where he was and they said, "Fast asleep on the bench."'

After Sandra met John's folk – Uncle Thomas, the Lord Provost of Musselburgh, officially welcomed her into the family 'in spite of the fact you're English' – she and John spent a few days on their own. They drove around Fort William and Oban – 'pretending we were married because that was the only way you could have a double room in a hotel in those days'. After that, fate pushed things along. In mid-September, while John was away with Spurs – it was the preliminary round of the European Cup, against the Polish club Gornik Zabrze – Sandra decided to see the club doctor because she had started being sick in the mornings. When she confessed to Alma she was pregnant, Alma's response was fairly traditional: 'Oh dear, I don't know what your dad's going to say.' Sandra remembers sitting on her bed, trembling as she waited for Harry to return from Poland with the team, but he was, she says, 'lovely – he came in and put his arms round me and said, "You don't have to marry him if you don't want to"'.

She did want to. 'I'd been out with boys but nothing serious. John was my first love. It was one of those times in your life when everything feels right. He was who I wanted to spend the rest of my life with.' They married on 16 October 1961, at the register office in Bromley, the London suburb where Alma's mother lived.

They kept the wedding quiet and didn't even ask anyone down from Scotland. 'Nobody realised he was a footballer. You couldn't get away with that today. They asked what his profession was and he told them he was a joiner, so he wasn't recognised. But then we went to the Trocadero in Piccadilly afterwards, and they played the Spurs tune 'MacNamara's Band' as we walked down the staircase. John was really embarrassed and came out in a sweat, and yet he'd play in front of all those crowds.'

They didn't have a honeymoon. There wasn't time; apart from John's club commitments, there was the Scotland v Wales international at Hampden on 8 November. Sandra flew up from London to watch. 'John was meant to tell his mum that we'd got married and that she was going to be a grandmother. I sat next to John's cousin Margaret at the football and from something she said it quickly became apparent that John hadn't said a thing. Well, he probably didn't like to after the other one.'

Scotland's 2–0 defeat of Wales – Ian St John scored both goals – was looked on as a good omen for their World Cup play-off against Czechoslovakia in Brussels later that month. John was picked along with the two other Tottenham Scots, Bill Brown and Dave Mackay; so was another Anglo, Alex Young of Everton. Denis Law, then playing in Italy for Torino, was also in. The play-off was due to happen on 29 November, by which time injury had picked off several members of the sixteen-strong squad. Alex Scott and Davie Wilson had gone. Dave Mackay, named in the squad five hours after Spurs had announced he would be out for at least three weeks with a hairline fracture in his skull after the European Cup tie against Feyenoord, failed to make the miracle recovery the Scottish selectors hoped for. Bill Brown dropped out as well, leaving John the only member of the Spurs trio to make the team.

A draw was going to be enough for the Czechs, who had a better goal average; Scotland needed to win, and a lot of hopes rested on Denis Law. The Wednesday-morning preview in the *Scottish Daily*

Express gave the forward line: Ralph Brand, John White, Ian St John, Denis Law, Hugh Robertson. In the opinion of their columnist, John Mackenzie: 'It is a line up that could get goals . . . I am convinced Crerand, Baxter, Law and White can keep us on top in the middle of the field.'

In fact, the game turned out the way a lot of Scotland's games have done before and since – a triumph of disillusionment over certainty. The headline in next day's *Daily Express* says it all:

CHILE, BYE-BYE!
SAD-FACED FANS WATCH CZECHOSLOVAKIA CRUSH SCOTLAND
IN WORLD CUP DECIDER

At 2–1 up – Ian St John scored both Scotland's goals – with less than ten minutes to go, they lost 4–2 in extra time. Denis Law and John took the most flak: 'only shadows of the players who did so well in the last game at Hampden'; 'Heads will roll and the blond head of Denis Law will be the main target'; 'Close behind Law for ineffectiveness was John White. The slim Tottenham man, harried, heckled, hustled and intimidated by the crunching Czechs, lived up to his nickname of the "ghost". He floated in and out of the game, mostly out of it.'

'He understood and carried out to the letter his instructions about the tactics,' said Scotland's manager Ian McColl later, 'even though it put him in the position of carrying the can for mistakes. He never complained.'

'Historically and with very great respect it wasn't an ignominious defeat because Czechoslovakia went on to be beaten finalists against Brazil,' says Rodger Baillie. 'If John had been spared to 1966, most of that team were still around, but, without him, and to our eternal shame and fury, we failed to qualify. Still, it's purely hypothetical, isn't it? Now there's hardly any in the Scotland international squad who play in the Premiership. Most of the Scotland to

England transfers now are to teams in the Championship. Which is sad. Greater minds than mine would struggle to give an explanation.'

As Rodger says, it's purely hypothetical. But language and logic are one thing; how you feel about it is something else again. On the day England played West Germany in the 1966 World Cup final, Denis Law was so determined to ignore the whole issue that he played golf 'while 27,000,000 other Britons crouched at their televisions'. He was coming up to the seventeenth fairway, struggling three holes down to his opponent, when a passing player shouted: 'Have you heard? England won.' Law flung his club at a nearby bush. 'That just about completes my bloody day.'

And even now, to some, the loss of John and the waste of the talent that was the golden generation still matters an awful lot.

THIS WAS VIOLENT, SPORTING MURDER

Spurs 8, Gornik 1

Surely not since Joe Louis smeared the frame of Max Schmeling across the floor of a boxing ring in New York has sporting murder come more violently out of the night. As long as we live the 56,730 of us whose nerves stood up to the strain will remember those first 19 minutes as Tottenham, double champions of England, steamrollered 11 proficient Polish footballers off the field.

It was the start of an avalanche. It was the end of the match.

Now that the tumult and the shouting have died the people of North London must be bewildered that that Polish team could have run elegant rings round Spurs only seven days earlier. Permit Bill Nicholson, manager of Tottenham, to explain. 'My team tonight,' he said, 'were as great as they were bad last week.'

Ian Wooldridge, Daily Mail, 20 September 1961

19

Chasing the Treble

White Hart Lane, September 1961. The crowd's roar blasts into the empty sky above north London: something scary, more than enough to shrivel the morale of any inter-lopers. Eleven Polish players wait apprehensively as Danny Blanch-flower, the calmest man in sight, arranges the ball on the penalty spot.

There's a moment of absolute silence, somehow even more dimin-ishing to Gornik. Then, 1–0, and after that, Armageddon.

Spurs are chasing down a deficit incurred in Poland a week back. Expecting a match pretty similar to a normal top-end English League game, they were crushed 4–2 instead in their European Cup preliminary-round tie against Gornik in Katowice. Defeat was made worse by the way they had played. Ninety humiliating minutes of naivety and the crudeness that comes of desperation ended with them being jeered off the pitch. Two Gornik players – one was said to be 'crippled by an attack from Mackay' – were taken to hospital for X-rays on leg injuries. *Trybuna Robotnicza* (the *Workers' Tribune*) used its front page to censure them: 'We do not want to see Tottenham again on our pitches. We have heard a lot about British fair play, but judged by Tottenham's tactics it is just a myth. We understand the desire of professionals to win their matches as much money is at stake. But we do not expect them to win over tombstones.'

But tonight changes everything. Danny's penalty starts the goal rush. Cliff Jones lets rip – a hat-trick inside seventeen minutes. Between these, a lone Gornik goal from skipper Ernst Pol makes the score 6–5 to Spurs on aggregate.

When Bobby Smith's header goes in just before half-time to make it 5–1, it's obviously all over. In the second half, Bobby heads another for 6–1, Terry Dyson gets a seventh, and then a minute from the end John does what is by now becoming his usual thing – having set up goals for everyone else he finishes off by scoring one of his own. In the *Daily Express* the next day he will be described as 'the master of inside-forwards'.

After the final whistle, the Gornik players sit in the dressing room with heads sagging, still trembling with tension. 'They were broken within twenty minutes,' says their coach. 'As I looked at them I knew it was all over. Our men had nothing left.' Next day's papers carry a picture of the Gornik goalkeeper Hubert Kostka, head in hands, wearing an expression last seen on the figure in Edvard Munch's *The Scream*.

Cliff Jones, whose brilliance played such a large part in destroying the opposition, is unequivocal about who to thank. 'After the first leg, Bill wasn't very happy, big time,' he says. 'Giving us a lot of stick. Words at training. But in the home leg we walked out and we'd never experienced anything like it. We were really up for it and so were the crowd. Sixty-five thousand people all craving for us to really take this team.

'At Gornik's ground the pitch was within a running track and a ditch. The crowd was fifteen yards away. At Tottenham they're right on top of you. The atmosphere was indescribable. We could see the Gornik players thinking, "What the hell is this?" Right away we broke away, Les Allen hit the bar and the crowd went mad. Gornik were intimidated. The supporters just picked that up. We tore into Gornik – they never stood a chance. For ninety minutes it was a continuous roar. We'd have taken anybody apart that night.'

A few weeks later Spurs go to Rotterdam for the first leg of their second European Cup tie. This one is against Feyenoord. Frank Saul, an eighteen-year-old from Canvey Island who is standing in for Bobby Smith, scores two goals – one made by John – that are 'elegant,

maturely taken and a financial fortune to his club' as Spurs notch
up a 3–1 victory, with John's assist also providing a goal for Terry
Dyson. The Dutch team are arguably a greater challenge than Gornik
but Bill is dismissive. 'We muddled our way through,' he says. The
next day, though, the papers enthuse about John: 'White the impeccable'; 'Much of [the glory] belongs to John White'; 'White certainly
again was the main creator . . . full of balance and change of direction, always accurate and inventive every time he was in possession,'
says Ian Wooldridge in the *Daily Mail*. John is 'the most cultured
attacker on the field'. The message is clear; John, picking up where
he left off last season, is entering his prime.

On the return leg at White Hart Lane on 15 November, a 1–1
draw takes Spurs into the quarter-finals. It's a result that would have
left a residue of disappointment – newspapers describe it as 'dreary'
– but for a performance by Dave Mackay that contains courage,
commitment and a touch of madness. Stretchered off with concus-
sion after a collision with Feyenoord's Kraay, he sits up ten minutes
later, says, 'What am I doing here?' and rejoins the game spattered
with blood like a butcher's apprentice. He plays on with what is
thought at the time to be a fractured eardrum. Later it's discovered
to be a hairline fracture of the skull.

Elsewhere, Spurs are chasing more than the European Cup. Up-and-
down form in the League is keeping them in fourth place and Bill,
who announced at pre-season training in July that he wanted to go
for the Treble, is getting ready to make a sensational signing.

Jimmy Greaves is a player Bill has wanted since 24 August 1957,
the moment he saw him as a seventeen-year-old scoring on his Chelsea
debut at White Hart Lane. 'He wears his pants long,' commented
Bernard Joy of the *Evening Standard* that day, 'and has all the cheek
of an East London cockney . . .' '[Jimmy] beat three defenders before
stroking the ball into the net,' recalls Bill later in his autobiography.
'It had all the hallmarks of his game, improvisation and genius.'

Here's a player whose modus operandi is later depicted by the *Observer* sportswriter Peter Dobereiner as 'suddenly popping up through a trap door in the penalty box to score, having a quick snog with his mates and disappearing again'. 'Convivial' is how Brian James describes him: 'He enjoys the company of friends, other footballers, journalists.' But the most lyrical portrait of Jimmy in action comes from Joe Mercer, the Manchester City manager: 'All of a sudden, when the chance arises, Jimmy is gone. He had left his shadow standing.'

In December 1961, Jimmy is a long way off the great disappointment of his career – the place in the 1966 World Cup final that should have been a showcase for his gifts but went instead to Geoff Hurst. He's even further off the battle with alcoholism that nearly destroyed him in the 1970s and his resurgence as a TV personality of considerable wit and charm. He is simply an engaging lad who at just twenty-one is already the most phenomenal and predatory striker of his era.

He scored 132 goals in 169 games for Chelsea before AC Milan bought him for what was at the time a mind-boggling £80,000 in April 1961. Jimmy had barely unpacked his suitcase before he realised the move to defence-choked Italian football was a mistake, implying as much to Bill during a function in London that summer. In his book, Bill records:

We . . . happened to visit the toilets at the same time.

'Why didn't you join a better club than Milan?' I said. 'You should have come to Tottenham.' I meant it as lighthearted banter to start a conversation, but he retorted: 'I think I will next time.'

Jimmy was a very witty man . . . and though his reply was typical of him I thought it might have serious undertones.

It's entertaining to think that Bill defines tapping up someone in the Gents as 'lighthearted banter'. His opportunistic pee pays off, though. Jimmy's signing from AC Milan costs Spurs £99,999, Bill knocking £1 off the fee to avoid his being burdened with the label of the first £100,000 footballer.

The effect Jimmy has on Spurs is noticeable from the beginning. On his debut on 16 December he announces himself with a hat-trick in the 5–2 defeat of Blackpool at White Hart Lane. The headlines are predictably effusive: SPURS ATTACK IS REVITALISED; YES, HE'S WORTH THE FEE; FAIRY-TALE RETURN BY 3-GOAL GREAVES; SPURS INSPIRED TO OLD FIRE.

Ten days later, on a bone-chilling Boxing Day, Jimmy returns in a Spurs shirt to his first club, Chelsea. Playing conditions are challenging but inevitably he scores in Tottenham's 2–0 win. But he isn't man of the match. That honour, according to the *Daily Telegraph*'s Donald Saunders, is 'awarded on this cold and frosty morning to John White. The elegant Scottish artist was the only player who was never embarrassed by an awkwardly bouncing ball and a treacherous, almost dangerous surface. He was still able to employ his subtle touches with something like normal consistency.'

Looking back at this moment in the Treble-chasing season, when John is still only twenty-four and continuing to develop as a player, it goes without saying that having Jimmy as a team-mate will enrich and sharpen his game. Actually, though, to ask what effect Jimmy had on John isn't really the right question; it's what did John give to Jimmy?

John was, says Jimmy now, 'like Bobby Moore – he had an inbuilt radar that took him into spaces that nobody else had seen. He had an instinctive feel for being in the right place at the right time and it was the front men who benefited. His positioning and passing certainly made me a better player. I played with and against some of the greatest midfield players of the era and John was definitely among them.' It's a gracious assessment and you can bet John would have reciprocated in kind.

As for John, one thing he got out of this new midfield/front-man partnership was surely gratification. How good it must have been to play to someone like Jimmy, a man with the genius and ruthlessness to do justice to what John had set up for him. As Jimmy himself comments later: 'I was born with an instinctive, natural gift for sticking the ball in the net. I just get in as close as I can and let rip.'

NON-STOP SPURS KNOCK OUT BRAVE BIRMINGHAM
Spurs 4, Birmingham 2
The equaliser had to come. And what a gem when it did! Blanch-flower took a throw a yard from the right corner flag, played tiddlywinks back and forth with White, who, finally, in a lazy half-turn, floated the ball to the far post where the fair head of Medwin climbed up and up to hit the ball with all the authority of Finney in his heyday . . .
Sunday Telegraph, 11 January 1961

After Christmas, the serious fixture pile-up starts as Spurs – they're second in the League now – compete for both domestic prizes and the European Cup. They make it harder for themselves by failing in their first attempt to get past Birmingham in the third round of the FA Cup, then going a goal behind after sixty seconds in the replay; the equaliser and two of the subsequent three goals are made by John.

But later this month it takes his absence to emphasise just how valuable John has become to the team. In the League he misses two games while he recovers from flu, and without him Spurs can only draw 1–1 away to Cardiff and 2–2 at White Hart Lane to Manchester United. This point is brought home even more strongly when he returns for the FA Cup fourth-round tie at Plymouth Argyle.

'White underlined once more,' comments the *Daily Telegraph*, 'how much Spurs are coming to depend on his spindly legs and darting brain. Against Manchester United the previous week they were without him and there was no controlled build-up of attacking moves; this week the line flowed smoothly, and always along unexpected lines.'

The 5–1 win means the possibility of not just a repeat of the Double but a groundbreaking Treble is indisputably on. But as February begins, an obstacle looms in the shape of Wolves. A 3–1 defeat at Molineux sees Tottenham dropping to third behind Burnley and Ipswich. There is, though, a description – it's by Brian Glanville in the next day's *Sunday Telegraph* – of their solitary goal, scored by John: 'White, trapping the ball outside the penalty area, calmly stopped, drew a bead on the goal then smashed a remarkable left-footer, in off the bar, near the far post.' It's impossible to believe that anyone who saw him that day could have come away feeling anything but absolutely amazed.

Spurs go on the following week to beat Nottingham Forest 4–2, but for John it's what happens away from football which is more important: his daughter Mandy is born. The Evanses' house in Berkeley Gardens is now home to two sets of parents and two infants. Quite possibly these are not ideal circumstances for a footballer in the whirl of domestic and European competition, but you can tell from the confident way John is playing that the love and stability he has found with the Evans family means as much to him as any amount of prizes.

SPURS TRIUMPHANT LOSERS
Dukla 1, Tottenham Hotspur 0
Superb, sophisticated Spurs became the magnificent failures here this afternoon – the team who finished one goal down to Czech champions Dukla in the first leg of their European Cup tie and turned that failure into a wondrous triumph.

After what I thrilled over this afternoon I am convinced Spurs will win the second leg handsomely on February 26 and go on into the semi final.

Desmond Hackett, *Daily Express*, 14 February 1961

In Prague, it's a bitterly cold afternoon in the Dynamo stadium and women shuffle around the pitch clearing off the snow with brooms as fast as it's falling. The going is sodden – you can sink a pencil six inches into the turf without difficulty – and in football terms, it's not going to be an inspiring match. Spurs play an ultra-defensive game, pulling six men back in front of Bill Brown. Tony Marchi, having played in Italy, explains the tactics to reporters: 'The correct title of the tactics used by Spurs is *contro piede*, which means "wrong foot". It aims to draw the wing-halves forward and traps defenders on the wrong foot with a counter-attack.'

According to Bill in his autobiography, 'Even John White was given a specific job to do, a job which restricted his freedom as a forward somewhat, and made him conscious of the fact that he was to be our very first defender. He was doing very well, and our plans were successful.' Spurs concede just the one goal. There can be relatively few occasions when a side is delighted in defeat, but this is one of them. 'It was,' says Danny Blanchflower afterwards, 'an Irish victory.'

Together with Dave, Cliff and Bobby, John is deemed 'outstanding' by the Czech paper *Obrana Lidu*. But Spurs are too involved in getting on with the next job to revel in favourable reviews. The team are flown directly on to the Midlands for their FA Cup fifth-round tie against West Bromwich Albion. They beat West Brom 4–2, with John making the first of Bobby Smith's two goals, and the first of the pair from Jimmy Greaves.

The focus switches briefly to the League. The fixtures are starting to pile up now. A goalless stalemate away to Aston Villa – who they will shortly meet in the FA Cup sixth round – is followed by a 2–2 draw at home to Bolton Wanderers; wear and tear is showing, and five reserves shore up a side deprived of Bill Brown, Danny Blanch-flower, Peter Baker, Dave Mackay and Cliff Jones.

And the pace doesn't let up. Two days later, on 26 February, Dukla show up for the second leg of the European Cup quarter-final. Ten minutes after kick-off, the White Hart Lane pitch is sodden with evaporating snow – it's still falling – as Danny Blanchflower's free kick skids into the penalty box, where John pushes it sideways for Bobby Smith to place it in the net. According to the *Daily Telegraph*, '[The 60,000 crowd] had scarcely digested it when Mackay controlled a pass from White and hammered the ball past the diving Kouba to put Spurs in front for the first time in this tie . . . White has played many a fine game for his club and country but rarely has he so frequently opened up an opposing defence.'

Dukla get one back – Tony Marchi's over-optimistic long back pass over the marsh to Bill Brown is intercepted by their winger Jelinek. From then on, the game belongs to Spurs. Bobby meets John's assist – 'that perfect John White centre came floating across' – to head Tottenham's third, and Cliff Jones heads on Peter Baker's free kick for Dave Mackay.

Spurs 4, Dukla 1. The chairman Fred Wale is already calling them world-beaters. But in the semi-final Spurs have drawn the cup-holders, Benfica, whose side includes a magically talented nineteen-year-old called Eusebio – four years from now he will be one of the sensations of the 1966 World Cup. The first leg, at the Estadio da Luz, sees Spurs fall two behind in under ten minutes and a final score of Benfica 3, Spurs 1 (it's Bobby Smith's goal).

Bill Nicholson thinks they can overhaul the deficit at White Hart Lane. His prediction is a draw, followed by a play-off. But what happens on 5 April will always be thought of as one of those nearly games; it might be wishful thinking, but Spurs are frustratingly close to reaching the European Cup final. After they go one down in fifteen minutes, Jimmy Greaves scores what looks to be the perfect goal. The Danish referee disallows it, but with thirty-five minutes gone

John lays on the pass for Bobby Smith's equaliser. Spurs now need three more goals for an outright win, and two for a replay.

This is Spurs! They can do it!

One goal is provided two minutes into the second half when a Portuguese defender shoves John in the back and Danny Blanchflower delivers the penalty. For the remaining forty-three minutes, Spurs play football that would crack any other defence on the planet. Here it isn't enough.

Spurs have to face up to the knowledge that another Double is beyond their reach too. Maybe they're suffering a hangover from missing out on Europe; whatever the reason, form deserts them in the first half of March, when they lose 6–2 away to Manchester City and are defeated at White Hart Lane by Ipswich Town; they also drop a point to Burnley at Turf Moor. Ipswich are the champions, Burnley runners-up. Spurs finish third, a point behind. Over the last few months they have played some of their best football, to a standard higher even than the Double season. It's hard to think of a more frustrating outcome.

There is still the FA Cup. The 10 March sixth-round tie against Aston Villa has been successfully negotiated 2–0, with goals from Danny Blanchflower and Cliff Jones. 'White, picking his way as carefully as a parson down a wet country lane, was quieter than usual, yet as vital as ever,' says David Miller in the *Sunday Telegraph*. At the end of the month there's the semi-final against Manchester United at Hillsborough. It's 3–1 to Spurs, with goals from Jimmy Greaves, Cliff Jones and Terry Medwin. But you don't need to guess who plays a huge part in this crucial win: 'White delicately weaved his way over the pitch, always one move ahead of the trailing Stiles'; 'Blanchflower saw White move into an empty space and pushed a pass to him. The frail Scotsman juggled the ball from one foot to the other, then sent it curling over United's defence to the far post, where Jones soared . . . to head a spectacular goal'; 'Over came a perfect centre from White and Medwin quietly headed in . . .'

Spurs are going to Wembley again.

English football in 1962, still parochial about Europe, regards the FA Cup as only slightly less important than the League trophy and Tottenham are desperate to rescue something from their pile of dashed hopes. They've lost the Treble, they've lost the Double. This is the last chance of glory.

But Burnley, their opponents at Wembley, remain one of the dominant sides of the era. This is a team that boasts four England internationals and a captain, Jimmy Adamson, whose reputation as thinker and sage almost rivals Danny Blanchflower's; he has just been named Footballer of the Year. Having just handed over the League title to obscure, provincial Ipswich, Burnley have something to prove too. Somebody has to win this head-to-head of the mighty, and it's no certainty that it will be Spurs.

That said, you can't get a much better start to a final than Jimmy Greaves's third-minute goal. Burnley, having spent the rest of the half playing catch-up, equalise five minutes after the restart through their big ball-playing number 10 Jimmy Robson. Less than a minute later, John picks up a ball from Cliff and centres it for Bobby Smith to put Spurs back in the lead.

Two–one. Enough to win by hanging on. Not enough to feel comfortable. Jimmy Robson finds the net again but this time he's offside. Wave after wave of Burnley attacks beat down on Spurs. Maurice Norman plays the game of his life.

Seven minutes to go.

Terry Medwin's on-target drive snicks the hand of Burnley's central defender, Tommy Cummings.

Penalty.

According to Dave Mackay in his autobiography, Danny Blanchflower, with 'that manic grin on his face', picks up the ball and offers it to him. The FA Cup is within Tottenham's grasp and he, Dave, has the chance to take hold of it.

In his mind's eye, Dave makes the mistake of looking down from the mountain top. What he sees is himself messing up his penalty kick. He sees Burnley on the counter-attack . . . an equaliser . . . extra time . . . a Burnley winner . . . Spurs not in Europe next season.

Most uncharacteristically, Dave loses his bottle and with a shake of his head runs back towards his half. But Danny doesn't mind. Unfazed, he places the ball on the spot and sends Adam Blacklaw, Burnley's goalie, the wrong way. Three–one. The FA Cup is back at White Hart Lane.

Delightedly, the statistics are reeled off. The best final since Manchester United beat Blackpool in 1948. The first club to win the Cup in successive years since Newcastle in 1951–2. The first southerners to win it four times. Even better, Spurs have found themselves another ticket to Europe.

Which prompts a question. How much has playing in Europe impacted on John's game? To begin to answer that, you have to go back to that second leg semi-final against Benfica, and a rare moment afterwards when John sticks his head above the parapet to criticise. 'I don't think we found our feet as we did in previous rounds,' he comments. 'I'm terribly disappointed. Benfica had very good forwards but a suspect defence and if we'd used the right tactics in front of goal we might have scored more.'

From a distance of nearly half a century, you wish you could have carried on the conversation. What did he think the right tactics would have been? Why did they not find their feet this time? Perhaps it's foolish to read too much into a single quote, but you wonder if he's already thinking far ahead into the empty space of the future when he will be a captain – a coach, even. As it is, the lessons he's learnt from playing against giants like Benfica will be put to good use when Spurs are back in Europe in a few months' time.

MACKAY THE MIGHTY
Birmingham 2, Spurs 3
28 April 1962

MACKAY THE MARAUDER SAVES DAY FOR SPURS
Spurs 1, Sheffield Wednesday 1
17 November 1962

DAVE THE DANGER MAN ROARS IN TO RESCUE SPURS
Spurs 4, West Ham 4
22 December 1962

20
Derby Days
Rob, 1973

It's midday on a frosty Saturday and Mick Levy is leading my twelve-year-old uncle Andrew and me through the foyer of the Hyde Park Hotel, which is opposite Harvey Nicks in Knightsbridge. We're off to Chelsea v Derby County at Stamford Bridge. Dave Mackay has just taken over as manager of the Midlands club after the resignation of Brian Clough and he's invited Andrew and me along.

Mick, bachelor and family friend, is our minder. He's one of the mainstays of the Spurs Jewish community who stepped forward when Dad died and said, 'Whatever you need.' Intriguingly, there's also a slight frisson between him and Alma, though it's accompanied always by the impression, enjoyed by both of them, that they each could do better for themselves. Which results in nothing happening. With the best will in the world neither of them is a particularly good catch so I don't know what either of them is waiting for.

I'm all dressed up in my best slacks, shirt, pullover and beetle-crushers; in my pocket is the autograph book with orange cover. I've got a drink – it's my first freshly squeezed orange juice ever. This is big time. All I've ever had before is concentrated crap from Sainsbury's. For a kid like me from the suburbs, hotels have always meant package-tour veal crates or the Ravelstone in Musselburgh where Granny White would have a sherry and we'd have a warm Britvic. Here there's a fantastic smell of opulence. Mirrors. Velvet. Wood. Staff everywhere, in burgundy uniform with gold braid. It's the first time this kind of sumptuousness has come on to my nine-year-old radar. It's how I imagine Paris would be.

We're shown into a private dining room where the Derby players are. They're sitting around a TV set in one corner watching *Grandstand*, wearing flares and shirts with big floppy collars, turning the place into a temporary Midlands version of the King's Road. My eyes zoom straight to Archie Gemmill, because he's my hero. I'm a Scottish London boy and Archie's everything Scottish. He's not got a lot in his favour on paper – he's a short stocky guy with wispy blond hair, he's not Sean Connery – but it's his attitude you warm to, a kind of 'Fuck it, I won't give in, I will succeed'. Next along is Bruce Rioch, who possesses the hardest shot in football, then Roy McFarland, who's big and rugged, just how you want a sportsman to be, and Colin Todd with his pudding-basin haircut. In fact, there's a spattering of very bad seventies haircuts all round, with Welsh international Leighton James the top mullet. And there's David Nish and Alan Hinton and Colin Boulton the goalie and they're all . . . *men*. Raised by my mother and nan, I find it unusual to see such a *collection* of males, genuine blokes who are great, who are interested in *me*.

We ride on the team bus from the hotel to Stamford Bridge, and it's motorbike outriders going through red lights! It's like being a celebrity! It's Dave Mackay making time for me! He's only five foot eight but a big, powerful presence, a barrel of a man, with dark, wild, warrior's eyes. It wouldn't take too much of a leap to imagine him with blue paint on his face, in a kilt. He'll always try to be smart but it's like when a guy buys the most expensive clothes and puts them on and he might as well not have bothered. Dave's in blazer, slacks, Cuban heels, big knot in his tie, and at the end of the game the shirt buttons will be coming undone and the tie'll be down. He never looks comfortable. He looks like the coach driver, all rumpled.

In the three-and-a-bit seasons during which Dave manages Derby, we get to go to all their games around London – from League games at Highbury and Upton Park to Luton and Peterborough in the Cup.

It never seems like we're in the way. Time is made for us. And for me this insight into behind-the-scenes football is crucial. It's another Panini sticker in my book about my father. We get to go everywhere. I get to know how the smell and feel of a changing room alters. Before a game, before anybody goes in, there's a sort of calm spirit that sits in there, and gradually it winds itself up before your eyes as the guys get changed, go through their rituals – putting tape on, and jockstraps, and liniment, and getting massages, or wandering around happily in just a shirt. We get ushered out into the corridor five minutes before the team comes out, by which time the level of stress and tension has risen and risen. A few minutes later the door opens and Dave and Des Anderson and Gordon Guthrie the physio come out: 'Come on, boys,' and there's that fantastic noise, the clatter of studs.

We get to sit in the dugout. We're the only boys in the world allowed to do that. I sort of feel the envious eyes of other kids in the ground: 'Who's he? Pushy git.' Walking out as a kid with a whole load of players onto a touchline – that's scary. I don't like being in the spotlight, though I do feel tremendous pride.

But here's the bit I really like, because it gives me a glimpse of my dad's world. At half-time Andrew and I wait outside the dressing room, bouncing a ball against the wall, consuming orange slices and a cup of tea like the players get, and listening out for the raised voices behind the dressing-room door. General male volume. General *Dave* volume, actually. And after ten minutes the door opens again with a waft of warm air. It smells of liniment, sweat and turf. It smells of *football*.

The first season, Dave takes Derby to third in the table. The second season, they win the League and he's a miracle worker. The third season, Derby are in the running for the Double, though they get knocked out of the Cup in the semis and end up in fourth place. Less than three months into the 1976–7 season, after a bad start, he's sacked and heads off to manage Walsall.

It's not the end of the road for me and Andrew. We just go down the divisions with Dave and have a year watching Walsall. And then Dave's off to coach in Kuwait from where he doesn't come back till 1987, by which time Andrew's a banker and I'm through college and living with Cara, who's going to be my wife.

But coming up to forty years on from that first Chelsea game I only have to go past the Hyde Park Hotel and suddenly it will all come back into my head: the orange-juice taste, the *Grandstand* signature tune, wintergreen, mud, sweat, cigars: the smell of my dad's life.

Sometimes I wonder if I'm being a bit sad, hanging on to scraps like these to put together a portrait of my dad. But what else can I do? It's only the people who shared his world that can help me overcome the limitations of his absence from it, and give me an insight into the essential John White.

To help carve the openings for Greaves – and the one-time blacksmith, centre-forward Bobby Smith – Spurs depend on John White, nicknamed 'The Ghost'. White, who constantly pays tribute to the benefits he found in National Service with the King's Own Scottish Borderers – 'I learned to concentrate and how to take orders' – is one of the few soccermen who believes in overtime without pay. Twice a week he returns to White Hart Lane's indoor gymnasium to practise with Dave Mackay. 'If a footballer is to keep at his best he must be prepared to practise,' says White, 'and I'll always remember an old-time international remarking, "It's harder to keep at the top than it is to get there." I intend trying to keep on top form and so give Spurs the best of my ability.'

Topic magazine, May 1962

21

It Was Definitely John White

M anchester, March 1963. It's Saturday morning, and one of the busiest parts of the city crawls with traffic, human and mechanical. On the second floor of the Midland Hotel, a window flies open and a lad leans out as white as a ghost. 'Help! Help, help!' he wails.

Twenty minutes later, as John and Cliff sip their early-morning tea, John answers a knock on the door of their hotel bedroom. It's two policemen, the hotel manager and a raging Bill Nick in the hole.

'Is everything all right, sir?' the hotel manager asks John.

Bill comes storming through. 'Call yourself a professional footballer? You're a stupid ****.'

When people want to give you a take on John's character the first thing they usually mention is the pranks. 'I roomed with Terry Dyson,' says Les Allen, 'and we used to make sure any connecting door between each room was locked because of the number of times you'd find water in the bed otherwise. Anything was wrong, John used to get the blame.'

'We were at a private party at Flanagan's in the West End, hosted by a big Spurs fan called Sidney Brickman,' remembers Isobel Mackay. 'Cliff and John rode in on an ice-cream seller's bicycle and started selling ice cream – they must have gone out into the street and borrowed it. I think we got banned that night from going back there.'

'There was always this smile about him,' says Cliff. 'He was wonderful, a funny man who lifted the whole team. He was great in the dressing room. I never saw him down. Every time I think of him I laugh.'

Cliff and John were pals from beginning to end. Most footballers have little superstitions; Cliff was no exception. 'Mine was: Always come out with John White. Wherever John was, I had to be.' That's true. Almost every portrait that has Cliff in it seems also to have a beaming John at his side, usually on his left, as if they're unconsciously replicating their starting positions on the pitch. When Bill gave his tactical talks, they sat together in the dressing room like two mischievous boys at the back of the class.

'Bill would finish and we'd all be ready to go and then Bill would say, "Danny, would you like to say anything?" Us: Oh God. Danny would bang on for half an hour, then: "I'm going to finish on this." Bobby Smith would half rise from his seat because he wanted to get to the bookies. Then he'd have to sit down again. Another half an hour would pass.'

As to how the Cliff and John partnership worked on the pitch, it's best to quote Julian Holland in *Spurs – The Double*: 'Blanchflower and Mackay asserted their authority in the no-man's-land of midfield, linking attack with the ubiquitous White or the menacing Jones. Usually the complex approach would be constructed within the Blanchflower–Mackay–White triangle. Jones would hover on the fringe of the operational headquarters ... waiting for the sudden semaphore that would set him free on one of his long anarchical runs.'

But it's the antics the two of them got up to off the pitch that everyone gets around to sooner or later. In Dave's book, *The Real Mackay*, he records how John would 'be sitting next to a stranger in the pub, and would rest his head on their shoulder as the other man shuffled along the seat warily; or take a crysanthemum from a vase and casually eat it'. Terry Dyson sums it up more succinctly: 'John and Cliffie were crackers.'

What happened at the Midland Hotel in Manchester is a case in point. It's also classic John, in that it was completely unanticipated. 'I'd got up and as usual I had to make him a cup of tea – that was my role,' says Cliff. 'Sat around drinking it. General chit-chat. Then suddenly he just gets up and opens the window and starts shouting. Bill was not best pleased – "I'm fed up of you two." We were split up and I was sent to room with Jimmy Greaves for a while.

'Once we put pebbles in the wheel hubs of Bobby Smith's car. Bobby couldn't work out what the problem was. He kept saying, "What the hell is that rattle?" Eventually he took it to the garage where they told him what was wrong. He never worked out how it happened.'

There's more. 'It was coming back on the train from Birmingham,' says Terry Dyson. 'We were sat in the dining car waiting for our food and John and Cliff turned up with a serving trolley. They go to Ron Henry and lift a lid off a plate and on it is a pack of Trill, because Ron used to breed and show budgies. They'd borrowed white jackets and everything. He was such a funny lad, the tricks he played.'

'We'd played Benfica away,' says Cliff. 'Drinks after the game. There were a couple of decorative swords hanging on the walls. We put a couple of tablecloths on as Roman gowns and came down the stairs, fencing. Errol Flynn impersonation. Swashbuckling. Bill was not at all impressed.'

This time it was John who was sent to room with Jimmy Greaves, though that arrangement proved short-lived as Jimmy and Terry Dyson were both smokers. Cliff and John were soon back in partnership. 'Bill Nick just did it to teach them a lesson,' says Jimmy. 'It was just harmless pranks. If you get fifteen young, fit, keyed-up guys together they're not just going to sit around drinking tea.'

Somewhere else to look if you want to shed light on John's character is Spurs' training ground at Cheshunt. Sandra recalls the way he'd always go back after lunch and join the apprentices' training session in the afternoon. 'He was a hard worker. He felt he was so lucky to do something he loved and get paid for it.'

'He used to stand out to us in training. He always wanted to do a little bit extra,' agrees Cliff. 'Seven balls lined up in the penalty area, he'd chip seven out of seven against the crossbar. Right *and* left foot. He was fanatical in his approach, so focused. Particularly pre-season, when a lot of it was based around legwork. Danny Blanch-flower, who could have been a marathon runner, was in his thirties and still nobody could keep up with him. Then along came John. And then John was starting to overtake him – Danny was trying to keep up with John. Danny wasn't too pleased about that.'

What comes over almost every time is the sheer joy and energy of the man. Here's Ian St John: 'A really funny guy, always taking the piss and messing about. Him and Mackay were always up to something, some sort of mischief, maybe throwing your boots out of the train window or some such thing. John was always one of the guys at the front, having fun, enjoying life.' Here's Terry Medwin: 'If there was any trouble – not aggressiveness-type trouble, not wickedness, but mischief – he'd be involved.' Terry Dyson remembers the time Spurs were playing Juventus in a friendly, '. . . and the hotel in Turin had this massive ceiling. Cliffie got an orange and started keepy-uppy, trying to hit it up to the ceiling. Everyone else managed about six. John wouldn't stop till he'd finished the orange off.'

Put that way, it makes John seem no more than a fitness-obsessed joker. Scratch below the surface and, as in most cases, there is a more complex personality to discover. Here was someone who was at ease playing in front of 60,000 crowds, but who was mortified when the band announced his presence as he and Sandra walked into the Trocadero for their wedding breakfast; who was so shy when he arrived at Tottenham that he spent his first season virtually mute in a dressing-room corner, but with a couple of drinks inside him lit up the whole room. 'He'd do really daft things, funny walks and funny faces, oh my God, he was so full of fun,' says his brother Tom. 'He could drink anything. You could see him at a party drinking a gin. A whisky. A beer. A cup of tea. And just continue. He wasn't some-body who just drinks pints of lager.' Then again, he wasn't always that relentlessly buoyant character. Cliff may never have seen him down, but it's a good bet that John was prone to winter depression.

He also retained a strong sense of his filial duty, continuing to support his mother financially. 'When John became who he was with Tottenham, we were in rented accommodation,' says Tom. 'John wanted to buy it for my mother, though she wouldn't allow him because she didn't want him to take the debt on.' He was intelligent and perceptive, too. 'John was slow to join in the conversation but once it got going he'd have something to say,' says the journalist Brian James. 'He was sharp in his observations.'

'I think he would have become a coach,' says Cliff. 'He was always into the football, and it's not always the hard approach that gets results. John was always respectful and he would have been respected in turn. He had a way with people which was always good.'

'After a sports function at the Russell Square Hotel, I came out into the daylight with John, Frank McLintock, a couple of other guys,' says Brian James. 'We'd had a skinful. We were looking for a taxi and I started to wave: "Taxi! Taxi!" when someone – it might have been a street person – said: "You've got a fucking big mouth, you have," and took a swipe at me. I was ready to get involved. John was the smallest guy there but – the sheer speed of his reaction – he pushed him up against a fence and quietly calmed everything down.'

Yet in contrast to that, there are times when the considerate, hard-working, fitness-conscious John White comes over as – OK, a bit of an airhead.

'He was a bit scatty at times,' is Les Allen's assessment. 'Once we were on a trip to Israel and it was bloody hot. Bill Nicholson said to us, "Don't be stupid with the sun, it's different to how it is in England, you'll get burnt." John and Jonesy went out in the sun, swimming, and John ended up with blisters as big as horseshoes. He had to hide 'em out of Bill's way and he suffered all that trip. To this day I've never seen burn blisters like that. Unbelievable.'

'We went on holiday to Jersey,' says Sandra. 'John forgot the tickets. Then he left us without any money after lending all his to a female family friend who had arrived from Scotland. So he spent the time sending telegrams from the hotel to get more when he wasn't off playing golf.'

There are a lot more stories about his spontaneous generosity and kind heart. When his daughter Mandy was born John gave the flowers he'd brought for Sandra to the woman in the next bed who didn't have any. 'The first Christmas he was at Spurs, he gave me a coat, a lovely white coat,' says his sister Janette. 'My mum said, "Look in the pocket," and there was a fiver.'

'He was a man's man,' says his friend Jim McAlister. 'He liked male company to play golf. And to go out with as well. He didn't drink during the week at all – neither did Dave Mackay. Not after Monday, but on Saturdays – footballers' night – he liked brandies, with ginger ale or Coke. He was at peak fitness, and he used to sweat like hell when he was drinking. In those days the pubs would close around ten, ten thirty but the landlord would keep us in with him. John would say, "Give us a solo," and I used to get up and sing "A Scottish Soldier". Then we'd go back to Church Street and play Kenneth McKellar albums very loudly.'

There was only a year's difference in age between John and Jim, an Ayrshire Scot who was one of the original Butten Boys, young British golfers sponsored by a management consultant called Ernest Butten; another was Tony Jacklin. They met when Jim was an assistant at Enfield golf course. 'It was a stag night at the Watersplash in Walthamstow. I was twenty-four. I'd been in London less than a month. It was the beginning of the 1962–63 football season. They'd won the Double the year before. I was friendly with Bill Brown, and he invited me and John. We just hit it off in friendship straight away. I was dropped off in Essex Road. With a bottle of whisky left on the table. Next day John came up to Enfield golf club and played a few holes.' The afternoon golf sessions became a regular thing. 'Sandra would get quite annoyed: "Keep away from that so-and-so." I was the bad one. Well, she'd probably want to go somewhere with John.'

Jim paints a picture of a softly spoken, young-looking man – 'he had a great head of hair' – who was neat and well dressed. 'He always had a suit when he went out. Mohair, browns and greys, the straight trouser with fourteen-inch bottoms over brown shoes. He got them from a tailor in Tottenham – either given or he got some fantastic deal. He had what I'd call the footballer's voice. Dave Mackay had it. A little bit of English in there. English sayings, but Scottish accent. Tom, his younger brother – practically identical.

'It was a great time in our lives. Not a care in the world, doing something you love doing. We played a Middlesex Assistants v Sussex, at Ham Manor. Foursomes and singles. John took the four of us – including Tony Jacklin – down there in his Humber Hawk. An all-day thing. And an all-night thing as well. On the way back, John, who had had more than a few drinks, got stopped by the police. "Where are you going, John?" "I'm off to Pottersh Bar to drop off Tony Jacklin." "Off you go." Different times!'

John's golf? 'He had a slicer's grip. His right shoulder was always forward. He was a fourteen handicap. He wasn't as competitive as he was on a football pitch. He would play well for five holes, then one bad shot and' – Jim shrugs – 'it'd be all nonsense after that. The concentration had gone out of his effort. That's what a golfer does – concentrates for eighteen holes. John was a master at what he did, which was football. Golf was just something he loved. He loved getting out there. He just liked to play and if he played well that was a bonus.'

The impression is of an even-tempered, easy-going man – 'He was much better with babies than I was,' says Sandra, 'he had much more patience' – whose reputation as a benevolent lord of misrule has survived him as long as his deeds on the football pitch. Or as Terry Medwin puts it, 'John was no problem at any level, was he? He enjoyed a bit of fun, he liked his golf, he just liked doing what he was doing.'

When people talk about someone long gone, it's easy to morph into hagiography. Who's going to be unkind about a young guy at the top of his game, whose life was discontinued by the abrupt intervention of a bolt of lightning? But that said, what comes through strongest is that not one single person has a bad word to say about him. 'He didn't have an enemy in the world' is a pretty trite phrase but in John's case it rings true.

'He always felt he could be better,' is Cliff's summing-up. 'He didn't underestimate himself but he wasn't complacent. He didn't get upset. He had a very good temperament.'

Which leaves only one question to be asked. Which of the two of them actually thought up the pranks?

'It was definitely John White,' says Cliff. He flicks a glance heavenwards. 'Sorry, John.'

John White, 24, Spurs and Scottish international inside forward, was admitted to a London hospital last night for observation.

He is in the University College Hospital, Euston, for a thorough medical check up.

Spurs now have two stars in hospital. Skipper and assistant manager Danny Blanchflower is recovering from a cartilage operation that is expected to keep him out of action for two months.

For some weeks White has been worried by his failure to hit the form that carved out countless goals for Spurs when they scored sixty-one in sixteen games last autumn.

But since scheming the double defeat of crack Scottish side Rangers in the European Cup-winners' Cup, White has failed to click.

Ken Jones, Daily Mirror, 23 January 1963

22

Winter Blues

For footballs buffs in the 1960s, it's the Charity Shield at Wembley that signals the start of a new season. Revenge is the theme as Tottenham inflict a 5–1 defeat on Ipswich, who beat them twice last season on the way to the championship. John scores the fourth goal in a Spurs performance which has the old-style sports journalists dusting off their fruitiest prose: Spurs are 'like master magicians mesmerising an enthralled audience'; Bill Nicholson has 'trapped the elusive butterfly of Ipswich's success and put it into the killing bottle' and his tactics 'worked with the precision of a Guards' present arms'. 'With Mackay, White, Smith and the rest producing their old magic,' they conclude, Spurs obtained 'the perfect revenge'.

Weeks of high-scoring games follow. John's game always seems to flow well in the autumn, especially this year when there have been positive changes in his personal life. He and Sandra have moved into their own home. 'After Mandy was born we were still living with my mum and dad,' Sandra explains. 'Then Mum said, "You've got to move before the Cup Final." I suppose I was a bit of a spoilt footballer's wife – the club bought a house for us in Friern Barnet and it smelt, and I said: "I'm not moving in here." So we ended up in Len Duquemin's old house in Church Street, Edmonton.'

There, John occupies himself with DIY, taking the banisters out and replacing them with metal rods, and building units in the sitting room. His joinery training also comes in handy on another occasion. 'Dave led him astray sometimes,' says Sandra, 'and one night I said,

"If you're not back by eleven, I'm locking the door." I'm a very heavy sleeper and didn't wake up when he rang the doorbell. He went round the back of the house, chipped the putty out of the window frame and lifted the pane out. It broke, of course.'

The odd night spent carousing hasn't affected his form. When Spurs show Nottingham Forest off the premises after dishing them out a 9–2 beating on 29 September, the press praise 'a superlative display of attacking soccer that swept through the Forest defence like an avalanche. Spurs' goals were all gems from an assorted cluster, clean cut and polished.' There are four from Jimmy Greaves and John scores Spurs' fourth.

October features the 4–4 home draw with Arsenal. Spurs, 'with the white-shirted magician, Scotland's John White, wrecking the Gunners' unset jelly of a defence at will . . . could – and should – have stood 6–2 up at half-time instead of a modest 4–2 after leading 3–0 . . . What a match! But the warning light is up, glowing a bright red, for Tottenham Hotspur. Watch that defence . . . it has a terribly insecure look when the going gets rough.' Even so, the players receive a rare tribute from Bill Nicholson: 'In that opening burst my forwards turned on the finest attacking football I have ever seen from them.'

Bill gets harder to please as October wears on. They beat West Brom 2–1 away and Manchester United 6–2 at home but his reaction to their 5–1 defeat of Leyton Orient at Brisbane Road – they're now top of the table – is: 'We're not playing so well as last year.' That said, in the *Sunday Express*, Denis Compton, former England cricketer and footballer turned reporter, praises 'this mighty Spurs steamroller' which has now scored twenty-six goals in their last five games. Spurs' third comes thirty seconds from half-time through what Compton calls 'White's magic . . . a long defence-splitting ball to Allen on the left', from whose cross Medwin scored. After fifty-seven minutes 'White received from Allen and went on unchallenged to shoot past Mike Pinner, England's amateur international goalkeeper'.

One game, though, stands out from all the rest this month. On 21 October, the *Sunday Express* previews the upcoming European Cup Winners' Cup first-leg tie between Rangers and Spurs at White Hart Lane, calling it 'the greatest British club match of all time'. Spurs are tipped as likely winners and John is praised as 'that great artist'. Mention is also made of Rangers' erstwhile reluctance to sign John. The number of times Rangers had him watched has fallen victim to inflation: 'before White left Scotland Rangers must have watched him with Alloa and Falkirk 40 times'.

If John has any point left to prove, he does so as Spurs beat Rangers on the last day of October, heading them into the lead within five minutes and scoring their second from a Jimmy Greaves corner. But Spurs let a 4–1 lead morph into 5–2 and Bill's post-match under-whelmed assessment: 'I am not at all pleased. We can play a lot better than this.' There's a rare comment from John's father-in-law, though. 'I thought White and Mackay were magnificent,' Harry Evans tells Brian James of the *Daily Mail*. 'Why praise foreign footballers when we've got players like these?'

Three days later, Harry's question is answered as Spurs beat Leicester 4–0. 'With Gordon Banks in goal Leicester had the second-best defence in the First Division,' records the *Sunday Express*, 'but they were washed away by the individual and collective talents of the wonderful Spurs forwards . . . they have scored 35 goals from their last seven games and in poise, flexibility and sophistication must rank among the top six clubs in the world.'

There's another satisfying result at Fulham the following week, where Spurs win 2–0, but on 17 November they manage only a 1–1 home draw against Sheffield Wednesday, and the inadvisability of their having played a friendly in Egypt during the preceding week is discussed. A week later, there are 'boos for Spurs strollers' at Turf Moor, where Burnley win 2–1 and Spurs are accused by Leslie Duxbury, in the *Sunday Express*, of being 'slack and insolent . . . they left behind a sizeable chunk of their reputation in a game in which even Greaves and White found it difficult to put a ball where they wanted it'.

It gets worse.

SPURS HELD 0–0 BY EVERTON
White is missing – so is the rhythm.
London Evening Standard, 2 December 1962

On 1 December, there is no sign of John at the home match – 'a dour, disappointing battle' – with Everton. He's reported sick 'with a chill' in the morning and the game ends 0–0 – the first time Spurs haven't scored in a home match this season. The *Daily Telegraph* comments that 'when White is out there is no one to do his job properly ... [His] importance to the Tottenham machine has never been better demonstrated than it was by his absence ... Without someone to direct and harness their talent, these Spurs forwards can be mastered by a sound defence.'

John doesn't make it into training on Monday, though on Tuesday he's examined at home in Church Street by the club doctor and judged fit to travel the following day for the return leg against Rangers. In the end, though, he stays behind while the rest of the team endure a fog-delayed train ride to Glasgow. The press laments his absence: 'As he was one of the stars in the first match against Rangers, his services would have been of great value tonight ... without White they are likely to conclude that their first objective must be to hang on to their hard-earned three-goal advantage.'

Then the weather takes a hand. Smog paralyses most of the country, closing airports and stopping trains. At Ibrox you can't see one goalmouth from the other and the game is called off forty-five minutes before kick-off.

Freed from fogbound Glasgow, Spurs – without John – are 'laid flat by Bolton' according to Leslie Duxbury, as they lose 1–0 on 8 December at Bolton. 'It was a sad, grey week for Danny Blanchflower's boys . . . I know this sounds like treason but the drive has been missing from Tottenham on the two occasions I have seen them in the last fortnight.'

From Bolton comes the sound of barking as Bill addresses his team. 'General slackness' is the theme of the bollocking they get in the aftermath of their 1–0 defeat. Having scored sixty goals in seventeen games, they have managed only two in the last four and are, he tells the press, 'suffering from too much success. I am very disappointed in them. Obviously we missed White. He is a good player. But we are supposed to have lots of them.'

John returns for the rearranged Cup Winners' Cup tie in Glasgow and the day before the match pays a visit to Alloa. 'What's going to happen tomorrow?' asks the kit man.

'I'm going to fucking stuff 'em,' says John.

True to his word, John helps Spurs beat Rangers 3–2, making their second goal, scored by Bobby Smith. The aggregate scoreline of 8–4 puts them in the quarter-finals. 'In these prestige games my players produce everything asked of them,' says Bill. 'But we won't get these games if we don't pave the way by winning the League or the FA Cup.'

The win comes at a price – Spurs lose Danny Blanchflower with an injury to his right knee. 'I was nearing my thirty-seventh birthday and feeling I could play until I was forty,' he writes later. 'I was playing well until I was struck from behind. My knee felt like the twisted strings of a harp.' It's harder to recover from injuries the older you get and Danny sits out the best part of the next three months.

Meanwhile, on a day of what the *Sunday Express* of 12 December describes as 'dribbling murk', it's Birmingham 0, Spurs 2 at St Andrews and John is considered to be 'below his best'. Two weeks later, it's Spurs 4, West Ham 4, and the *Daily Telegraph* notes that 'the injured Blanchflower sat next to Bill in the dugout . . . the grim expression on this dour Yorkshireman's face suggested he was not singing the praises of his team.'

Snow, fog and ice wipe out a lot of the football programme over Christmas but the Boxing Day game between Ipswich and Spurs goes on. It finishes up Spurs 5, Ipswich 0, and in the *Daily Telegraph*, David Miller comments that 'no one but Spurs could have played with such breathtaking poise on such a treacherous surface . . . Spurs are not as others, and we marvelled at a first half of contained wizardry. As against Dukla last year, White's skill on a surface most people would think twice about simply running on, overwhelmed Ipswich. He, Mackay, Greaves and Jones . . . anticipated the pace with uncanny accuracy.'

Donald Saunders's 'Monday Soccer Commentary' for New Year's Eve reports 'the worst blizzards for years sweeping across much of England' and Spurs' FA Cup third-round tie with Burnley is postponed till 16 January. EXIT SPURS – IN SHAME and BLACK DAY FOR SPURS are among the headlines when they finally get to meet at a snow-carpeted White Hart Lane. With Danny Blanchflower in hospital getting over a cartilage operation, it's an attritional game which Spurs lose 3–0 while evoking comments such as 'lost their reputation as a sporting, all-weather team'; 'farce of a match'; 'Never has a mighty team gone out so shabbily', and 'crude brutality'. There is, in addition, 'no excuse for players who, when action has passed, punch and hack at their opponents'.

The trouble starts when Bobby Smith sticks it to the Burnley centre-half, John Talbut, who collapses dramatically onto the pitch. It is, apparently, 'a grim mystery' why Bobby isn't sent off. There's more: 'The shame of Tottenham continued as Dyson went into a brawl with Blacklaw . . . It was the signal for a free fight.' Study a photo of the incident and John can be seen quietly trying to calm Terry Dyson and Blacklaw, the Burnley goalie, as everyone else comes roaring in.

Some football is played and the *Sunday Express* of 20 January reports Spurs 2–0 defeat of Blackpool when they regain the League leadership 'in farcical conditions' in which 'the players' faces, heads, eyelashes and hair were so caked and powdered that Spurs . . . looked like off-white ghosts as they skidded and tobogganed on the Blackpool goal'. Along with Dave Mackay, Jimmy Greaves and Danny's replacement Tony Marchi, John is applauded for 'controlling events in their customary manner'.

By the middle of the following week, though, John is in University College Hospital. For the last two weeks he has been unable to sleep – an unheard of condition where he is concerned – and is suffering some serious pains in his back. 'Things haven't been going right for me for some time,' he tells the *Daily Mirror*'s Ken Jones. 'I expect to be here until the weekend for X-rays and an examination. I'm sure everything is OK. It's just I want to settle my mind and then get down to showing some form.'

White's subtle skill, adds Ken, is 'probably the most decisive factor in Spurs success. And it is significant that when he is not in top form their performances lose some of their glitter.'

In the wider world, Christmas 1962 is remembered for the Boxing Day rail disaster, which killed eighteen people and injured fifty others when the midday Glasgow–London Express ploughed into the back of another mainline train near Crewe. For John and Sandra, adversity struck from a different direction. Step back to consider what was going on as the winter of 1962–3 dug in, and John's absences and erratic form start to make total sense.

At the end of November, Harry, who had been suffering abdominal pains, went into hospital to have an ulcer treated. Instead he was diagnosed with inoperable cancer. He died on 22 December, the day Spurs drew 4–4 with West Ham while Bill sat grimly in the dugout. It was Alma's birthday and Harry left her a card which said, 'Sorry, mate.'

Alma was left on her own with Sandra's three-year-old brother Andrew. 'It was an awful winter, a very difficult time for her,' recalls Sandra. 'Then John went into hospital with terrible pains in his back. They said it was psychosomatic. Because Dad had died.'

People express emotional pain in differing ways, from full-on dramatic outbursts through stiff-upper-lip stoicism to mute despair. It doesn't take much analysis to understand that the loss of Harry, the man who gave him encouragement and friendship at the start of his Tottenham life, seems to have affected John deeply. In those days men thought it was a weakness to cry, even if they had the strongest excuse in the world. John dealt with it the best way he knew how, by just getting on with things, but his body let him down.

It leaves you wondering just why Harry's death produced such a strong and unexpected reaction. The only person who could supply an answer to that is Sandra and even she remains puzzled. 'I don't know,' she says. 'Perhaps Harry meant home.'

BEST WISHES FOR A HAPPY AND PROSPEROUS NEW YEAR
from
THE CHAIRMAN, DIRECTOR, STAFF and PLAYERS OF THE SPURS

Tottenham Hotspur Football and Athletic Club
Official Programme, 26 December 1962

23

Absent Fathers
Rob, 2010

If there's one thing that links all the men in our family, it's the missing dads. Andrew growing up without his. Me growing up without mine. Tom, Eddie and my dad growing up without theirs. I don't know what it was like for them but this is how it is from where I'm sitting.

Take some of the functions of a dad. The other day I was talking to a friend whose father died when he was fifteen. He says he still misses the guy, and it's not necessarily for the big things dads are meant to provide – approval, authority, discipline. 'I miss being able to ask him what kind of mortgage I ought to take out,' said my friend.

And he's right. When I'm playing football, I'd like a dad who says, 'Hit that ball with this part of your foot.' It's the dad-instructions, that's what you long for. What you've got is a hole where all those mundane, comfortable, everyday bits of man-advice that dad hands on to son ought to be. What makes my friend heartsick is not having his dad's guidance about the best central heating boiler to install.

And there's something else my friend misses. He can't perform his role as his dad's son any more. So, OK, I can't miss what I've never had but I've just realised why I always feel so pissed off around Christmas. I'd always thought it was because the sheer chaos of the festive season gave me the hump. But it's about much deeper issues than that. It's to do with not being able to give my dad a present or receive one from him.

I guess I look at my case as slightly different from the other men in my family. They were all left with a few memories, even fleeting ones, of doing dad-and-son things. I've got none. But it's not only that. I lost the chance to have a dad who was this fantastic man revered as a football genius. It's frustrating.

But nevertheless it's not weird. If you're born with one leg, that's what you know. Having one leg is normality. Which is probably the weirdest thing about it. I've always had this defence mechanism: 'It doesn't bother me.' 'I haven't suffered.' But I have. Emotionally it's been limiting. Always keeping quiet, not really talking about it. I've not allowed myself to think that it *has* been different for me, not having a father. And the father I didn't have was John White, football god.

Which throws up two problems.

The first is that when I play football I can spend an entire ninety minutes working out how he could do what he could do. I'm stupidly trying to measure myself against someone when I don't have the measurements to hand, only a collection of facts and stories about a genius.

The second is that for most of my life I didn't know the biggest fact and story of all.

For a twelve-year period, from my twenties to mid-thirties, my dad's brother Tom would get drunk and to my bemusement tell me what a crap uncle he'd been, to a point where I'd get really annoyed and tell people not to leave me alone with him.

Then one day, at my auntie Janette's sixtieth birthday party, Tom got drunk, told me he was a crap uncle, then gave me the amazing, punch-in-the-gut news that my dad had another son. That he'd been caught out – this is the official family version – by the local man-trap when he was just a naive and foolish boy, and that it was devastating for him but he'd done the right thing all round. He'd behaved impeccably and honourably. You could expect nothing less from John White.

Obviously I felt threatened. My dad's mine! Now suddenly, somewhere, someone is my older half-brother. And of course I felt foolish too. I was the last person to know. How come I didn't guess? How come nobody felt it right to tell me?

Here's what I think.

I don't know enough to pass judgement either way but I reckon what happened must have been more devastating for the woman than for my dad. But I guess Tom presented the whole episode in the way he did because he wanted to show my dad in the generous light he'd always shown him to me.

Therein lies the problem. I don't want to go into some self-regarding navel-gazing thing but I'm hard-working to the point of being obsessional. I want to be hugely good at what I do. Which has been my way of trying to measure up to this guy, this perfect man.

So the information Tom had about Dad's human frailties would have helped enormously. Knowing he was an ordinary, fallible person, not a god, would have been great. I remember listening to Jim McAlister relating the story about John giving him and Tony Jacklin a lift and being excited by my dad being drunk and getting stopped by the cop. John White wasn't perfect! He drank and drove. He did fuck up. He fathered a child and didn't stick around. He did panic. He was irresponsible and a shit sometimes.

And there's another thing. This other son, my half-brother, hasn't even got the consolation of being *the* son of John White. There's a shared reality for both of us – we're both the sons of the same absent father. But at least I've got acceptance from the family. I am who I say I am.

It's scary, though. There's always that fear . . . what if I meet this other guy and it's completely crap? What kind of Pandora's box gets opened? What if I find things out that I don't want to know? But oh yes, maybe I do want to know. Subconsciously maybe it's one of my motivations for doing this book. Maybe I *want* him to come out of the woodwork.

There you go. We all keep these secrets that are sometimes easier not to talk about. I've been saying I really don't understand why I wasn't told so much earlier, but what I do see now is how very difficult Tom found the prospect of telling me. Here's this little lad who's lost his dad, he would have thought. At least let's build the image up so he's got someone to be proud of. Let's give him the consolation of being this football god's representative on earth. How can I shatter his world by telling him he's got a half-brother?

The poor bugger, carrying around this boulder of guilt all the time, knowing he really needed to tell me, knowing it was something I wouldn't like to hear. If he'd had a dad, he could have asked his advice about how to tell me. But he hadn't.

THE LITTLE MEN STAR AS SPURS ROMP TO CUP

Spurs 5, Atletico Madrid 1

Spurs tonight hold high the European Cup-Winners' Cup. They hold it aloft with pride as thousands of Londoners and neutral Netherlanders join in a song of salute. Spurs wrested the trophy – the first major European soccer prize to come to Britain – from the holders Atletico Madrid, here at the Feyenoord Stadium.

This is the moment of greatest triumph not only for Spurs, who had planned this day for three weary years, but also for British soccer and British sportsmanship. For tonight, Spurs won not only a slim silver cup. They won the hearts of the phlegmatic Dutchmen, who came just to see a match but stayed to cheer 11 skilled fighting professionals.

Spurs have never been a better team.

Brian James, Daily Mail, 16 May 1963

24

Oi! Remember Rotterdam

'**B**it unfortunate, today's teams,' muses Terry Dyson. 'Because they're always compared to us. We were the best. We were the first.'

Terry is a short, sturdy powerhouse of a man, with greying hair that still contains a touch of the russet colour that made him so easy for the crowd to pick out on a claggy day at White Hart Lane fifty years ago. Then, charging along the wing and flinging himself into the goalmouth, he was described by Julian Holland, as a 'berserk rogue mouse', and though there was nothing the remotest bit timorous about the way Terry played it's certainly true that as a flank man he was flamboyantly energetic and uncatchable, not to mention seriously diminutive. At five feet three inches he was the smallest man in the club – and yet if you saw him jump for a high ball you'd swear he was a Goliath.

Bill Nicholson sang his praises as an enthusiast, a player who was prepared to run for the whole ninety minutes and never let himself be bullied out of a game. 'If I had to nominate a player who had the attitude I wanted, it was Terry,' he wrote. 'He needed no motivation.' Terry was also, notes Cliff Jones, 'one hell of a footballer, a good passer who scored important goals'. You could argue that the most important were the two he stuck past Atletico Madrid one night in May 1963.

Tottenham's season in the League had pursued an increasingly familiar course till then. Burnley had knocked them out of the FA Cup and it was looking as if the old pattern of getting close to the championship but no nearer was going to repeat itself. The one thing that would prevent 1962–3 being – by Spurs' standards – a write-off would be winning the European Cup Winners' Cup, a much bigger deal than it might sound now. No English club had ever won a trophy in Europe. First, though, they had to reach the final.

John was out of hospital by the end of January. Three weeks later, after the 3–2 away defeat of Arsenal, the *Sunday Express* described him as 'the most exquisite artist on view', though there's no sense of him imposing himself on the game and after that his progress was fitful. Against West Brom at the start of March – Spurs beat them 2–1 – the verdict of the *Daily Telegraph* was that 'Spurs can possibly afford to have one forward off form, but when Greaves, White, Jones and Medwin are all out of touch on the same afternoon, their attack falls a long way short of the slick machine we expect'.

Three days later came the first leg of the Cup Winners' Cup quarter-final against Slovan Bratislava. Danny Blanchflower, still injured, sat out a match played in conditions so bitter that, according to Ken Jones, the Danube had frozen into a white avenue. 'Bill Brown had the game of his life,' says Ken. 'Spurs lost 2–0 and it would have been 10–0 if it hadn't been for him, so halfway through Bill Nicholson sent Danny down to talk to him to keep him going.' Afterwards, Ken asked Bill Brown what had been the content of Danny's sinew-stiffening speech. It was, '"There's a great nightclub under the hotel. Look out, they're coming again."'

In his book, Bill Nicholson recorded: 'We were lucky to escape with a 2–0 beating.' The report Ken filed for the *Daily Mirror* began: 'Spurs report for early training this morning knowing they are ALL on the carpet.' It was John, though, who bore the brunt of press criticism: 'Colourless White'; 'the saddest disappointment was White, who sank almost without trace in the mud and with him all hopes of cohesion'; 'John White was the most ineffective'; 'John White fiddled and lost the ball in midfield'.

The disparagement continued after the 9 March League game at

Old Trafford: 'Spurs were not spectacular. White took too small a part for that'; 'With White seeming to lack confidence, Greaves took much of the midfield work on himself . . .'

This isn't necessarily to say that John was as unimpressive as people made out. For a start, Spurs beat Manchester United 2–0 that day. They were also top of the League, albeit only by goal difference. But, as ever, it was a by-product of John's peculiar gift that spectators, whether paid or paying, weren't always able to appreciate just how influential he was. Dimitar Berbatov isn't the most obvious player to compare John with – the former languidly sauntering in a relatively small area of play whereas John was mobile and ubiquitous – but he resembles John in one significant department: the ability to get about with the minimum of air disturbance. 'That type of player carries a mental picture of the game around,' says David Lacey. 'You can see when the ball comes to them they know exactly what they're going to do with it. Great positional players. It's only when you see the TV playback of a goal that you realise it was started by a three-yard pass from Berbatov somewhere else. White was that sort of player – a chess man. But they didn't have TV playbacks then.'

It's a good idea, therefore, not to take at face value some of the comments John inspired during that phase of the season. When the *Daily Telegraph*'s 14 March preview of the Slovan tie observed that 'much will depend on whether John White, the man who has often turned their attack into a devastating goal-scoring machine, is back to form', it was at least partly right.

John was on form, and then some. Spurs overwhelmed Slovan, with a ten-minute, three-goal burst just before half-time and another midway through the second half. SIX-GOAL 'MURDER' SWEEPS CZECHS ASIDE was the headline in the next day's *Daily Mirror*. In the *Daily Mail*, Brian James wrote: 'Like brilliant flashes of light-ning, the 11 white-shirted men of Tottenham struck a new high in sporting achievement last night . . . Slovan, their conquerors by two goals on Czech soil last week, were annihilated.'

If you still need proof of just how essential John was, you only have to sift through reports of the goals. Dave Mackay's – the cross came from John. Jimmy Greaves's first – a pass from John in midfield. Bobby Smith's – a move begun by John. Jimmy's second and then Cliff Jones's – John initiated both moves. The sixth and final goal was scored by John himself.

The championship continued as an on-off affair. On 23 March Spurs drew 2–2 away to Leicester. Burnley, though, continued to be their bogey team as they drew 1–1 at White Hart Lane on 31 March. When they drew 1–1 at home to Fulham on 14 April Spurs were top above Everton by a goal difference of 0.25. Then they went to Goodison and lost 1–0.

GREAVES SENT OFF – BUT SPURS STORM ON
White and Dyson leave Jugoslavs trailing in first leg tie
OFK Belgrade 1, Tottenham 2

The Cup Winners' Cup semi-final punctuated the end-of-season run-in. Spurs won in spite of playing for the last half-hour with ten men; Jimmy Greaves was sent off – a career first – for what the Hungarian referee Aranjosi called 'not acting like a gentleman'. John scored their first goal after twenty-six minutes: 'Marchi pushed the free kick to Bobby Smith, whose side-flick was hammered into the net by White from 20 yards.' He started the build-up for their second, too: 'With 20 minutes to go, White collected the ball near the right corner flag and curled a centre accurately into the penalty area. Smith leapt for it and the goalkeeper . . . suddenly dropped it. Up popped Dyson to drive the ball into the back of the net.'

Back in England, Danny reappeared for his first League game since crocking his knee in December as Spurs beat Bolton 4–1 on 27 April; John scored again. Four days later, he laid on two of Tottenham's goals when OFK Belgrade came to White Hart Lane for the return

Earning his Spurs: John was brought to White Hart Lane by Bill Nicholson in 1959 for £20,000

Those glory, glory days: Bill Nicholson (*centre*) and the rest of the Spurs team celebrate winning the league in 1961, the first half of their Double

Tottenham Hotspur. The 1960–61 Double-winning team with their trophies (*from back left*): Bill Brown, Peter Baker, Ron Henry, Bill Nicholson Danny Blanchflower, Maurice Norman, Dave Mackay, Cliff Jones, John White, Bobby Smith, Les Allen, Terry Dyson

John training with
Dave Mackay (*right*)
and Jimmy Greaves
(*centre*) who arrived
from Milan in 1961
for a record fee
of £99,000

'O Captain!
My Captain!':
Danny Blanchflower
pictured (*centre*)
with John White
and Cliff Jones

The Ghost of White Hart Lane:
John scores against Rangers
in the 1962 European Cup

John and Maurice Norman
hold aloft the FA Cup in 1963

The trophies keep on coming
as Spurs land the European Cup-
Winners' Cup in 1963

Playing for laughs: (*Clockwise from top left*) John and his wife Sandra with Dave Mackay; John, Dave and Cliff Jones experiment in a photobooth; John indulging in one of his favourite pastimes at the Crews Hill golf course

John and Sandra celebrate their engagement

John overcomes his shyness away from the football pitch to dance with Sandra

John with his daughter Amanda (*above*) and his son Rob (*below*)

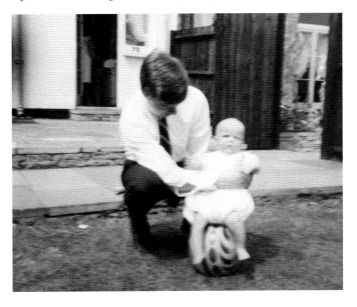

SPURS STAR KILLED BY LIGHTNING

A Bloom chief in 'good news' riddle

By ROBERT HEAD

HOPES of an eleventh-hour reprieve for 5,000 shareholders in John Bloom's crumbling Rolls Razor washing-machine empire were raised—then dashed—last night.

A message on stockbrokers' ticker machines quoted Rolls director Irving Jacobs as saying: "The good news we have been expecting all day will, if it comes, be later to-night."

But last night Mr. Jacobs told me: "I cannot understand how it happened. I made no such statement at all."

Mr. Bloom appeared at the door of his Park-lane flat shortly after 10 p.m. to say: "I will be making no statement tonight."

Meeting

Mr. Bloom's day began at 7.30 a.m. when he left his flat to meet accountants, bankers, and creditors at his Cricklewood headquarters.

The talks continued back at Mr. Bloom's flat.

On the Stock Exchange, Rolls Razor shares worth more than 47s. each at one time had last year—started the day at 1s. 6d. perked up hopefully to 2s. 7½d. then slipped back to 2s. 11d.

Bills

Hopes centred on prospects that—

CREDITORS might be persuaded to give Rolls Razor another year or two to pay bills believed to total £1,000,000.

FINANCIERS might be found to put up an extra £1,000,000 working capital to keep the firm running until it can develop new washing machines, increase sales and slash costs.

But it seems certain that no agreement were to ... who bought shares ... to give them ... trol of the company.

By MIRROR REPORTERS

SOCCER international John White, 26, star of the Spurs and Scotland forward lines, was killed by lightning yesterday in a storm which flailed a wide area of Southern England.

A flash struck him as he sheltered from the rain under an old oak tree at Crews Hill golf club, Enfield. He had been playing alone—and two groundsmen found him lying dead.

White, who was regarded as one of the finest inside forwards of recent years, was sometimes called "The Ghost" because of his will-o'-the-wisp play.

He played for Scotland twenty-two times and it is reckoned that it will cost Spurs an £80,000 transfer fee to get a replacement of his calibre.

Mr. C. F. Cox, a Tottenham director, said last night: "White's death is a tragic loss to Tottenham and football in general. He was a vital link in our successful run in recent years."

Weeping

Soon after White was found dead, his 24-year-old wife Sandra arrived at the golf course with their six-month-old son Robert. She intended to pick up her husband in the family car—but was met by police officers at the entrance to the club.

They broke the news to her, and fifteen minutes later she was driven away in tears.

Mrs. White, who has a two-year-old daughter, Amanda, married John in June, 1961.

Club steward Albert Burr, 58, said last night that Mrs. White had but wanted her husband to play golf, because their son was ill.

"But he decided to have a round while she went shopping," Mr. Burr added.

Sudden death came to John White—"a true man of Soccer," writes Ken Jones on Page 22—on the Bron fairway. A one-minute cloudburst sent him scurrying for cover under a tree at the side of the course.

As he sat beneath the tree with his golf bags by his side, lightning struck. It is thought that he died instantly.

John White and his wife Sandra with their daughter Amanda and baby Robert—in one of his father's international caps.

IT'S DANCING CILLA

LOOK who has joined the chorus . . . SINGING star Cilla Black, 21, DANCING in a glittering costume. Cilla, who has been taking dancing lessons, was rehearsing for "The Night of 100 Stars," the big charity show which is being staged at the London Palladium tomorrow to help orphan children of actors and actresses.

Great storm holds up the rush-hour trains

yards from where he was found. I could smell burning in the air, and there was a tingling in my fingers.

The savage summer storm held up rush-hour trains in London . . .

Floodwater built up in a tunnel just outside King's Cross station and halted all trains, an Eastern Region spokesman said last night.

Jams

The centre two tracks of the station were flooded, and within fifteen minutes all outgoing tracks were swamped.

After a while, single-line working was started. "We are getting trains away, but up to seventy minutes late," said a railway spokesman.

Later, services were back to normal.

The last of the three Royal Garden Parties given by the Queen and the Duke of Edinburgh in the past week ended in a thunderstorm and torrential rain last night.

Huge traffic jams built up in several areas—the longest stretched almost eight miles from Hoddesdon to Waltham Cross.

People waded through 3ft. of water outside Chislehurst Park Tube station.

Round the South coast, ships were battered by high winds and rough seas . . .

A record-breaking rescue was made off the Kent coast.

Less than thirty minutes after being blown into the sea when their yacht capsized near the River Swale, three men were landed for treatment at Margate Hospital, after being saved by helicopter.

Flood pictures—Back Page.

leg and were beaten 3–1 in what was described as 'one of Tottenham's less distinguished performances'. It was a rufty-tufty encounter in which, observed the referee afterwards, 'the players seemed to be more interested in each other than the ball'. Who minded? Spurs were in a European final for the first time.

The championship eluded them, though. To have any chance of containing Everton, they needed to beat League stragglers Manchester City at Maine Road; they lost 1–0. John missed that game, but was fit for the final in Rotterdam. Dave Mackay, who had also been an injured absentee against Manchester City, was less of a certainty, and by the time they arrived in Holland for the final, a lot of the side – drained from a long and unrewarded season – were apprehensive.

Dave, it transpired, was a definite non-starter, and Danny's knee was like a cannonball with blood vessels. The choice, then, said Danny, was 'me on one leg or John Smith on two'. Danny got the job. They needed him. Atletico were the Cup holders; some of their players were legends, and Bill Nicholson went on to give one of the most depressing pre-match talks of his life about how good they were while the players got gloomier and tenser.

Danny raised them up from their depths with a speech of wit, passion and belief. Then Atletico's bear of a centre-half, Griffa, bent Bobby Smith double twice in the opening minutes, and the next moment John got whacked, then Cliff, then Jimmy. It was the final goad they needed to plunge into defiant contention. After sixteen minutes, the first goal. Tony Marchi, Dave's stand-in, began the move and the ball passed from John to Bobby to Cliff, then Jimmy picked it out of the air to score. Another seventeen minutes, another goal. This one was John's – a shot rapped in off the underside of the bar after Terry Dyson's defence-busting cross. Two up by half-time – winning looked like a certainty.

It wasn't.

Two minutes after the restart, the Spurs defence was in a tangle.

Unmarked, Adelardo banged a shot goalwards and Ron Henry only kept it out with a punch. Penalty. 2–1.

Spurs went through fifteen minutes of gripless defending that made Atletico look good. Almost too good. But as Rivilla was squaring up to shoot, Terry Dyson told himself that Dave Mackay would have scorned to protect himself in the line of fire no matter how much it hurt, so he threw himself in the way, the shot hammering his foot so hard he was nearly crippled.

But it worked. And then the almost instant segue that turned the match Spurs' way again – Terry's curling centre from the left that took a last-minute ride on the breeze and went in between the goalie's head and the crossbar. 3–1. Then 4–1 – Jimmy, from another centre by Terry. And then Terry himself, belting upfield, limping like a crazed animal, to score from twenty-five yards.

Tottenham Hotspur 5, Atletico Madrid 1. Afterwards there was Dave sobbing in one dressing room because he hadn't been part of it, and the Atletico goalie weeping in the other because he had been. Dave wasn't only crying because he'd been left out, though. No one was fooled by Danny's parting comment: 'We're going to be the Cup Winners next year as well.'

Even the reports of that final, read today, have an elegiac feel. Like Dave, Brian James knew that what he'd witnessed that night was the last of the Double side. 'Tonight, suddenly, this was a team free of tension,' he wrote in the *Daily Mail*, 'a team taking its pace from the quiet skills of Blanchflower and White, the aggression of Smith, Henry and Baker. *Simply . . . this was a team.*'

'I think they were all very nice people,' says Brian now. 'Manchester United have more outstanding players on the bench these days than Spurs had on that team, but the thing I remember most about them is that there was a lovely relationship I've never experienced before or since in a football team. The warmth there was like being in a family. There was huge admiration for each other, less sniping than in another team. You were in the company of solid, sensible, professional men who knew the value of what they did and knew the value of what the others did.'

'There's something about that era, maybe because they didn't get so much money,' says Ken Jones. 'Players were different. There was rarely any difficulty in making contact with them. When you look at them giving interviews on TV these days, they're pulling away.'

'What was so frankly beyond comprehension was this intimate relationship between footballers and football journalists,' concurs Brian. 'At the Bell and Hare there was a lock-in after every match. It wasn't a notebook occasion, just players and a handful of journalists. Plus fans like Allen Lansberg, the jeweller, and Morris Keston – people who asked nothing of anybody, always paid their own way, but every time you pitched up at a football match they were there. I have the greatest respect for them. Then there were people who you didn't mess around with, but a lot of them were matey, like One-Armed Lou.'

'One arm was on the fringe of gangsterism,' says Ken. 'He knew the Krays very well. Terrific, but he was a ticket tout. Danny was a particular mate of his and would always see him right. I can't remember anyone having a go at Danny for mixing with One-Armed Lou.'

The Bell and Hare was a corner pub. To get into the car park you'd have to drive across the pavement – not so easy with 60,000 fans pouring past. The players' territory was a small back bar. 'Often very noisy' is Brian's description. 'People gesticulating. Chat about the match: lucky bastard, had to be a penalty, that sort of thing. Racing. Golf. Films. But slightly better informed than most pub chat after matches.

'You had to be given the nod to get in there,' he continues. 'Probably by Dave Mackay: "He's all right." The first thing you'd hear would be Jimmy Burton, Dave Mackay's business partner, funniest man who ever lived, screeching with laughter. Cliff Jones had plenty to say for himself, too. Jimmy Greaves was life and soul. Bobby Smith – a bit full of himself though not to the extent of being obnoxious. No need to tell him he'd played well – he'd tell you.

'Ron Henry – one of the quiet types. Enjoying the company. Not the slightest danger he'd start dancing with his knickers on his head. Maurice Norman – a big man who didn't need to demonstrate how big he was. The confidence of someone who knew he was the tallest around. People clearing a path for him when he made his way to the bar. Bill Brown – a bit of a gent. You looked across. Whitey, not talking very much. Trapped by a fan. So you'd go over. He'd generally have something interesting to say. Sharp in his observations. What he said, he meant.

'After the Bell and Hare, they'd go their different ways. With some of them, it was girls. But I think the scandals were limited because the players were getting £20 a week. There's precious little mayhem you can get up to on that.

'Tuesday or Wednesday morning, you'd go to the training ground. You stood there and waited and walked off with them. Relationships did develop. Geoff Hurst, Alan Mullery, George Cohen, they treat me like an old friend. Geoff Hurst came and mowed our lawn after I'd done my back in. Today it couldn't happen on a number of levels. Training ground? Not let in unless it's a bloody press conference. You could never establish a relationship.'

'We were closer to the supporters, too,' says Terry Dyson. 'Players couldn't care less about them now. There's no connection between them and the people who see them play. Kiss the badge! What a load of crap. Another £10,000 a week and they'll be gone.

'When the club were celebrating one hundred years of Tottenham, me and Danny Blanchflower were invited back. Danny said, "I tell you, Terry, they can have their money, today's players. They'll never have our memories." I said, "That's true, Danny, but I'd like their money." Flipping useless some of them. Wouldn't have got in our reserves team.

'We were still ordinary people. Mess about in training. Mess about with each other. You come into the changing room. You've won, and you've done well yourself. That minute or two when you sit down. Them three or four minutes. That's a wonderful feeling. Great, that. You can't describe it to people. Then you're chatting away. This and that. Guys going round talking to people. Shower the mud off then you'd get in the big bath. You're sat there.

'That's what it's about, really. The feelings you get. Danny described it in his book as "the rapture of the game" and I think he described that very well. Rapture's when you're elated. Caught up in it. That's what I would miss about football now. After a game. Crap if you'd lost of course. But we didn't lose often.'

That European final was Terry's apotheosis. He remembers Bobby Smith saying as they left the pitch that they should retire straight off, because they'd never play like that again. Two years on, he was transferred to Fulham, so ending a Spurs career that had started in 1954 when he signed for them in a cafe opposite the Royal Artillery Barracks during his national service. But even now if Terry gets any stick from his old team-mates he'll wag his finger and say, 'Oi! Remember Rotterdam.'

Maybe you need to have been part of that era to understand the affection and loyalty and pride they felt. Maybe people who watched football before the mid-eighties were the lucky ones. Those players were their gods come down. They took their buses, rode on their trains, drank in the same pubs. They had to answer to the supporters who paid their money, and they gave those supporters not just entertainment, but something more – glory, rapture, elation, thrills and sometimes transcendent beauty. They also got it in a way modern players don't. They were never going to be rich beyond anyone's wildest imaginings. Equally, they were never going to be despised and envied as often as they were worshipped and rewarded.

A football team, as Danny Blanchflower once said, is a mysterious thing. These days players arrive and go more quickly. Teams fall apart sooner. The intimacy that bonded the Glory Boys isn't there any more. That makes the alchemy harder to perform, and the connection between supporter and player seems as quaint and formal as courtly love.

Strange turnabouts happen, of course. But it's hard to imagine that the ties that bound the Double side and their followers could ever be replicated in the narcissistic, profit-driven culture of the modern game. Even so, it's pleasant now and then to dream that some day not far off our present and future gods will turn their backs on the rapacious individualism of their era and think of football again as a game where they belong to each other, and to us, as incontestably as their families and ancestors.

As Terry Dyson would say, Remember Rotterdam.

Bill Nicholson would like to be able to go out and buy players that would add up to a better team than the one he has got. If he could get 11 new players to improve on us he would not hesitate to do it. If he could replace me tomorrow with the complete satisfaction that it would be better for the club he would do so. It is not that easy.

Danny Blanchflower, *Sunday Express*, 1 September 1963

25

The Last of the Glory Boys

July 1963. The scene: the lanes of Hertfordshire, bordered on each side by arable fields crisped up by the sun. It's just after two thirty. A group of men, walking fit to bust, sweep round a corner. 'Run for a couple of hundred yards!' barks the trainer.

A middle-aged man, damp-haired and red-faced with effort, fights his way to the front. He's hurting. They make you do the road walk at half past two after your muscles have stiffened up at lunch. It's hard to drag yourself up off your chair these days.

One knee doesn't work properly any more. There's no cartilage left, so bone chafes on bone. But Danny pushes on, faster and faster because he can hear the footsteps hammering up behind him.

Soon this is a full-on run. He knows the pace is killing, ridiculous, but he's got to be first. His stomach is almost turning over. The intake of air finds the decay in his teeth. The pounding of his weight on his knee sends shock waves all the way up the back of his thigh and it's all he can do not to moan out loud.

A younger man glides alongside him. 'Keep going,' says John, then patters off into the distance.

It's 24 August, first day of the season. It's a veterans' head-to-head at the Victoria Ground where Spurs play Stoke City. Stoke, the oldest club in the Football League, also have its hoariest player; Stanley Matthews is now forty-eight but thanks to a fitness regime that includes a pint of hot sweet tea every morning retains enough lead in his pencil to have helped bring the club back into the top flight.

Excepting that Jimmy Greaves now wears the number 10 shirt in place of Les Allen, the Spurs team that loses to Stoke is the Double side; compared to Stan, Danny and his men are practically juvenile, but even so, they're beaten 2–1 and the press start knitting round the guillotine.

'White and Jones played hard but Greaves had a wretched match . . .' 'Danny Blanchflower could never contain McIlroy . . .' 'Dave Mackay had to play like two men . . .' 'Henry and Baker were often struggling . . .' 'Only the drifting White had much to say for himself in Spurs' attack . . .'

The press are already advising Bill Nicholson to buy the Scotland international Jim Baxter: 'What is £100,000 when your team may be starting to slide?' Bill's solution comes cheaper – a change to a 4–2–4 system with Danny confined alongside Maurice Norman and John having to drop back deeper in midfield.

At first the new formation works. The midweek game on 28 August sees Spurs beat Wolves 4–1 at Molineux. It's Spurs 4, Nottingham Forest 1 the following Saturday ('Danny Blanchflower, never a great tackler in the Dave Mackay tradition, fitted neatly into the rear line without looking the least like a centre-half . . . perhaps his covering will improve') and Spurs 4, Wolves 3 on 4 September; 'Tottenham, using with devastating effect the 4–2–4 system which had seemed such a burden to them on Saturday . . .'

Three days later, at Ewood Park, there is a less impressive performance; Blackburn Rovers beat them 7–2. People wait for them to fold. Instead, what happens is a 6–1 thrashing of Blackpool, in which John opens with 'a cracking goal' and Jimmy Greaves comes up with one of his hat-tricks.

On 16 September, it's Aston Villa 2, Spurs 4. Phil Beal plays in place of an injured Danny Blanchflower and Spurs 'drew the applause, polite and ungrudging, for the elegant tapestry worked by White across the lush grass'. On 21 September, it's Chelsea 0, Spurs 3.

What's impressive is how well Spurs' ageing workforce are doing.

Towards the end of September, Nottingham Forest lead the table but only by a point above an agglomeration of five clubs. Spurs are among them. And what comes over equally clearly is the increased burden of responsibility that John has taken on in midfield, and how successfully he is dealing with it. That's emphasised in the last match of the month, when he's the driving force in the 3–0 defeat of West Ham and is being hailed as 'the key man of the Tottenham team' and 'now playing deeper and better than ever with the vast spaces at his command'.

Yet looking back at these old reports, it's hard not to feel puzzled. The win against West Ham is Tottenham's fourth in a row, and their seventh in nine matches. They've also scored thirty-one goals, more than any other attack in the country, but you wouldn't guess that by the tone of the commentary. Here's the verdict on their 4–1 defeat of Forest: 'Spurs forwards played as though they had never met before.' Here's the headline over the 6–1 crushing of Blackpool: 'SPURS SCORE SIX BUT STILL EARN CRITICISM'. It's open season when it comes to defeat by Blackburn: 'Spurs were the width of a pitch slower in thought and deed . . . the towering power of Maurice Norman was a pillar of straw.'

To maul a cliché taken from another sport, for Spurs they set the bar higher than for anyone else. In his *Sunday Express* column on 1 September, Danny Blanchflower writes of 'a growing demand to knock the Spurs' and asks: 'But can anybody really say for sure that it is not capable of winning something again this year?'

It's a question that seemed to beg a positive answer. The 2 October home game against Birmingham finishes 6–1 and puts them on top of the First Division. In midweek they draw 3–3 away to Sheffield United, unleashing a familiar grudging note from one journalist on the subject: 'the uncanny ability of the Spurs forwards to find goals gave them a lead they scarcely deserved'.

Still, they're second to Manchester United in the table, level on points, and autumn is always a good time for John. The 15 October away game against Arsenal – it finishes 4–4 – has Brian James, in the *Daily Mail*, praising as outstanding 'White and [Arsenal's George] Eastham, the skilful little men in two teams of giants'. On 19 October, when Spurs draw 1–1 at home to Leicester, John is deemed in the *Sunday Express* to have had 'a quiet game' but against Everton the week after – they lose 1–0 – he is 'Spurs' best forward'. November opens with a 1–0 home defeat of Fulham when 'John White was in his element on the treacherous surface and his superb passing was a joy to watch'.

In the League table, it's still Manchester United on top with Spurs a close second. Their meeting on 9 November is, it follows, a match of high significance – more so since they are drawn to play each other again in the European Cup Winners' Cup in December. It's also where the problems really begin.

Manchester United 4, Spurs 1. MARCH OF TIME CATCHES UP ON TOTTENHAM; LAW (3), MOORE PUT SPURS TO THE SWORD; SUPERB LAW SHATTERS SPURS are the headlines. The finger of shame is pointed at Danny: 'Law pounced on a long clearance and ran round Blanchflower . . . Law shot United's fourth goal following a move in which Blanchflower again missed the ball . . .'

'I had the feeling that the team was going to last forever,' says Brian James. 'Brilliant one-touch football based on those mad five-a-sides in the White Hart Lane gym. Then it became painfully obvious that Danny was slowing up. Spurs lost at Old Trafford quite comfortably. Ken Jones and I were in the corridor when Matt Busby came out of the dressing room. We asked him what the game plan had been and he said, "Quite simple. I told the players to run at Danny."

'Bill Nicholson waved this at Danny. All the skill, delicacy and elegance he had on the ball were no use. But he was such a charismatic figure. I wouldn't have thought even Dave Mackay would have wanted to tell him. It's a thought you don't want to think because these people are such a *delight* to watch and you can't bear to think you won't see it again.'

On 1 September 1963, in his column, Danny had written: 'Why should I retire? I shall continue to play as long as I feel I am of some use to Tottenham . . . I'll stay at the party until they throw me out.' For 'they', read Bill. What follows when they meet after the fateful game at Old Trafford is a mercifully brief conversation. He tells Danny, 'I'm thinking of leaving you out this Saturday and bringing in Tony Marchi,' and Danny's response is, 'Well, that's up to you.'

Danny doesn't retire, not straight away, even though he knows too well that 'this week' is a lace handkerchief over a corpse. It's only Bill's innate caution that prevents him from saying anything more finite, in case he needs Danny again. Danny's column the following week is headlined: 'I'LL STAY FIT IN CASE SPURS ASK ME BACK', and he takes himself off to the shadowlands of reserve-team football. It's hard, now, not to think of him as a rejected lover hanging on in the hope that the girl will change her mind.

With Tony Marchi in Danny's place, Spurs look to be doing all right. They beat Burnley and Ipswich and draw with Sheffield Wednesday. When December begins with the second round, first leg of the European Cup Winners' Cup, Manchester United arrive at White Hart Lane to be beaten 2–0 with goals from Dave Mackay and Terry Dyson. Job done, it appears. 'It will be an awfully hard job for United to get three goals in the second leg,' says Bill.

Bill's optimism is shored up four days later when Spurs win 3–1 at Bolton. One of the goals is Jimmy Greaves's two hundredth. They are third in the table behind Liverpool and Blackburn and in the next day's *Sunday Express*, Stuart Hall describes them as 'a class in front . . . moving fluently, rhythmically into attack, with John White flitting shadow-like among statuesque Bolton defenders'.

So there's nothing to prepare them for what happens next. The symmetry must be blackly funny, for anyone who hates Spurs. Two months back at Old Trafford, Danny Blanchflower met his nemesis – time – in the form of Denis Law. This time it's Noel Cantwell, the United defender, who takes the role of agent of what is literally a Tottenham player's downfall when he and Dave go for a fifty–fifty ball and, according to the account Dave gives in his book, 'I got to the ball and Cantwell got to my shin. I heard the crack and . . . so did half the crowd.'

Dave ends up on the ground with the end half of his leg towards his face. 'John was physically sick when he saw it,' says Jim McAlister. Dave, though, acts cool. 'He was sitting up on the stretcher, leaning on one elbow, pushing people away,' remembers Brian James. 'No way was he going off a fallen hero.'

As Dave is having the break set in hospital, the game rages on. It goes into extra time and ends up 4–1 to United. The aggregate score is 4–3. Spurs are out of the competition.

Dave faces six weeks in hospital; it's a bad break and he is told he might never play again. (He does, of course, but that's way into the future.) 'John set off to see him, and he was legless,' says Ken Jones. 'He was driving a Humber Hawk by then and he crashed it into the gates at White Hart Lane, then carried on driving to the hospital. I arrived to find Dave sitting on the seat, Tommy Harmer perched on the arm of the seat and John lying in the bed where they'd had to put him.'

You can see why John is finding the need to put away what is probably more liquid happiness than is good for him around this time. Between Dave, Tony Marchi and himself, they've managed to do a great midfield job over the previous few weeks, adapting to the loss of Danny so well that Tottenham are still very much in contention for that season's championship. But Tony would be the first to admit that at thirty years of age and what might be termed ring-rusty – he's spent most of the best seasons of his life in the stiffs, albeit as a first-call, highly valued substitute – he isn't best equipped to keep up the midfield creativity. With another reserve, John Smith, in Dave's place, the burden for keeping up Spurs' high standards of creative attack is now all John's.

But Spurs don't collapse straight off, not even now. The next fixture is away to Bolton; with John Smith in Dave's place, Spurs win 3–1. Two goals by Jimmy Greaves a week later ensure a home win over Stoke. They're still second in the table. Even so, the carping comments in the press begin in earnest. 'The whole Spurs attack, with the exception of that tiny tornado left-winger Terry Dyson, was slow thinking and slow moving . . .' is one. 'John White flitted about like a white-shirted wraith – and unfortunately with about as much impact . . .' – that's another. And on 21 December, in spite of their handing out a 2–1 defeat to Nottingham Forest at the City ground, the verdict is: 'This Spurs half back line will not do. Maybe years of reserve team soccer have taken the edge off Tony Marchi and John Smith . . . Maurice Norman often wrong-footed . . . only Bill Brown and Mel Hopkins can look back on this afternoon with much personal satisfaction.'

What do they have to do to win back approval? Not draw 4–4 to West Brom at the Hawthorns, then lose by a couple of goals at home to them just two days later, that's for sure. John, injured, misses out on that one, the last game of 1963, when headlines announced 'MIGHTY SPURS ARE IN REAL TROUBLE'. Jimmy Greaves, said to be 'feeling the absence of White', has 'no impact on the game'. More disturbing is the response of the crowd. 'Howls of derision and the slow handclap broke out at one stage in the second half . . . it emphasised the sorry state of Spurs in their first home defeat of the season . . . the long term reserves are no longer able to step in and maintain the pace and rhythm.'

Things get even worse. The first game of the new year is the FA Cup third-round tie with Chelsea at White Hart Lane. It's a 1–1 draw. John, still injured, sits it out. Bernard Joy of the *Evening Standard* comments: 'Without John White, Dave Mackay and Danny Blanchflower, Spurs lacked authority and cohesion in midfield and played football far below their usual standard.' Four days later, they meet Chelsea again in a midweek fixture at Stamford Bridge. With John still absent and six reserves in the team, they lose 2–0.

Danny's *Sunday Express* column of 12 January 1964 bemoans the 'huge waves of disapproval' that have been 'surging around White Hart Lane, threatening to engulf the survivors of a recently great team. The pressure has been on Tottenham since the beginning of the season . . . When it was apparent that our team were in decline . . . few stopped to ask: But is it not still good enough to keep pace with the others?'

Danny has a point. Considered impartially, the side has coped fantastically well while the blows rain down on them. But the Tottenham crowd can't see it that way. What they are watching is the last of the Glory Boys. Their reaction is born out of something more intense than boredom and disappointment. Put simply, they're in mourning.

NOW SPURS TOP THE LEAGUE
John White Gamble is a Master-Stroke
Tottenham Hotspur 4, Blackburn Rovers 1
Baker's long ball reached White from a full 40 yards. The phantom Scot, lurking on the left, pivoted and swung the ball across goal where Dyson, belting up out of nowhere, lashed it past the helpless Else.

Sunday Express, 12 January 1964

There's nothing like being carped at in the press to infuse a spirit of defiance in a struggling team. John Hollowbread stands in for Bill Brown in goal and other regulars are still missing, but yet another Jimmy Greaves hat-trick brings Spurs a 4–1 victory at home to Blackburn. Bill Nicholson's decision to bring back John even though he is only half fit is claimed to be an act of managerial genius. Spurs are top of the table. If a sound of chewing is heard at White Hart Lane, it's probably the press eating humble pie.

But soon comes Chelsea on 1 February. Tommy Harmer, once of Tottenham, then Watford and now – in his football dotage – on the strength at Stamford Bridge, must have the phrase 'sweet satisfaction' running through his head if he reads the next day's paper: Spurs 1, Chelsea 2; 'TOMMY HARMER FOXES SPURS ... In contrast Tottenham's hard-working White could seldom escape the ruthless Upton.'

Just when they don't need it to happen, John is sinking into his usual winter blues. At Upton Park on 9 February, West Ham humiliate Spurs by four goals to nothing. That said, Spurs still head the championship table, with a game in hand over Blackburn, and John is still a force; in the 0–0 home draw with Sheffield United, 'overworked John White seemed to be the lone, creative midfield man'. Against Arsenal on 22 February (Spurs win 3–1) he's 'at his most elegant and artistic best' and 'played with the fluency which has always been an integral part of Tottenham's peaks'. At the end of the month comes a 2–1 away win over Birmingham.

But then they lose 4–2 to Everton, the team is accused of lack of fight, and 'John White and Les Allen were virtually blotted out by Everton's uncompromising half-back line'. That's followed up by another home defeat – Spurs 2, Manchester United 3. 'John White was eclipsed', it seems. They draw 1–1 to Fulham at Craven Cottage, when 'John White certainly looks as if he has temporarily lost confidence'. On 27 March, it's Spurs 1, Liverpool 3; 'White still brings the ball under control with graceful ease, but his pass too often goes to an opponent.'

Bill drops him.

The end-of-the-month game is a return clash with Liverpool who by now are working up a realistic challenge for the championship. Liverpool's 3–1 win confirms their position as leaders.

If John is playing way below his best, it's hardly surprising. Not only does he have the extra pressure at Spurs; there are new responsibilities at home, too. His son Rob has been born at the end of January, and he and Sandra are also having to support Alma, who in her forties is struggling to adapt to widowhood while coping with her own child of three.

There is, as ever, nothing to be gained from focusing on these difficulties – John just has to get on with it. That he does, scoring twice on 4 April as Spurs beat Ipswich 6–3: 'White played better than for many weeks.' Cliff Jones bags a hat-trick and Spurs' other goal comes, promisingly, from Jimmy Robertson, a young winger who has just arrived from St Mirren. But Liverpool are racing clear in the championship, and even a 1–0 defeat of Bolton at White Hart Lane in mid-April can't lift Spurs any higher than fifth. It's the day Liverpool clinch the title.

WHITE SNATCHES WINNER
Leicester 0, Spurs 1
The element of surprise was supplied by John White who scored a great goal in the 72nd minute. With everyone else expecting him to pass, he let go a tremendous drive from the edge of the penalty area and it zoomed past Gordon Banks.

Sunday Express, 26 April 1964

April is nearly at an end when Spurs play their last game of the season. It's at Leicester's ground, Filbert Street, and John scores the only goal to give them victory.

Perhaps John's story should end here, at the end of a season he must be glad to see the back of. It's spring. As John darts forward towards the edge of the penalty area you are aware of the colossal roar rising from the stands, enough to blow the lid off the sky. This season you've often heard that same massed hopeful bellow before someone's shot goes the wrong side of the netting or over the bar, so you've trained yourself to stare at the ground where your expectations are firmly nailed. But this afternoon you keep your head up and look at it the way John does: as a reaffirmation of intent, a promise of resurgence.

Jimmy's pass is perfectly timed. Nobody is expecting what happens next, least of all the Leicester defence. Instead of knocking the ball on to someone else, John quickly drives it into the roof of the net.

What a difference Mackay has made! From a middling, muddling, erratic team last season, Derby have been transformed by his experience. He bristles with authority, he shouts, he gets results from his younger colleagues. To see him pace his game, to recognise danger where none is clearly evident, and then, in averting that danger, spring his forwards into animated creativity, is a delight.

Guardian, 1969, quoted in *The Real Mackay*

26

Still Mackay
Rob, 2009

'I'm glad I didn't go that early.' Dave looks at me with the benign but skewering gaze that is pure Mackay. 'I'm sorry he went that early. I always thought if I could reach seventy I'd be delighted with it. When I was eleven or twelve I thought seventy was a fantastic age.' We are in the sitting room of Dave's house in a peaceful Nottingham suburb, where Isobel, his wife, has dished up scones topped with strawberries and clotted cream. Dave has just returned from the kitchen bearing a cup of tea; Isobel has made him brew his own. It seems an instrinsically, wonderfully Scottish thing to do. And Dave remains intrinsically, wonderfully Scottish.

In his mid-seventies, the man who played such a big part in my life at a vital stage of my development remains upright and inde-structible-looking; he carries himself as he always did, as if he has steel bands around his chest – put there, obviously, because his heart is so big it might otherwise come bursting out. He has a scar on his upper lip, the only residual evidence of the skin cancer with which he was diagnosed (and which was successfully treated) while in his final job in football, that of manager of the Qatar youth team. The wild Scottish curls of his youth and middle age are now white and brushed stiffly back from his forehead, but underneath them the fierce eyes still burn with alertness and, to my relief, recognition.

Just why I feel relief requires some explaining. The last time we met was five years back at Hampden, where Dave had travelled to present my dad's Scotland Hall of Fame Award and I'd had to tell him who I was. There was good reason for the lack of recognition

– in the intervening years since he'd last clapped eyes on me I'd turned from a schoolboy with a blond moptop into a balding middle-aged guy. But since then I'd heard his memory was failing.

That was confirmed first hand when I'd phoned to arrange the visit. Dave had answered – with the old familiar 'Aye?' – and I'd told him about the book and how I was hoping he'd talk to me.

'Aye, son, only we're away to Scotland.'

They were going towards the end of the month and we agreed that I'd check the next day if it was OK to come to Nottingham before that. When I followed through, it was Isobel who picked up. I told her I'd spoken to Dave the previous day.

'Oh, did you? He didn't tell me.' Isobel sounded slightly embarrassed. 'You see, Robbie, it's his memory. It's not so good. I'm trying to get him to write this sort of thing down.'

We settled on a day and I spent the intervening time facing up to the possibility that Dave might not have the faintest idea why I was there. But there was no way I could do a book about my dad and not talk to The Man. He was one of my true-life heroes. Every boy should have a Dave Mackay to follow and learn from. I hoped he'd still be able to remember stuff and not only – not even most importantly – for the book, but for Mackay.

His record is long and peerless: four years at Hearts, with whom he won all three Scottish domestic honours; the Double with Spurs, plus two more FA Cup winners' medals in 1962 and 1967; a cheap transfer to Derby where under Brian Clough and Peter Taylor in his first season he got them promotion to what was then the First Division and then in his second stint with them – now as manager – winning the 1975 League title. But that doesn't convey *how* he did it, with heart and skill and unsparing courage; this was the man who sat up on the stretcher at Old Trafford with the broken bones of his leg showing through, his whole demeanour resisting the idea of being carried off horizontal. He was, said George Best, 'the hardest man I've played against, and the bravest'.

For me, of course, it's more than simple admiration that I feel. Dave understood instinctively what I needed as a boy – knowledge of the world my dad had lived in, the man's world of professional football. So the privileged journeys I would have made to football grounds with Dad had he lived, to travel on the team bus and sit in dugouts and inside dressing rooms, became journeys I made with Dave instead.

I've brought along some old pictures and cuttings that I hope will help, along with the Macbook, which has more images but not the impact of old pictures which demand interaction and sensory input. Touch, smell, even hearing – the rustle of old documents stimulates the senses in a way pictures on a laptop never can. One photo, of a now incredibly old-fashioned-looking car parked outside the main entrance at White Hart Lane, arrests his attention. 'The Jaguar,' he says. 'It was silver. I got it sprayed maroon, for Hearts, when I signed for Tottenham.'

Hearts remains the place that he speaks of with the nostalgic happiness of first love. They were, he says, his favourite club, growing up. 'Tynecastle. I'd slip under the turnstiles. That was easy. I was a skinny wee laddie. Me and my brother went early – twelve o'clock, get the tennis ball out and kick it. I'd always been a Hearts supporter. Didnae want to go to Tottenham but if I'd said no, I'd have upset two people – Bill Nick and Tommy Walker. It was in March. So quick. It just happened one weekend. The Hearts supporters were all gutted. Some said they would never go back to Tynecastle. But they got £30,000 for me and built a stand with the money.'

He focuses on another photo. 'Bobby Smith and Terry Dyson, they liked the dogs. I used to like the dogs too,' he adds.

That prompts a question from me. Did they really all get on as well as legend has it?

'You've got to really,' he says. 'If you have a team where everyone falls out you haven't really got a team.' Dave hasn't lost his wisdom.

'I got on with them all. But John, Cliff Jones, Terry Dyson were the guys I'd go about with. John and Cliff were big pals. After training we'd go to the pub. Which was always nice when we'd won and we usually won.'

Isobel, a small, vivacious, friendly woman, breaks in. 'John was so nice,' she says. 'He was shy, I think, but easy to talk to. I remember one time I was travelling up to Scotland with the children, on the train. It was an eight-hour journey and Valerie still had a baby's bottle. John was on the train, too, and he went away to the buffet car and got the hot water and everything else I needed.'

She and the children had been heading for Whitecraigs, the village a few miles from Musselburgh where she grew up. Later on, it was there, at her family home, that she last saw my dad, in July 1964. She had gone back there to wait for the birth of their fourth child – all Dave's children had to be born in Edinburgh, so if boys they would qualify to play for Scotland – and a week before the baby arrived Mum and Dad – together with Mandy and me – had popped in to see her. 'It was a bizarre week,' she says now. 'Your dad told me he couldn't wait till pre-season training started. He said, "Bill Nick's took me in and says he's giving me a rise. Imagine, him building a team around *me*."'

'I went in to have Julie. The day I came home was the 21st, and that same day a reporter came to the door asking for me. He asked me where John's mum lived and then said, "How well did you know John White?" I said, "What do you mean, *did*?" But he left without answering. It was so weird I phoned through to Dave in London but I couldn't get a reply. I sensed inside that something was wrong and it came over on the six o'clock news – John had been killed. He had been sitting there not long before. I will never, ever forget. My daughter was born on the 14th. But the 21st is on my memory for ever. Every 21st of July I think of John White, and Sandra. He was such a lovely guy.'

'He was always cracking jokes,' says Dave. 'He was a really nice guy. Everybody liked him. It was lovely to have another Scotsman down at Spurs. I could understand him. Most of the people down there couldn't understand me. I shared with Cliff Jones and he couldn't understand what I was saying and I couldn't understand what Cliff was saying.'

Dave's still in demand from journalists wanting interviews and he always comes up with the goods; I find myself wondering if he learns these lines so he can give them the performance as Dave that they're looking for. And I think, too, of the great pride and affection with which we look at the fantastic images and articles, although there is a sense of his disconnection.

Yet Dave's essential spirit is still there. He hasn't lost what I picked up on as a kid, the way he seems totally sure of himself – and there are times when I still feel like a small, insecure boy. And there are other moments when I feel the sheer strength bestowed by his warmth and confidence. I could sit here for hours in a schoolboy dream, feeling absolutely secure as I listen to the tones of 'Mackay', those echoes from the past.

Perhaps, I suddenly think, this is how Dad felt in Dave's presence. The other players always used to say that Dave was so ferociously combative that even in games during training it was imperative to be on his side and – following on from that – that if you were on Dave's side anything was possible. That strikes a chord with me. Being on Dave's side was the single most important thing that happened to me growing up. And now as I sit there with him, thirty years on, it comes to me that Dave's gifts to me – time and interest – didn't dry up once I stopped being that fatherless boy. Instinctively he still knows what I need – not time, interest and affection now so much as insight. He hasn't just taken me into my dad's world, but into my dad's mind.

It's mid-afternoon, and as I leave I brush past the small family saloon occupying the space for off-street parking in front of the house. By the look of it, it's not been driven for a while.

I study it and see it through Dave's eyes – a symbol of what he is now compared to what he was as a young guy. To have lived that magnificent life, and not to be able to relive it in memory, seems a crushing prospect. To have lost the tape of those winning thirty-yarders belted through the fog at Goodison, of barrelling through the mud to gain points at Craven Cottage and Villa Park and Highbury, of those mad eyeballs-out five-a-sides in the gym at White Hart Lane, and of the day in 1967 when he raised the FA Cup in triumph at Wembley three years after a second broken leg seemed to signal the end of his career, is an unbearably painful thought.

And yet it would insult him to be sad. The essential part of him – the warmth and kindness, the confidence and empathy, the sense of a man still completely in control – is as imperishable as rock. He hasn't lost his winning instinct and severe focus. The opponent to which he is now bringing all that fierce competitiveness, that valour *in extremis* and refusal to admit defeat, is his fading memory.

Still Mackay. No way will he go off a fallen hero.

WILL THE SPURS EVER BE GREAT AGAIN?

Although one knows it will come, it is still fascinating to watch how time ravages a team. Just last May we were holding triumphantly the European Cup-Winners' Cup, the first British team to win in Europe. Now the ranks are sadly diminished.

First Medwin and then Mackay broke a leg. I called it a day. And now Bobby Smith has fallen from the high regard of an England centre-forward to the humiliation of a low fee on the transfer list.

During the past season most of the team have had a spell on the sidelines. Bill Brown was dropped. Ron Henry was left out after an injury. Terry Dyson . . . and even John White were rested . . .

Bill Brown, Peter Baker and Ron Henry are nearing the end of their careers. Maurice Norman and Cliff Jones may wither, too, before Tottenham's turn for greatness comes round again. John White and Jimmy Greaves could be the foundations on which it is built . . .

John White is a great player. I have watched him this season with growing interest. He is a delightful, delicate ball artist, a joy to my eye. He has his bad games, like everyone else, but his style continues to please me. I would love to have him in my team.

Danny Blanchflower, Sunday Express, 10 May 1964

27
July, July

Tottenham's close-season tour of South Africa in 1963 is remembered for two things mostly. One is Cliff and John tying their ties round their heads and pretending to be invaders when the team visited Table Mountain. The other is that Terry Medwin broke his leg.

'It was five days after we'd won the Cup Winners' Cup,' said Terry Medwin. 'We flew to Cape Town for the first of three friendlies. First minute of the game, somebody crossed from the right, I've gone into the six-yard box, Cliffie's headed, I've gone off it to stick it in the net but it's not there. The goalie came out and dived across me. Once I've gone over and over into the side netting off the pitch I knew it was gone, painful, a bad one. A spiral fracture – like when it twists – at the front of the leg. Tib and fib. That was my career more or less ended as it turned out.' 'Five in the morning, the doctor's wife knocked on the door to tell me in case I heard it first on the news,' says his wife Joyce. 'I thought he'd died.'

If you were making a film about the last days of the Double side Terry is one character you'd focus on. Back from Cape Town, he had to learn to walk again, spending a whole month simply getting to the point where he could hobble around. By November 1963, six months after the leg break, he had become so apprehensive about the future that he dropped ten pounds in weight through worry alone. Much of his anxiety centred on the big family he had to support – 'Joyce used to say Terry only had to hang his trousers on the bedpost for her to get pregnant,' says Linda Baker. By July 1964, he was nerving himself for the last two weeks of the month when pre-season training would demonstrate with merciless impartiality whether he had a hope of making it.

The last half of July was a target time for another of Tottenham's walking wounded, too. Dave Mackay had devoted the first part of the year building up the leg he'd broken at Old Trafford. When the plaster came off it was half the size of the other one and he was working out with Bill Watson, the weightlifter, to get a matching pair again. The *Sunday Express*'s 14 June edition reported that 'Dave Mackay has his first "game", a 5-a-side in the White Hart Lane gym with a soft ball'. Dave was quoted as saying, 'It was a start and I feel marvellous. I have been running up and down the terraces at White Hart Lane . . . I aim to be as fit as the others when they report back for training next month.'

If this really was a film, it'd probably jump-cut from Dave dragging himself up and down the terraces at White Hart Lane to Bill's office where you'd see him crouched over a phone call to Watford, sticking in a bid for their young Irish international Pat Jennings. Bill Brown had been a brilliant goalie for Spurs; now he was just one of the vintage players that had to be replaced with someone younger. With the transfer deadline approaching in March, Bill hadn't signed anyone since buying Jimmy Greaves from Milan. That had been more than two years back.

This isn't to say he hadn't tried. Among the players Bill had gone for were Ray Wilson, Alex Hamilton, Bobby Moore, Jim Baxter, Billy McNeill, Willie Henderson and Mike Summerbee. Blackpool had invited offers for the England defender Jimmy Armfield, who then withdrew his transfer request more or less as soon as he'd closed the manager's door behind him and headed off down the corridor. During the 1962–3 season Bill had tried unsuccessfully to jemmy Alex Scott away from Rangers.

One problem, he had told the *Evening Standard* reporter Bernard Joy, was that 'clubs don't want to let good players go if they can help it'. Spurs could become an ordinary club again any time if they bought ordinary players, but there was no way a rival like Manchester United or Everton was going to sell them a star. But the biggest problem of all was that you can't relight a rocket that's already been fired. 'Where,' he asked Joy, 'is there another Blanchflower? I may be able to get someone who will be a superficially adequate replacement but will he have the spark of genius to lift others?'

By the end of the 1963–4 season, Bill had made a start on the reconstruction work but it was slow going. A speedy nineteen-year-old winger called Jimmy Robertson had arrived from St Mirren. That spring he had spent an eye-boggling amount of money on an Arsenal centre-half, Laurie Brown, who, deployed by Bill as a centre-forward, scored on his debut – which was, as it goes, against his old club. Sadly, the beginning of Laurie's Spurs career was also its zenith – after a string of blank games, he hardly ever appeared again.

In March, Alan Mullery had arrived from Fulham to take over Danny Blanchflower's shirt. Here was a player no one could describe as ordinary. But though he was destined eventually to captain Spurs and lead them to another European triumph, Alan's prospects of winning over the crowd, let alone collecting trophies, had looked dismal during his first weeks there. 'It was bloody awful taking over from Danny,' he says. 'The expectations were impossible. I was nothing like Danny. I was more like Dave Mackay.'

A third character who features at this point is John's brother Tom. Some background is needed here, too. Laurie Brown's failure to follow through meant Bill was still looking for Bobby Smith 2.0, a rugged, free-scoring striker who could combine proactive self-protection – in other words, he could dish it out before it was dished out to him – with classically skilful distribution of the ball. Tom ticked at least some of the boxes. He was a high-scoring basher – during the season just gone his front-line partnership with Willie Wallace at Hearts had produced forty-eight goals – but his progress had recently hit a brick wall. Or to be absolutely accurate, a lorry.

'It was April,' Tom says, 'and I was out with my girlfriend Irene and my friend Dougie Johnson and his wife. We'd been at this little hotel in Wallyford which wasn't far from where we lived. We'd had a few drinks, the four of us, and Dougie and I had had a little tiff, as you do.

'I'd just got a Ford Anglia, spit new, not a thousand miles on the clock by then. Dougie would have been in the front with me but because we'd had a little tiff he's in the back with his wife and Irene was in the front. And about fifty yards from the hotel is a round-about, and it was nearly eleven o'clock Sunday night and I sprinted away from the hotel. And I thought I was quite a good driver, see. I'd had a few drinks and assumed there wasn't any vehicles coming. I didn't see any headlights. This is the A1 coming up and I've allowed my car to go over the central line. I went straight into this big lorry which only had two little sidelights on.

'No seat belts then. I remember bending the steering wheel and my head went out of the side window, smashed the glass to bits. Both Irene and I had the coats put over our heads, it was that bad, they thought we were gone. I must have been still drunk, I could see all the news reporters in the Royal Infirmary, all going up in the lift. I remember shouting out to them: "Is Irene OK?"

'We were in for a couple of days. Tommy Walker the Hearts manager comes in: "The selectors have asked me if you'd be available for Scotland–England, at Hampden." I said, "Can we not say to them I'll be fit? Just so as I get selected. For the kudos." Tommy said, "Oh, we can't do that, Tom." That was my chance gone.'

Tom soon got back into training but he still wasn't quite right. John had told him that Tottenham were looking at him but it couldn't have come at a worse time. The accident had left him with sciatica. 'I wasn't quite able to get back straight away. It's the sort of bloody thing that just niggles you, but it really does undermine your confidence. And these are the kind of things that happen in your life.'

While Tom was struggling back to fitness in Scotland, down in

London John had just heard what Cliff called 'those dreaded words from Cecil Poynton – "Bill wants to see you in the office"'. Bearing in mind that the last season had been relatively poor for him, John wasn't exactly singing and dancing in the street on the way to White Hart Lane, but it was to be the meeting at which Bill informed him that he was upping his pay and making him the player the new Spurs team was going to be formed around. One of the first things John did was arrange to buy the Church Street house off Spurs. He'd just put the first deposit down when he set off to Musselburgh with Sandra and the children for a summer break.

Something Tom remains happy about is how well he and John got on during that holiday up in Musselburgh. Over the previous few years he had begun to feel keenly the disparity in status – perceived or otherwise – between Scottish and English football and while there had never been any estrangement between him and his brother, he suspected they'd lose the closeness they'd shared in the days when they were both ambitious young lads starting out.

'John was pretty private that way,' says Tom. 'He would never talk about Tottenham up in Scotland when he was with us. John was a great guy, he would never do anything to harm, or keep anything away from his mum or me or Edwin, but he wouldn't say a thing about Tottenham unless you asked him. I choose my words carefully but I wondered whether there was a snobbery, bearing in mind you're talking about the Manchester United of the day – they were the top boys, they were the best side in the world. So you're looking at a fair difference. But that holiday it was just like the old times, we got on fantastically well. What footballers need are targets and because John was at the top it made me strive and strive and keep going for that. And he said to me again, Tottenham were watching me.'

While all this was going on, John's pal Jim McAlister was back in London and also focusing on his career prospects. His contract with the Butten Boys was up for renewal but meanwhile he'd been offered the post of golf pro at Crews Hill. The last time he and John ever met up was on Monday 20 July, when he remembers John still in high spirits about his pay rise. 'I had this little Morris 1000,' says Jim. 'The reverse gear wasn't working and John was pushing it to get it out of its parking place. He said: 'Can you play tomorrow?' and I told him I couldn't because I was going to see Mr Butten to finish my contract.'

There's a song by The Decemberists' Billy Paul called 'July, July' – about memories of teenage first sexual experience in a chicken slaughterhouse, as it happens – which carries a repeating vocal riff. It is:

> July, July, July
> It never seemed so strange

They're words that can stick in the mind when you come to what happened over the following twenty-four hours. Later on that day, John and Sandra were due to go out to a function. Joyce and Terry Medwin lived five minutes away and after settling the babysitter they arrived in their finery at Terry's.

'It was a big sports dinner for the Double side and the Australian cricket team,' says Terry. 'There was a knock at the door and I opened it. John with Sandra, all dressed up. I said, "John, have you read the invitation?" "Yes?" "Look again. It's men only."'

'Driving up to town in our dinner jackets we talked about how sad it was Sandra was missing the occasion,' says Terry now. 'But we had a great night. Tony Marchi, Mel Hopkins, all the players were there, even though they hadn't been regulars in the Double side. Richie Benaud and that cricket crowd were there – different to us altogether but very friendly. We drove home and I dropped him back at Church Street – "See you tomorrow."'

Sandra hadn't been back long herself. 'After John and Terry left for the dinner Joyce and I chatted for a bit, but when I got back in the car I didn't go home straight away. I just drove for hours and hours, all around north London. Everything looked a bit different. It wasn't as strong as a premonition, but I felt very unsettled.'

The impulse to read meaning into small incidents that precede a big event is often irresistible and if you make too much of them you run the risk of sounding crazy. All the same, if you did believe in signs and portents, it's hard not to look on what had happened that night as a message. Which was that John was going somewhere and she could not go with him.

GOLF COURSE TRAGEDY

Scots soccer ace is struck by lightning

John White, brilliant young Spurs and Scotland star, was killed by lightning yesterday as he sheltered under an oak tree at Crews Hill Golf Course, Enfield, Middlesex. Playing alone, he had driven his first ball when the thunderstorm broke. He left his clubs at the fairway and ran for shelter.

Scottish Daily Express, 22 July 1964

28

What Football's Like

'John was a frail sort of player,' says Tony Marchi reflectively. 'You looked at him and thought, "My God, someone's going to knock you out of the game." He was very, very slim. But he could run all day long and not get puffed out. He could create mayhem, hanging back behind the forward line. And he was always laughing and joking.'

Tony, in his seventies, is still rangy and tough-looking, like the big defensive midfielder he was. He lives in a pleasant modern house in the small Essex town of Maldon, where till retirement he ran a painting and decorating business after his football life was over. It's a far cry and forty miles from traffic-blasted north London where he was born in 1933, in Edmonton; his grandfather was an Italian who emigrated to England as a boy. White Hart Lane was practically his back garden. He was always going to be a Spur.

He crossed paths with Peter Baker, another Tottenham lifer, when they were schoolboys, when Peter was playing for Southgate Grammar and Tony wore the shirt of Enfield Tech; it was the last time they were to meet as opponents. He signed for Spurs at seventeen, the age at which he made his League debut for them. That season he played with Bill and all the other golden oldies – Alf Ramsey, Ronnie Burgess, Eddie Baily. And he was Tottenham from the beginning to the end of his seventeen-year career but for two in the middle.

It's always been something of a mystery why, halfway through the 1956–7 season, when he was Spurs captain and on the edge of inter-national stardom, he suddenly took off to play in Italy. This is how it happened. 'I was on a high,' he says. 'Everything was hunky-dory. They had a good team at the time – runners-up to Manchester United and we thought we had a chance of beating them the following year.'

With the club, he went on a close-season tour of Canada, followed by the family summer holiday in Jersey. 'Suddenly the phone started ringing. It was Gigi Peronace. "I want you back here because Juventus want to sign you."'

Peronace, described as the first real football agent in England, was famous for negotiating headline transfers; over the course of a few years he was to shift John Charles from Leeds to Juventus, Jimmy Greaves from Chelsea to AC Milan and Denis Law from Manchester City to Torino. He was a small, limpid-eyed, exquisitely clothed Calabrian wheeler-dealer with slicked-back hair who started out as a goalkeeper. To chop a long story, by 1956 Italy had a semi-embargo on non-national players; teams were allowed one foreigner, plus another foreigner of Italian descent. Which is why – you've guessed it – Tony, with his Italian grandfather's DNA, was such an attractive target.

Peronace's phone calls to Jersey were so relentless that Tony got fed up with them, but he'd seen nothing yet. The day after he got back home from Jersey, the wooing began in earnest. Peronace flew Tony and his wife to Italy, showed them round, and expatiated upon the riches that would come their way. 'I suppose it was the £42,000 Juventus were putting on the table that interested Spurs,' says Tony, 'but they never said either "We don't want to lose you" or "We want you to go". Jimmy Anderson never took me on one side and explained what was going on. They just left me alone to make the decision. At Spurs I was on £20 a week, £4 win bonus, and I suppose I felt, Well, let's go for it because I'll never earn in England what I'd earn in Italy.'

The £7,000 that went to Tony as a signing-on fee was unarguably handsome compensation for his experience out there. Juventus already had their permissible two foreign players so he was loaned out, first to Lanerossi and then to Torino. It was an eye-opener. 'Before I went, football to me was English football – both teams wanted to win. In

Italy you had a different kettle of fish altogether.' What he encountered was *catenaccio*, defensive football as only Italians could play it. 'My first game for Lanerossi was against Milan, the champions. Everybody was afraid of them. I didn't know anything, I was a newbie. I started off left-half. The whistle went. Off we go, temperature of ninety degrees, absolutely boiling hot. After five, ten minutes of this I thought, What's different? I looked around. We had two full-backs, three centre-halves, another wing-half like me, one bloke in midfield and two people up front. And this was a home game. All us blokes packed at the back trying to prevent Milan from scoring – just playing out the game. It was a right struggle. It was always a struggle, to go out and enjoy it, because you always had to have six or seven defenders. When you got the ball and attacked there was hardly anybody to pass the ball to. It was a total culture shock, coming from Tottenham.'

Two years went by, during which Spurs had made a signing which didn't work out – Jim Iley from Nottingham Forest. When Bill Nicholson took over from Jimmy Anderson, he went to Italy and bought Tony back, for half what Juventus had paid for him, to take over Jim Iley's place.

'I thought, Danny's only got another year because of his age,' says Tony. 'While I was away, he'd had a bad season and been dropped, too. So my expectation was that I'd continue where I left off.' And so he returned to White Hart Lane.

'But just before I came back Bill went up to Scotland and signed Dave Mackay. He became a folk hero. Then John White arrived, Danny got a new lease of life and played his best football ever aged thirty-six, and I got left on the sidelines.'

For such a magnificent talent, it was rotten luck. Condemned, in the days when there were no substitutes, to be a jigsaw piece to be forced into a vacant space in defence or midfield, the label permanently attached to him like a piece of chewing gum stuck to the underside of his boot was 'Britain's most expensive reserve'. In

November 1961, the *Telegraph* journalist Gerald Williams described him as 'the complete professional, skilful, undemonstrative, utterly reliable. He would be a regular in almost any other First Division side.' Though he filled in a couple of times in the Double season and received the medals like everyone else, the general impression was of a career that hadn't reached its potential.

'It was hard,' he says now. 'I played right-half, left-half, centre-half, left-back, inside-right.' Which prompts, of course, another question. If he was still in his mid-twenties when he came back, with possibly his best years in front of him, why didn't he leave?

'I don't know,' he says. 'I can't explain the feeling. By this time I'd had the experience of going away from Tottenham. I was born and bred a Tottenham man and I really didn't want to leave again, and year after year went by.'

And he had his moments. In the 1961–2 European Cup, Spurs went to Gornik. 'We were 4–0 down by half-time, got back to 4–2 and beat them 8–1 in the return leg at White Hart Lane, but Bill decided we couldn't play five forwards, five defenders in Europe, and that's where I came in.' He played in the Lisbon semi-final against Benfica – 'They had a hell of a side' – when Spurs lost 3–1. 'When we came back to Tottenham we had to have a team to score goals so I was left out. I sat on the line and watched.'

But in the 1962–3 season, when Danny and Dave were both injured, Tony reappeared in the first team. He played in a lot of the Cup Winners' Cup games: 'Funnily enough, the tactics were four forwards and six defenders. I was sixth defender, alongside Maurice Norman.' The following season, Dave broke his leg and Tony became captain for a while. But the big chance had come too late. 'I was thirty,' he says. 'When you look back on it, really and truly I was getting on.' After Spurs' 3–2 defeat of Burnley in mid-November that year, one reporter commented that 'Marchi, understandably, did not get into full stride after a long absence from League football'. By the end of the year, as Spurs lost 2–0 to West Bromwich Albion at White Hart

Lane and were slow-handclapped by supporters, Tony was the main focus of their disaffection. And so, come July 1964, when pre-season training was about to kick off with the traditional first-team photo call, he wasn't wanted for the line-up.

'So that morning I decided to go to the golf course to practise – get two or three balls and follow them because I was on my own. I finished about lunchtime and went into the locker room and there was John. I said, "Hello, John. Who are you playing with?" and he said, "I'm going to play a round with some friends." We sat having a chat. I packed up – "See you then. I'm off."'

He left John in the locker room and drove home. 'I remember the old dark clouds coming over and I thought, John's going to be lucky.'

Most of that morning John had been at White Hart Lane; after the photo call was finished he'd headed into the ball court. Terry Medwin was already there, working up a sweat under the dark, bare rafters. 'I was having this trouble getting back into condition and Bill knew John always liked to carry on training so he handed John a tennis racket and told him to hit a few balls with me,' says Terry. 'John stripped down to his underpants and we started a knockabout against the wall. Then Cliff came in.'

'John saw me and said, "Fancy a game of golf?"' says Cliff. 'No, I didn't fancy it. So I said, "See you, lads," took John's trousers and went home with them.'

'John asked me if I wanted to play golf,' says Terry, 'but I couldn't because I was going down to Tonbridge where Sidney Brickman was holding a function. He was a builder – George Cohen was part-time with him. Lovely daughters he had. And a thing that made him twitch all the time. But when I broke my leg, every day he brought salt-beef sandwiches to the hospital. So I couldn't let him down and, not knowing what was going to happen, I left.'

John seems to have extracted a half-promise to partner him from Jimmy Robertson, the little left-winger newly signed from St Mirren, though Jimmy later told his fellow Scot Jim McAlister that when he noticed the threatening weather he'd decided against it. 'He said, "I'm not going out there. It's going to pour,"' says Jim. 'John hunted for his trousers everywhere, then decided to drive home in his training kit, get changed there and go straight on to golf. He and Sandra had a row: "You're not going golfing" – but in the end she agreed to drive him to Crews Hill and pick him up later on.'

Jimmy Robertson never turned up. The storm still hadn't broken. There were people out on the course, the lady members about to contest a trophy. John bought three Warwick golf balls from the pro shop and thinking to get going before the women teed off, started going round on his own.

'Sandra and I used to see each other quite a lot because our children were around the same age,' says Linda Baker. 'She'd dropped John at Crews Hill and brought Mandy and Rob along to our house at the Ridgeway in Enfield to have a cup of tea.

'I remember we started talking about the pill and Sandra was saying: "We shouldn't take it because we don't know what the long-term effects are going to be." And then she said: "But why should I worry? Could be under a bus tomorrow. Oh, it's starting to rain. They're going to get so wet."

'Mandy performed. She didn't want to leave with Sandra to collect John. She wanted to play with Brandy, our dog. So I told Sandra, "You go and collect John. Leave Mandy here and I'll give her her tea."'

'The sky was completely black,' says Jim McAlister. 'Alec Patterson, the captain of Crews Hill, was going up the ninth when the lightning struck. It knocked the brolly out of his hand.'

'I was having a bite to eat when the phone rang,' says Tony Marchi. 'It was Vic Railton from the *Evening News*. "What do you think of John White then?" "What do you mean?" "Haven't you heard yet? He's dead." "You're joking. I only met him a few hours ago up the golf course." "He got struck by lightning while he was sheltering under a tree and he's dead."'

You can speculate for ever about why John sheltered under that tree. You can't, for a start, help recalling Les Allen's comment about the scattiness that led to John getting badly sunburnt on that Israel tour. Did he really just not think about the danger he was putting himself in? And then you wonder if it was simply that he was young – at twenty-seven, most people still think of themselves as immortal. There can't be many males who when they were that age didn't drive a car too fast or dive off a high ledge into shallow water but survived with nothing to remind them of the moment but the exhilaration and terror of a near miss.

And then you think about the If Onlys. If only he hadn't stayed so long at White Hart Lane. If only he hadn't waited around in the locker room. If only he'd teed off a minute later so he would have been in a different place when the lightning struck. But that's the way it is. Most of us *don't* dwell on how close we might be to a sudden end to our lives, otherwise we'd never get any of that life properly lived. We take for granted the small incremental decisions about where to be in what place at what time – those unacknowledged fragments of luck that protect us from harm as we go through the world.

But nearly half a century later Tony Marchi still finds himself puzzled. 'Ridiculous. Why did John go and sit under a tree? Why didn't he go back to the clubhouse? I couldn't make it out. I suppose it was pouring so hard he just thought, I'll get under cover. What do you do when it's pouring like that? You think, I'll get out of it as soon as possible.'

The old footballer rests his angular elbow on the table and gives the matter some thought.

'Maybe he didn't know the lightning and thunder were coming,' he muses. 'Maybe it was the first flash of lightning that got him.' He searches in his mind for an analogy. 'You know what football's like. One kick and it's over.'

HE WAS A TRUE MAN OF SOCCER

It couldn't be true. It mustn't be. But it was. 'Whitey' was
dead. Somehow the stunning news, telephoned to me at my
home late yesterday, wouldn't sink in. Lightning doesn't strike
down your friends. Not people you know . . .

Ken Jones, *Daily Mirror*, 22 July 1964

29
After the Storm

When Sandra went back to Crews Hill with Rob to pick John up, she noticed the car park was full of police. 'I remember thinking, Ooh. Something not quite right,' she says. 'Then they came up to me: "Are you Mrs White? Can you come into the office?" so I went inside with them and they said words to the effect of: "Your husband has had an accident."'

Some accident. John had been found in a ditch that ran alongside the oak tree under which he had been sheltering. Spun there by force of the lightning strike, he had scorch marks on his backside and heels, and the hair on the back of his head was singed. Jim McAlister thinks he must have been sitting with his elbows resting on his knees and his hands clasped together. They were still clasped when he was found; the lightning was so powerful that the two rings he always wore, on the fourth finger of each hand, had fused together.

The Crews Hill groundsman had caught sight of John sitting under the tree around three o'clock. He and a workmate were elsewhere on the course when they registered the flash of lightning some five minutes later. He thought no more of it till he left the storage sheds at around four thirty, and noticed scorch marks on the tree a couple of feet from the ground. Alongside it in the ditch was John's body. The GP member who was called out urgently from the clubhouse could do nothing. He thought John had been dead for some time.

'When they told me, the first thing that came into my head was, How will we manage?' says Sandra. 'I really can't remember how I got back or even where I went. I haven't got a clue who took me away. The only thing that's stayed in my mind is going to find Mandy and saying to her, "Daddy's not coming back." And Mandy saying, "We'll be all right, won't we?"'

Someone who has a strong recall of what happened is Linda Baker, who was waiting at her home with Mandy when Sandra, with baby Rob in his carrycot, was brought back from Crews Hill. 'Peter and I always left the back door unlocked for people to walk down the side of the house and come in that way,' says Linda. 'I'd made Mandy a boiled egg and I was feeding her and my Sarah when I saw Sandra walking past my window between two policemen. I was flabbergasted. I looked at the policemen. Whaaaaat?

'Everybody at Crews Hill had been trying to get hold of her to tell her what had happened. There weren't any mobiles then. She wasn't at home. She'd just walked in on it.

'I actually just grabbed Sarah and ended up going with the policemen and Sandra and the kids to her house. I rang Peter at Enfield Golf Club: "Come to Sandra's. It's a dire emergency." So Peter was there. Alma was there. Someone from the club was there. She was in shock. Losing your husband. She was twenty-two.'

Bobby Robson, Fulham and England wing-half: 'Of all the inside-forwards I've played against, he rated as one of the very best. You could never get near him. I often muttered to myself when marking him: "Why can't you stand still for a moment?"'

Daily Mirror, 22 July 1964

When the Tottenham police rang Bill Nicholson to tell him, he thought the call was a hoax. Within the past fortnight there had been two similarly claiming that Jimmy Greaves had been killed in a car crash. His first reaction, it followed, was fury, and he ordered the caller to give him his number for verification. It was indeed the police station number – he was already familiar with it – and when he dialled it back the same voice answered. This was no hoax.

Sandra clearly couldn't have borne the ordeal of identifying John's body. Bill was going to have to do it. He had never been to a morgue before, and asked the Spurs trainer Cecil Poynton to come along with him for moral support. In his book, Bill wrote:

The body . . . was undoubtedly that of John White. He looked exactly as I had known him.

Outside, I said to Cec: 'From the expression on his face, you'd think he was up to one of his skylarks.'

'I know,' said Cec. 'I felt the same way.' John liked a practical joke. 'Did you see that burn mark down his back?'

I had to confess I hadn't. I was feeling too shocked to notice details like that. Even though I had seen the body, it was difficult to accept what happened . . . It seemed such a brief, almost wasted life. He had so much more to give.

By then, naturally, the news had reached Fleet Street. In the Long Acre office block in which the *Daily Herald* shared headquarters with its far more successful stablemate the *Daily Mirror*, Peter Corrigan, a young Welshman in his first London job, had been left to mind the sports desk when the phone rang. 'It was a fella saying, "I hear that John White has been struck by lightning,"' says Peter. 'You get a terrible lot of these calls, so like a stupid boy I thought, I'll ring his home. You're a reporter. A bit of news, you want to get reaction. People said to me, "How could you have rung the bloody home?" I wanted it dismissed as a load of bollocks, that was why.'

It was Alma who picked up. 'Oh, he's not here,' Alma said. 'He's out playing golf, imagine that. In this weather. Silly boy, he must be mad.'

'My stomach turned over,' says Peter, 'so I rang Cliff Jones to see if he knew anything. Cliff just said, "Christ, I've got his trousers in my car boot."'

Peter rang White Hart Lane, where he was told that Bill had had to leave urgently. 'I began to get suspicious,' says Peter, 'so I rang the golf club, and they confirmed what had happened.' After that, unpleasant though it was, he had to ring round the players; he had a story to write. When he got through to Dave Mackay, the man was crying so hard he had to put the phone down.

'I remember someone telling me later he was holding an umbrella,' says Peter, 'which is something you shouldn't do. Don't stand under a tree. Don't put up an umbrella. Just get bloody wet.'

Every summer Musselburgh's Olive Bank stadium was home to a five-a-side tournament for local teams. Tom White had been roped in to play a part. 'I was there as a Known Footballer,' he explains. 'I had to stand on the terraces and sign autographs if people came up to me. Well, John had told me Tottenham were looking at me, and one of the ways for a manager to approach a player back then would be to get a reporter to tap him up first, see if he's interested in coming, so when this guy came up and shook my hand, saying he was from the *Daily Express*, I genuinely thought: He's tapping me up! This is Tottenham! But the only thing the guy said was, "John's been killed."

'Well, I grabbed him by the lapels and I just said, "You'd better confirm that." I was angry. I've been thinking this is him tapping me up and he says that instead. And it was a terrible thing to do, to come up to me and say it in the middle of all those hundreds of people when I was signing autographs.'

Tom dragged the reporter out of the stadium and into his car. In complete silence, he drove him through Musselburgh to the public call box outside the town hall.

'I told him to get out and phone London for confirmation,' says Tom. 'And I can see him talking, and then he looks at me through the phone box, through my windscreen, receiver in hand, nodding: "Yeah, it's true."'

The reporter hadn't made it out of the phone box by the time

Tom drove away to be with his mother. He had to push through another group of reporters to get into the house. 'And my mum was in there, sitting in the lounge on this chair, and as I've hit the door to get in she's shouting: "Tell me it's not true, Tommy!" Well, I went down on my knees and put my head in her lap and I had to tell her it was true.'

'I was at the pictures when a notice appeared on the screen,' says Janette, John's sister. '"Would Janette White come to the foyer." My cousin Edward was waiting for me. "John's been in an accident," he said. I thought he meant a car smash and I said, "Are the kids OK?" Then he said, "It's a bigger accident than an accident but I don't want to tell you here." We got to my house. There were photographers, press and all sorts of folk outside. We went in and he told me.'

> Tony Marchi, Spurs' skipper: 'It's tragic. John was a great player and a fabulous character. If John had an off-day, the team had an off-day. That's how valuable he was to us. I'm heartbroken.'
>
> *Daily Mirror*, 22 July 1964

Jim McAlister remembers that day all too well. Earlier in the afternoon he had ended his contract with the Button Boys, and was phoning up a *Daily Express* golf writer, Ronald Haeger, who had asked if he could be the first to know. 'Straight away Ronald said, "I've got some terrible news for you." He went away and had it confirmed. Pff. That was it.'

David Lacey, in his first job at the *Brighton Argus*, remembers the news coming in on the agency machine. 'People were just stunned a bit. Mid-afternoon, quiet day at the office. Hang on – footballers don't get killed.'

'I don't mind admitting I cried,' says Jimmy Greaves. 'We'd lost a wonderful, humorous, mischievous, lovable human being. It was a senseless death, beyond a tragedy. It was a complete bombshell.'

'I was in hospital recovering from a ruptured appendix, which nearly killed me,' says Ian St John. 'Someone brought the evening paper to me. I couldn't believe that something like that could have happened.'

Terry Medwin's first reaction was the same. 'I was at the function in Tonbridge,' he says. 'The weather was bad so the phone lines were down and we were all sitting down to a meal when rumours started to circulate. I managed to get through eventually, and Joyce answered. I said, "I just don't believe it." "Terry, it's on the telly.' So we finished the first course, all got up and went home.'

Around nine thirty that night, Terry made his way round to John's house in Church Street where he found Tom and Eddie. They'd wanted to get to London as quickly as possible but neither had the money for the plane fare so they borrowed it from Tom's girlfriend Irene. Tom thinks now that he virtually sleepwalked through what followed. 'It's hazy,' he says. 'Sandra was in . . . I don't know how to put this . . . a sort of jovial mood. She was happier than she might have been but not because she was happy. She was just a young girl and she had the responsibility of looking after the children, Eddie and me. I think she'd been given something to get her through it. We went to bed and I remember lying there just listening to the silence.'

Alec Scott, Everton's Scottish international forward: 'I knew John when he played with Falkirk and I was with Rangers . . . And we have been room-mates on many Scottish tours. I don't know of a better positional footballer.'

Daily Mirror, 22 July 1964

Terry Dyson was in Yorkshire when he got the news. 'I was born in Scarborough and I'd go up there every close season. That Tuesday night I got a phone call from the family I'd been in digs with for eight years, Peter and Lyn Adcock. "Look, Terry, there's a rumour going round John White's been killed." So I came back. Went in for training the next morning. It was true.'

'When we all gathered at the club, Bill called everyone into the changing room and started to talk about what kind of bloke John was,' says Mel Hopkins. 'Then he broke down and ran into the toilets.'

'It was quite shocking,' says Terry Dyson. 'He wasn't that sort of fella. But he was really upset. He was so dedicated to Tottenham. When he came back out he said, "We're not training today. We're going out on the pitch and having three minutes' silence for John." All the staff, everybody came out. It was the most eerie thing I'd ever seen in my life. John was so well liked. Lots of lads were crying and Dave Mackay was the worst of the lot.'

Bill Brown, Spurs' Scottish international goalkeeper: 'John was my buddy for the last five years at Tottenham. He was one of the greatest inside forwards of his type and time. He had a dry humour, and was great company.'

Daily Mirror, 22 July 1964

That same morning, the police took Tom and Eddie to Crews Hill to show them where John had died. 'In the ditch were some newspapers that had actually been scorched,' Tom says, 'and on the tree was some of John's jumper, some little bits of wool that were his. One of the things that was sad for my mother was finding out that if someone had got to him soon enough, if it had just been a few minutes, he would have still been alive. Maybe that affected my mum. She didn't want to think about that.'

Eddie couldn't face the other duty, a visit to the funeral parlour. 'I didn't want to go either,' says Tom, 'but I felt a responsibility. I had to see John for the sake of my mother. He looked great. His hair was quite thick and he wore it short, crewcut-ish, and it looked like that in his coffin.'

Looking back, he recalls someone being with him but had no idea it was Cliff Jones keeping him company. 'I wouldn't have known that it was Cliff there. It really hammered me.'

'It was an awful day, that,' says Cliff. 'John looked like there was nothing wrong with him. He almost seemed to be smiling. I was in bits. Just absolute shock. We were soulmates. We got on so well together – we were like a couple of schoolkids, getting into mischief. Coming back from the funeral parlour was the first time I cried. And I'm not ashamed to say it because we were so close. I just broke down from seeing him. He was my pal, and he was no more.'

Crews Hill Golf Club

Originally designed in 1916, Crews Hill Golf Club is a parkland course set in rural west Enfield, once the hunting ground to the Crown. Modern Crews Hill is less open, with many oak and silver birch trees defining well designed golf holes. Situated at the northern tip of Greater London, the area is now surrounded by garden nurseries and farmland. Crews Hill is often referred to as 'The Jewel of the North' and considered the finest test of golf in Middlesex County.

www.geogolfcourse.co.uk

30

On the Ghost Train
Rob, 2010

Crews Hill Golf Club car park. A late afternoon in early summer. My windscreen wipers are going full tilt. As soon as I set off, the weather completely turned and I've driven here under this amazing dark grey sky while a picture builds up inside my head. It's 21 July 1964. The lightning parts the clouds and out rings the voice of God: I want that number 8! And my dad's body is lying there. Another player for that incredible Subbuteo team God's building up.

This is the first time I've been to the place since I was five months old and in the carrycot Mum took with her when she went to pick Dad up. But I've always known where it is. Mum used to take Mandy and me walking up at an area of woodland called Whitewebbs. On the way I'd see signs to Crews Hill and I'd think, Don't take us there! It's been a bit like the ghost train at the funfair – part of you does want to go on it but all the same you daren't.

Apart from anything else, I've been afraid it wasn't going to be a very nice place. Not a vision of hell or anything like that, but there are a lot of garden centres up at Crews Hill and if you go on a Sunday it's at the far end of a horrendous strip of nurseries, with grimy polytunnels and wilted tomato plants, whereas it should be Valhalla, where my dad's soul departed.

Let's confront it. This is part of my growing up. I have to let go.

One of my favourite movie scenes ever is the one in *Butch Cassidy and the Sundance Kid*, when Robert Redford and Paul Newman are on that ledge at the edge of the canyon and they realise all they can do is jump.

And I'm the Sundance Kid. Fuck it. Let's jump.

I get out and look around. I find golf courses weird anyway – not the most welcoming of places. In the end I head for the pro shop, a romantic vision in my head that I'll find this wizened old guy in there, the Scottish golf pro from Central Casting – Jim McAlister fifty years on. He'll have been there on The Day. He'll remember it all. I'll introduce myself. Yeah, that's right. *The* John White.

I'm the person he's been waiting for. He'll regale me with the tale of that day. And how pleased he is to be able to pass this story on. The last moments. To the son. Something he thought he'd never be able to do.

Then the juggernaut of real life takes over, in the form of a spotty youth in a Pringle jumper behind the counter. I force some strained conversation about whether you could play up there as a non-member.

While we've been talking, it's turned out to be one of those afternoons when it pisses down and afterwards it's actually quite nice. Almost a Disney scene. The birds start tweeting, the branches are dripping, it's fresh and peaceful.

I decide to take a little walk. Find the tree.

Which I do.

And I feel really . . . pleased.

Part of my fear has been that it wasn't a good place, that the ditch he'd been found in was full of broken glass and hubcaps, the kind you associate with tabloid headlines about strangled prostitutes. In my brain previously I'd leapt from the cacophony of the storm, a scene of *The Cruel Sea* – relentless rain, wind, thunderclaps – to the racket of discovery – sirens, police, crying children. But there's only peace. Like those moments just after you've been listening to a very stirring piece of music.

I stand by that tree and it's really nice to be at that spot. I feel a lull in which I can picture my dad's spirit leaving his body. Not with angels singing, trumpets and cherubs on clouds, but a sacred moment all the same. This is my King Arthur's Stone. My place of pilgrimage. And standing there on this summer's evening I find real solace.

THE FANS MOURN JOHN WHITE

The Sad Farewell to a Star

The world of soccer paid its farewell tribute at the Enfield funeral of Spurs' great Scottish international John White who was killed by lightning at Crews Hill golf course on Tuesday.

Thousands of fans who had idolised this gentle genius watched the cortege on its route from White's Edmonton house, and the service was relayed by loudspeakers to a big overflow outside the three chapels at Enfield Crematorium.

Many were unable to hide their emotion as they listened to the Rev. Maurice Bayliss, himself a Spurs supporter, during the service ... He referred to the slight figure bobbing across the pitch ... his skill and sportsmanship ... and all that goes to the making of a great player.

'White Hart Lane will be stricken,' said the Rev. Bayliss, 'much of its glory will pass away with the passing of this great player who thrilled us time and time again by his play.'

Evening News and Star, 25 July 1964

31
Last Things

Sandra experiences a blank when it comes to memories of John's funeral. Only a detail sticks in her mind – shopping in Edmonton for black clothes, and having trouble finding something suitable because they didn't make mourning clothes for young people. She can also remember her Greek neighbour shepherding her through the funeral day. 'She followed me round the house from room to room and every time I looked at her she started wailing,' says Sandra. 'Like Senna the Soothsayer in *Up Pompeii*.'

But few people who were there can do better. It's one of the kinder functions of time that it fogs recall of strange, shocking events like that. Richard Blanchflower remembers only that Danny, his father, took him to the funeral service; Jim McAlister that the streets were lined either side as the cortège went past, and that it was where he first met Jim Baxter. 'Jim said later in his book that he was badly affected by John being taken so young, and that's when he really started wiring into the drink.'

'Every club in the League seemed to be represented,' says Terry Dyson. 'Not everybody could get in, there were so many, so the service was relayed outside. Tom, John's brother, was in tears. He did well, because he was so upset.'

'The funeral, oh God,' says Janette. 'My mother didn't go. She couldnae. She couldnae have done it.' So Janette came down from Scotland with Eddie's wife, Nan, and Jim Lannan, John's pal from Musselburgh Union, and Jim Lannan's father. 'I cried all the time,' says Nan. 'When we went back to Sandra's, Janette and I went up to bed because we were all upset and Tom brought Jimmy Greaves up to see us.'

The obituaries appeared. In one of them, Bill Nicholson described John as 'a player's player' who would be 'missed by the boys more than they would any other'. There were no flowery sentences from Bill in his simple commendation, just the plain, blunt truth. 'He was,' said Bill, 'very, very likeable, as well as being a very good footballer.'

A schoolfriend, William Gibson, said, 'John was a fine, quiet lad and was very good to his mother. He didn't forget his schoolfriends either, because he gave me the tracksuit top he wore the day he won his first medal for Tottenham. When he was up here on holiday I kicked a ball around with him.'

There were many more tributes, but even so the journalist Peter Corrigan thinks that the impact of the news would have been ten times greater nowadays because modern players are ten times larger than life. 'There was no TV coverage then,' he says. 'It was only the true football fan who could recognise his greatness. Saying that, it was a major story, the equivalent of Cristiano Ronaldo getting killed today. It had a big impact on everyone, and it haunted me. I can still remember my bloody intro. "Football mourns for John White the slim Scot who graced our lives so tragically for a short time . . ."'

Tom went back to Scotland and rejoined Hearts for pre-season training. One morning, riding on the team bus, he got the twitches. 'It was an amazing experience – I've never had them before or since. It was like every now and again I was looking out of the window and I'd go shake-shake-shake. It must have been nerves but I wasn't aware that could happen. These days people get counselling but then it was just something you couldn't explain. You're just carrying on with life and getting on with things, and going shake-shake-shake every now and again.'

The coroner's report was published. It cited the 'very tragic case of this young man killed by lightning'. The coroner, one Dr A. P. L. Cogswell, said that death was due to electrocution. Asked by the coroner if anything could be done for people struck by lightning, a Dr Rushton said that breathing usually started again as soon as the current had stopped passing through the body. He added that the thing was to get the circulation going again, because the heart had practically stopped. If the heart could be compressed from outside, there was no reason why some people could not survive. It was a case, however, of doing this in two or three minutes.

'It felt as if I'd been in a fantastic film,' says Sandra. 'All these glamorous people. I don't know whether our marriage would have lasted. Betty Blanchflower came to my engagement party, early in 1961. She said, "If you have any problems, dear, come to me, because I've had them all." I was quite naive – "Ooh. What does she mean?"

'I remember girls coming up to him when we were out. It wasn't as blatant as it is now, but it was quite threatening. But what can you do? They were young men. I do remember having rows. Probably I felt insecure with the other footballers' wives, being so much younger. I don't know what would have happened in the long term. You don't know. But if anybody had said, "You're only going to know this guy for four years," I'd still have opted for four years. The fabulous, wonderful four years. We got on so well. It was like a magic time.'

'Peter was leaving Tottenham on a free and decided to go to South Africa,' says Linda Baker. 'I wasn't going to go. Sandra said, "Linda, if I thought my John was there I'd want to go." I remember Mandy being a naughty girl and Sandra saying, "If you don't behave I'm going to throw you out of the window." Mandy said, "That's all right, I'll fly to heaven and be with my daddy." You put it in the back of your mind. You don't want to remember these feelings and these things. We were so young. I went off to South Africa in 1965. She went back to college and trained to be a teacher. She really was strong.'

Jim McAlister started his new job as golf pro at Crews Hill. 'So I went past that tree twice, sometimes four, sometimes six times a day. It was a massive oak. It's still there.' He ended up not looking at it. 'You thought, This hasn't happened,' he says. 'You were always expecting him to come in. John was the best friend I ever had. I loved him as a human being, as a person. He was just a good bloke.'

The 1964–5 season has started. In the programme notes for Tottenham's first game – they're playing Sheffield United – an item headed 'The John White Fund' reports that 'the fund inaugurated for the benefit of the young widow and children of our late player John White . . . is meeting with a generous response' and announces that a testimonial match will be organised. 'Mecca Ltd., who are the Club Caterers . . . will be making available their Lyceum Dance Hall for four Friday evenings early in the season for dances to be organised for the fund.'

Bobby Smith has been transferred to Brighton, and Frank Saul wears the number 9 shirt. The number 6 shirt filled previously by Dave Mackay goes to Phil Beal. Nineteen-year-old Pat Jennings is in goal. Of the Double side, only Ron Henry, Cliff Jones and Terry Dyson play. Under the headline SPURS' DAY BUT NO FANFARE, Brian Glanville, in the *Sunday Telegraph*, writes of 'the new, pitifully depleted Spurs' winning comfortably 2–0, and singles out Cyril Knowles, from Middlesbrough, who in Peter Baker's place 'appeared leggily comfortable at right-back', and Jimmy Robertson who 'showed dash and ambition'. Alan Hoby, in the *Sunday Express*, describes Cliff Jones playing 'creative inside-left [in an attempt to] plug the gap left by the death of his dearest buddy John White'.

'The first match back after John died there was a huge gap,' says Cliff. 'He was so good in the dressing room and we missed that straight away. We'd never seen him miserable. And of course I always followed John White out. But John would have said, "You've got to try and get over it as soon as possible."'

'Bill told me I was taking over John's number 8 shirt and made a point of asking me if I minded,' says Jimmy Greaves. 'I thought it would be a great privilege to have the shirt, and I didn't mind at all. I took it as my responsibility to wear it. I went on wearing it till I left Tottenham and I was more than happy to do it.'

Meanwhile, the days start to shorten, the air becomes chillier. The programme for the evening game against Burnley on 2 September carries a list of donations over £20 to the John White Fund. Among them are: Celtic FC. – £105; Spurs Supporters Club – £100; Rose and Crown public house – £50; Danny Blanchflower – £26. 5s; Morris Keston – £25.

The *Sunday Express* for the second week of September features a match report under the headline SPURS ARE NOT YET GOOD ENOUGH FOR HONOURS. The byline belongs to Danny Blanchflower, reporting instead of playing in Spurs' 3–2 defeat by West Ham at Upton Park. He muses: 'The Tottenham team are still suffering comparisons with the recent past. But the question now is if they are good enough to survive in the First Division . . .' MOMENT OF AGONY is the headline over Ken Jones's report in the following day's *Daily Mirror*. Dave, making his comeback in a Football Combination game against Shrewsbury Reserves, has broken his leg for the second time in nine months.

The season wears on. Under the headline SPURS WITHOUT GLORY, Ken comments in his report on the home game against Stoke – Spurs win 2–1 – that the crowd have 'realised that the golden days have gone for their team. That this will be a winter of waiting.' Ten days later, it's STRUGGLING SPURS A SAD SIGHT and SPURS WILT AS LAW SHINES as Manchester United beat them 4–1 at Old Trafford.

But though they are down, they aren't completely out of it. Danny Blanchflower reports on 10 October that SPURS CRUSH SPIRITLESS, DISJOINTED ARSENAL. Spurs 3, Arsenal 1. Spurs are fourth in the table.

JOHN WHITE MEMORIAL MATCH
Spurs v Scotland XI
Souvenir programme
In memory of a great player

Tom got a call from Bill Nicholson at last. It was to ask him to captain a Spurs side against Scotland at White Hart Lane in John's testimonial game on 10 November. He had to be transferred temporarily from Hearts to do it.

'It was a bit daunting in a way,' he says, 'because again I felt the snobbery side – I use my own word there. Sandra's dad had been Bill Nicholson's assistant manager, they were upper crust on the football side. I had doubts whether I was good enough. I didn't want to make a fool of the family, of myself.

'I needn't have been bothered – I scored the first goal from a pass from Jimmy Greaves. It was a funny feeling, when I was running on to the ball – the adrenaline was running in me, the ball wasn't going to go anywhere else, it wasn't going to go there or there or there, it was going in the net. It was like – I can't describe it – I just could not have misfired that ball.

'I wasn't the most skilful player but then Bill Brown kicked a ball out and it had snow on it, up in the air it went and it came down and I controlled it and went past him. Just at the last minute I give it that little bit extra and it clipped the outside of the post. If I'd have stroked it, it was in.

'And Bill said afterwards, "If you'd knocked that in, you'd have been playing for us on Saturday." I mean, there was no way I believed it, that was just a throwaway, but I think I coped all right on the night. It was a big night for me.'

The final score was Spurs 2, Scotland 6, with Bryon Butler of the *Daily Telegraph* commenting afterwards: 'It was [Tom] White's first game at centre-forward for a month – he is still recovering from a car accident last March – but he still looks a most useful player.' The *Daily Mail*'s Laurie Pignon referred to Sandra 'sitting beautiful and sad-eyed in the front row'. In the *Daily Express*, Norman Giller recorded that 'Alan Gilzean, the transfer-seeking Dundee forward in whom half a dozen clubs are interested, sparked an incredible goal rush that staggered Spurs'. By the end of the year Gilly was making his debut for Spurs against Everton. The result was Spurs 2, Everton 2. Jimmy Greaves scored twice. The G-Men were launched. That same day, it was announced that Dave Mackay was to start training on Wednesday.

The 1964–5 season finished with Spurs beating Leicester 6–2 and the League table that night showed them in sixth place behind Leeds United, Manchester United, Chelsea, Everton and Nottingham Forest. To answer the question Danny Blanchflower had raised at the start of the season, they had done more than survive.

But the Double side broke up like a plane falling out of the air. Tony Marchi left to manage Cambridge City. Terry Medwin gave up his struggle for fitness and went into coaching. Terry Dyson joined Fulham and Les Allen transferred to QPR. Peter Baker went to live and work in South Africa.

'It's true that life goes on,' says Terry Dyson. 'We still thought about John. But we didn't play too well the following years. John was vital for us. People didn't realise how vital. He used to *float* around that pitch. And he was such a funny lad.'

'It was hard to measure up to, that early-sixties side,' says Jimmy Greaves. 'There's no modern equivalent. There's nobody who could be compared to John. The team had lost its navigator. He was the greatest off-the-ball player I've ever seen. Bill bought Terry Venables to replace him but good as Tel was, he wasn't in the same league as Whitey.'

'Bill tried to find someone to take his place,' says Tony Marchi. 'It was hard, very hard. Obviously the team missed him. But John had died and that was it. We had to get on with it.'

By the 1966–7 season, with Dave Mackay back, Spurs won the FA Cup and had a good shot at the championship, finishing third. But if you look at the League tables for the years directly after John's death another, less hopeful picture forms. 1964–5: champions, Manchester United; runners-up, Leeds. 1965–6: champions, Liverpool; runners-up, Leeds. 1966–7: champions, Manchester United; runners-up, Nottingham Forest. In 1970–1, Arsenal won the Double.

Tottenham, finishing third in the League, had to endure the sight of the enemy clinching the title at White Hart Lane on the last day of the season. And so to the drip-drip-drip of the seventies and the sacking of Bill Nicholson by a board of directors who felt he was out of touch and yesterday's man.

Cliff's last game for Spurs was against Manchester United in 1968. 'I had a chain of butcher's shops but I'm not a businessman and I got stitched up a bit,' he says. 'Bill knew I was having difficulties and at the start of that season he said, "Hang around. We've got a fixture pile-up. Once that's over I'll let you go on a free."

'By October I'd knocked in about ten goals. I was thirty-four years old but I was a good trainer, I was always in good shape. The ball comes, I smacks it past Alec Stepney. Two each. That was a Wednesday. Thursday, Bill sold me to Fulham.'

'John's death destroyed something a bit precious,' says David Lacey. 'They didn't evolve. They continued to win a few things but cups don't count. In terms of being League challengers, they were nearly men. It slipped away. The game became meaner and harder. Leeds came in, and Liverpool who were not mean but functional and methodical. The gift of glory went to Manchester United – Law, Best and Charlton – and Spurs didn't get it back.'

'John was definitely ahead of his time,' says Ian St John, 'and a lot of people didn't understand – or at least they underestimated – his contribution to the game. If he had lived, who knows what might have been.'

'John was unobtrusive,' says David Lacey. 'When people are remembering that side, they'll say, "Oh yes – there was also John White." Like Alonso at Liverpool – the back-room boy made people tick. No one noticed what he did till he'd gone. Mullery had just come in. Greaves was still very good but beginning to slide a bit – he'd peaked. The team didn't need a disaster. It's not something where you can just sign like for like.

'At Tottenham, players come and go, like they do at every club.

But if people from 1950 and 1960 came to watch Spurs now they'd still recognise the way they play. Pass and move. On Saturday I went to White Hart Lane and there was Tom Huddlestone feeding the ball forward as accurately as Danny Blanchflower and then Glenn Hoddle did. John was slightly built, and Luka Modric is another one – people were a little worried about how he was going to cope. Exceptional, almost old-fashioned – taking people on with the ball. I'd like to think there's still room in the game for people like that.'

'It was a magic time,' says Cliff. 'At White Hart Lane, you ran out on to the pitch from one corner with the East Stand in front of you, tiered, thirty thousand people, and you'd think, I'll have some of that. Let's go.

'Football is not work. It is a wonderful pastime. And now it is a highly paid pastime. But I wouldn't change it. I played in the glory years. We saw the Beatles. We saw England win the World Cup. You ran on to the pitch, there was a buzz. Everywhere we went. Full house. Anfield. Villa Park. Old Trafford. It was special, very special. Winning the first eleven games of the season is still a record. Not many records last for fifty years.

'Bill could never replace John White. Terry Venables and Alan Mullery were terrific characters who thought deeply about the game, but they couldn't take his place. It was a moment in time. That you can't repeat, either. You're never going to see that ever again. It was such a great side. Such a blend of players. We were something special and we responded to it.'

And, of course, there's a postscript. After John died Cliff went to see Sandra and confessed he'd taken the trousers, and she said: 'Oh, it's all right. You keep them.'

He still has them. And now he can look back with a smile at the memory of what happened that morning before the sky fell in: of John capering in his underpants round the ball court with Terry Medwin; of gleefully driving away with the trousers in the car boot. 'It sums up our relationship,' he says. 'Our players' world.'

SCHOOLBOY HARRY — MY SPURS MEMORIES

The 15-year-old Harry Redknapp watched on at White Hart Lane as Tottenham reached the European Cup semi-finals in 1961–62.

'I watched all those games. I was a schoolboy, used to train here and used to come down and watch the European games. It was a great atmosphere in those days. Against Gornik I remember Bobby Smith battering the Polish goalkeeper and they won 8–1. They were great nights, Benfica, we want European nights here again. John White, what a midfield player. Dave Mackay, have you ever seen a player like him? Bobby Smith, all these people . . .'

Guardian, 25 August 2010

32
A James Dean Thing
Rob, 2010

Why can't he just show me where they are?

I maul the receiver in my sweaty palm. I feel like I'm eight again, trying to think him into being and feeling that brief moment of exhilarated dread, as if I'm waiting for a massive firework to go off. And then . . . nothing. Lots and lots of nothing. And I end up with a really sore throat from holding all the tears in.

I've been sitting here for half an hour, putting off the moment of ringing the crematorium. Should I sound solemn? Or do I put on a slightly jokey tone? 'Hello. Is that Enfield Crematorium? I'm ringing to find out what happened to my father.'

It's not him. It's *ashes*.

Thing is, Andy Porter, the Spurs historian, has emailed to say he's been contacted by a 78-year-old fan who wants to know where John White's headstone is so he can pay his respects and tie up a few loose ends. Maybe he wants do some networking for the next life.

Which is where the fun starts. Dad doesn't have a headstone; he was cremated. Mum has always felt sad and a bit guilty because she doesn't know what happened to the ashes, though considering what must have been her state of mind at the time I can't see any reason for self-reproach.

But since then she's cherished a dream of relocating them – him? – to Musselburgh. So I disinter the cardboard box of treasures – these days it's kept in a cabinet in my studio rather than a loft – and track down an article written by Danny a week after the funeral, in which he claimed that the ashes were scattered over the pitch at White Hart Lane.

By now I'm half hoping no one will pick up. Then I can tell myself I've tried, and get on with the rest of my life.

Someone picks up.

'Erm, yes. My father was cremated in 1964 and I was wondering if there's a record of what happened to his ashes.'

I'm waiting for her to say, 'Have you tried asking your mum?' but she's very polite and asks his name. I tell her that it's John White and that the cremation was on 25 July 1964, at which I half expect a hand over the receiver and a muffled voice saying to her colleagues, 'I've got John White's son on the phone. Doesn't even know where the ashes are!' But instead I hear her checking on the system. 'What was his middle name?'

'Anderson.'

'Yes, we've got the details here but there doesn't seem to be any record of what happened to the ashes. I'll make some checks and get back to you.'

Then, after an hour, Tracey calls back with some news. She's checked with Upson's the funeral directors and they have it on record that the ashes were collected afterwards by a family member.

So maybe Danny was right. That, though, prompts another question – who scattered them? I ring my uncle Tom but he can't remember anyone collecting the ashes – 'though there's a vague memory of them being scattered at the ground'.

Then I ring my uncle Eddie and ask him if he remembers.

'No, but I liked the Blanchflower version so I'm going with that.'

Thinking about it later, I come to the conclusion that the whereabouts of Dad's ashes contain all the ingredients – confusion, false trails, mystery – that you'd hope for in a ghost story. Just as he did on the pitch, they've drifted away and no one can see them. Perhaps even now he's having what Bill would have called 'one of his skylarks'. Even when he's dead he's elusive and mischievous.

★ ★ ★

An early morning in August. I'm on the number 3 course at Gullane
Golf Club, eight miles south of Musselburgh, three hundred miles
north of Tottenham and in a different world.

If you didn't have a watch or a calendar you wouldn't know it was
2010. It feels timeless. It could be Scotland in the 1940s, 50s, 60s. The
sky is overcast – 'dreich', to use a Scottish word. Mist muffles the noise
of the greens being mowed and blurs the distant outline of the Pent-
land Hills. The whole place has a fantastic aura, the traces left by years
of golfers coming here to play on these links. It's the kind of energy
that emanates from a very old piece of furniture – the spirit of all the
people who have used it. The dunes are where Dad would come for
Scotland training camps and pre-season runs when he was up at Musselburgh on holiday. Those footprints on the sand could be his.

Third green to fourth tee. You have to cross a two-lane main road
to reach it. The odd car drifts past, with a long wait before the next
one. Not much of a place for playing chicken even if you're on a
Zimmer frame. Then you're hitting almost vertically up a hill to a
blind green at the top. You can see 2mm of flag if you know where
you're looking. But you're really hitting and hoping.

The fourth is a 250-yard short par 4 which still always takes more
than you think. But I guess most golfers tee up with ambitious expectations that are usually very quickly dashed. At which the realisa-
tion occurs that you're just going to play for fun, to free the mind
and contemplate rather than strive and battle.

In a way, I suppose, that's rather how the search for my father has
turned out. If I'm honest, I sort of half hoped, like when I was
growing up, for a sign that he knows I'm looking; just something
that will reassure me he's watching over me. That hasn't happened
of course, but what I want to convey is the sense I've always had,
that he *is* there, in my mind.

The air is damp on my skin, the kind of ambivalent dampness
that means the weather might dry up later. On the other hand it
might turn sultry and stormy, and whenever I'm out in the open

and hear thunder, the possibility flickers in my mind that I might get felled by a lightning strike.

Best not to think about it. If I was to start imagining a coincidence like that I'd never set foot on Gullane again, and though it would remove all risk of premature death my life would be a lot less sweet.

It's a sweetness that demonstrates itself when, at the top of Gullane Hill, the clouds break all around and the full magnificence of the landscape spreads out before me – a flat, calm, peaceful, amazingly lovely expanse that reaches down to the southern shores of the Firth of Forth under a vast blue sky. Old guys on the course stop and look at this thing they've seen for forty years, this vista of links and greenery and forest and sea, of deer and seals and gulls, this wilderness that stretches away across the hills and down to the Forth rail bridge, and across to the kingdom of Fife.

Behind me is the village of Gullane. London is so big and so busy in contrast. It has white-walled villas lining the side of the course, and the ruined old church of St Andrew with its neat, dignified graveyard, and an endless string of folk teeing off from number 1, with the clockwork regularity of fighter planes going off. It is east Scotland, the land of my ancestors, and it is absolutely beautiful.

After five minutes I walk on. Inevitably I find myself thinking about my dad. I'm reading John Steinbeck's *The Winter of Our Discontent* at the moment, which is a lovely book. There's one passage in particular which makes me think about the information that I have collected about my dad, and also about the people giving us that information, and of course about the story that is being told. 'A man who tells secrets or stories must think of who is hearing or reading, for a story has as many versions as it has readers. Everyone takes what he wants or can from it and thus changes it to his measure. Some pick out parts and reject the rest, some strain the story through their mesh of prejudice, some paint it with their own delight.'

I know as much – and as little – about my dad as a character as I ever did. The people who knew him can only tell you so much.

What I'll never have is the personal, first-hand experience. All I've ever known of him has been mediated through others. But it's not bad stuff that I've been told. He was unselfish, modest, generous, funny. He fucked up once or twice along the way, but who doesn't? He was a good team man. Intelligent – he thought about the game and tactics. He was respected. He talked sense. He fitted in. He was shy, until he got where it mattered – on a football pitch. Playing in front of 160,000 people at Hampden, or 60,000 at White Hart Lane week in, week out – that's a pretty good way to announce yourself.

I think of the affection in which he was held. I think of his gifts – the service he gave his team-mates, and the glory and excitement he gave to thousands of people who watched him. I think of how he's remembered and celebrated even now, nearly half a century after his death. That was him. That was my father, John White, of Mussel-burgh, Alloa and Falkirk, Tottenham Hotspur and Scotland.

And I only have to feel sceptical – reluctant to believe he was the paragon everyone makes out – to remind myself of one incontro-vertible fact. The people who wept for him were good people. Dave Mackay, Cliff Jones, Bill Nicholson – that's quite some line-up to shed tears at your passing.

Besides – and hard though this may be to credit – there is a kind of comfort to be derived from the fact that he died when he did. That came home to me not long back when I talked to Richard Blanch-flower, Danny's son. Richard – you can see his ten-year-old-head poking over the side of the open-top bus as the Double side parade with their trophies through Tottenham – is a tall, confident-looking guy in his late fifties who makes his living well away from football, as a char-tered surveyor. Here's someone who has never felt overpowered by kinship with one of the greatest footballers of the twentieth century.

'You don't make a lot of it,' he told me. 'I've seen through the illusion of fame. My dad died a broken man of Alzheimer's. End of career – your purposeful life is over, like a Hollywood actress whose looks go. The last three or four years, it wasn't worth him being there. There was this big guilt thing, people saying, you should be going down there to see him, this, that and the other. No point. He looks at me. Doesn't know who I am.'

And when I think of all the others who played alongside my dad, falling by the wayside one by one, it's possible to be overcome by melancholy at the way our gods have become mortal. Neither Richard nor I had any choice how our fathers went. But one moment, sitting there waiting for the rain to clear, next moment you're gone – it's not all bad, compared to some of the options available.

It's the James Dean thing – going before you start to decay. No If Onlys. No decline. No inkling it's going to happen. Just bang. Gone.

Fisherrow, Musselburgh, on an August evening. Like Gullane, it doesn't change much year on year. It's late in the day, but this is Scotland. The sky seems to stay light for ever. There's both a chilly breeze and a beautiful calm. Boats from the local sailing club are bobbing on the Firth. People, old and young, are out walking their dogs.

I push aside the thoughts of the drive back to London, the way everything closes in the further south you get, and walk down towards the harbour front, past the patch of green in front of Links Street where the washing lines still stand. I breathe in that fantastic smell of the sea and feast my eyes on the ravishing Musselburgh sunset, an inimitable display of blue and grey, silver and black, green, yellow, red and pink. The Firth is a glinting mosaic of pewters and granites; the lights of the kingdom of Fife are golden pinpoints on the green-black hills; and the little town is serene with the sense of another good day passed.

I think about all the years I've been coming here. More than forty have passed since I first stayed with Granny White in her flat overlooking the Firth. I have so many happy, simple memories, of sleeping on a camp bed in the living room, of Janette luring me to church on Sundays with the promise of an ice cream at Luca's afterwards, of drinking Britvic orange juice at the Ravelstone on the edge of town. And it's such a beautiful little town. It feels like home. It's as if no matter how many years pass, some part of your being never leaves.

And that leads me to another thought. It doesn't matter where my dad's ashes are scattered. They're not him. The thing that I've been trying to get closer to or to touch is indeed a ghost, but the world is full of these elusive spirits. I've been looking all around for something that is right here in front of me. In some bizarre way, this is him – Fisherrow, the Firth, the links, the sea and the seals and the deer and the gulls. And this is me. I am my father's son.

I walk past my auntie Janette's house. Here's the washing green that I used to rush around, doing the Olympic 10,000 metres with all the other boys who gathered to play in the fading light in front of the harbour. I hear echoes of our pounding feet, laughter, the bounce of a ball.

I look up and I see Granny White in her flat. I see Auntie Maggie and Auntie Cathy. Footsteps sound in the summer breeze, and the feeling he's around is so overpowering that I seem to hear him breathe, and the idea creeps into my mind that when the time comes for me to go home for good, when I'm bent and slow and grumpy and forgetful – and it's a happy idea, not in the least bit frightening – I'll meet him at last. He'll be at the end of Links Street, a tantalisingly ghostly figure at first, but one who becomes clearer and more and more real to me as, slipping this wrinkled skin, shedding the years, I run to join him. It's you! You're here!

And that'll be us, together at last in endless boyhood, kicking a ball around on the ash pitch till midnight, long after everyone else has gone home.

33

What Happened Next
Rob, 2011

April 2011. It's such a big thing to have to do.

I sit there hearing the phone ring out at the other end and stifle this massive temptation just to put the receiver down. I don't know how he's going to be and I'm wondering how I'll deal with it if he's angry with me. I've already rung the number four times this week, and been put through to voicemail. But I can't just leave a fucking message. Not with what I've got to say. It's like that time I rang the crematorium to see if they knew what had happened to Dad's ashes. In my head I'm trying out work out the right words.

I'm your half-brother?

We share the same father?

Then his wife picks up.

'Is Stephen there?' I say.

'Who's calling?'

'Can you tell him it's Rob?'

I'd best go back a couple of months. There was no Ground Zero day when all of a sudden this bomb of a book was going to explode. It was more like a fuse burning down. Just hoping and waiting. Hoping it didn't upset any of my family. Waiting to see if my half-brother would show up.

Maybe the fuse was lit when the publicity started at the beginning of February, and I did an interview for *Scotland on Sunday*. It was with Aidan Smith, who I talked to when I was up in Musselburgh for a funeral. My uncle Alec, Janette's husband, had died suddenly of a heart attack.

Despite the circumstances, I really enjoyed going in to Edinburgh to meet Aidan. We met in the Cafe Royal on West Register Street and just chatted for a couple of hours. It was good to meet somebody who really liked the book and got it on the level that was important to me. He said it reminded him of his relationship with his father, which he'd written about in his book *Heartfelt*.

The morning after was Uncle Alec's funeral. He got a big crowd, and at the wake afterwards it seemed like half of east Scotland was queuing up, waiting to tell me stuff about my dad. What struck me was that after years of silence they felt able to come up to me and broach the subject. My writing the book seemed to have flagged up to them that I was open to talking about it. Everybody was thinking, 'We'll tell you what we knew about him, we'll tell you all these stories.' They all added substance to the myth.

One of people who spoke to me was a really nice guy called Bill Hunter, known as 'Sim', who had been one of McGillivray's Boys at school along with my dad. 'McGillivray was such an inspiration,' he said. Bill had lived just round the corner of Links Street, near where the old Co-op used to be, and the two of them walked to school together every day. He'd arrive at Granny White's in Links Street of a morning and sit on the couch waiting for my dad to get ready. Then they'd set off and call for two or three more boys. 'John would have this tennis ball, he'd keep it up all the way across the road between the traffic in Musselburgh,' Bill said. 'But when we played on the cinder pitch he was never one of the guys who was picked first.' He was convinced, as well, that Dad would have moved back to Musselburgh at the end of the day. 'Whenever John came back here you'd never have guessed he was a pro. Not like some who were big-headed about it. The same John was back every time.'

I also paid a visit to Bonnyrigg Rose while I was up in Musselburgh, to watch them against Pennycuik. I met the former club secretary, a lovely old guy of ninety who'd come with his son. He was the person who'd signed John at Bonnyrigg, and who'd given his house key to my dad so he could stay the night before. He remembered driving him to that trial at Middlesbrough which came to nothing.

Nat Fisher was there too, and he introduced me to a guy called Mark Young, who used to play in the same team there as Dad, central defence/midfield for half a season. He reckoned they started calling him the Ghost there, because of the positional sense. 'John was always the player that stood out.' Mark remembered one game when Dad had crossed the ball for a corner. 'I went for it and got knocked out by the goalie.' But the most amazing image he fetched out for me was that of the massed games that used to take place at the back of the old gasworks behind Musselburgh racecourse. 'Twenty-a-side,' Mark said. 'And even when your dad was at Alloa and Falkirk, on Sunday morning he'd still go and play with his mates.' Then he recalled all the cars that would be parked up there, which gave a nice indication that they were no longer just kids.

A lot of the people who spoke to me said they wished I'd asked them about Dad's early days before. I wished I had too. When I was researching the book I thought I'd had everything covered, but as with most ghost hunts there always seem to be unanswered questions. Overall, though, it was just great to have this extra information about my dad, not just from Bill and Mark but from all the others who had known him, or seen him play, or whose lives he had touched in some way. I got emails, letters, even photos, from all over the world. To print them all would require a long chapter in itself, but it was fantastic to know how many people have good memories of him. And that he's an icon even for fans who weren't born when he was alive.

One letter was from a guy called Sandy Whitelaw, who'd been brought up in post-war Musselburgh. His aunt was friends with Granny White, who sent Sandy's autograph book to my dad for the team to sign. 'Your dad had gone to a great deal of trouble,' Sandy wrote, 'and had "got" everyone for me including Bill Nicholson and Cecil Poynton . . . It is one of my most treasured possessions and I can always say with great pride, John White got me those. He could have said to himself, "Oh, not another one," but he went to all that bother which says something of the person.'

Something similar happened to Tony Billington, who had been to watch Spurs against Blackpool at Priestfield Road, the year after the Double. 'I can remember it as if it was yesterday. Spurs won 2–1 and we went off happy back to Blackpool South Station for the Preston train. 'The Spurs team were in the buffet bar at the station so I went round with my scrapbook for autographs. I'd got a few and asked Cliff Jones if he'd sign. No, he said (tongue in cheek, I now realise). Your dad came over and said, "Come on, Jonesy, don't be so miserable," winking at me. He asked me if I needed any more and I said I hadn't got Danny Blanchflower or Maurice Norman who were sat with Billy Nicholson. Your dad went over and got them all, even Bill Nick's!'

David Pavitt showed me the letter he had received from Dad, handwritten from hospital in 1963, dated Thursday 23 January, thanking him for writing a get-well letter. Apart from scribbled words in a diary or the odd autograph, I'd never seen my dad's handwriting before. This was a whole letter! Another piece to put in the jigsaw.

Allan Balnaves told me Dad was his father's apprentice joiner at the building firm of Gibson & Milne in Musselburgh. He said Gibson & Milne had the maintenance contract at Musselburgh Racecourse and he remembered Dad calling in to see his father. 'I was lucky enough to be there that day and we played football in one of the bar areas. He was at the early stage of his international career, so I'm sure you can imagine the great thrill of exchanging passes with him (even with a tennis ball). I wasn't much of a footballer but he took a keen interest in my golf and gave me a bag which I would have kept to this day if it hadn't been stolen (with my clubs) from my locker at Monktonhall Golf Club.

'The last time I talked to him was just before he died. I had left school and was working at Brunton's Wire Mill in Musselburgh. I was out for a walk at lunchtime and met him and your mother pushing your sister on the swings in Lewisvale Park . . . It wasn't long after that when we heard the dreadful news on TV. My dad just walked out the house and sat in the garden for the rest of the night.'

Walter Moffat's mother Elsie was 'a dear friend' of the White family, especially May, with whom she used to babysit Tom, Eddie and John. He remembers Granny White, who he knew as Auntie Anne. 'She used to dish me extra custard at the Burgh school during 1961–2. She had a smiling, careworn face as I recall.' My auntie Janette, Dad's sister, now lives in the flat Walter's mother lived in as a child.

Tony Rosenberg emailed from Basle to say his father and uncle had been were Spurs fans from the 1920s on, and he first saw them play aged seven against Leicester in the Double season. 'Ironically it was the first home defeat but your dad scored so I was only half unhappy. In 1963, aged 9, I got a Red Rover all-day bus ticket which went from Ilford to the exotic (to us) Church Street, Bush Hill Park, to try and get his autograph by hanging around outside his house. Not only did John sign for us, he was worried we were lost (which we were really) and gave us a lift back to Edmonton where we got the 144 bus home. So a great player and a very nice man.'

A lady called Carol Davis emailed to say she'd been a Spurs supporter all her life and knew Dad way back in the 1960s when she was a schoolgirl. Those were the days when players were happy to socialise with fans; she had been babysitting for several of the players and was good friends with quite a lot of them. 'I remember that the breast pockets of his shirts were often torn, the reason being that he would display his ball skills with a golf ball, entertaining the eager throng of young autograph hunters to which I belonged. He would come out of the gates at the Lane and we would watch him bouncing the golf ball off his foot to his knee to his head, to his shoulder, back down to his knee and foot and then back to the chest, when he would pull open the pocket and the golf ball would pop in – and so the pockets would eventually get ripped.' Carol said she and her friend Jill were the two ever-present fans at the ground paying their respects that Danny Blanchflower wrote about in his column the week after Dad died.

And one email was a real gem. A guy called Colin Neill wrote: 'I was only 10, but I'm sure I attended a match in August 1964 at Hampden when Spurs played a Glasgow Select. This was a regular charity fixture. In my mind Spurs won 5–2 and Jimmy Greaves scored direct from a corner. However, I also remember that John White's ashes were scattered, I think at half-time. As I said, I was only 10 but if you'd asked me even before I read your book that is what I remember.'

So maybe that's one mystery solved. Or maybe not.

Doug Cheesman's review in *When Saturday Comes* was the first professional feedback I got. Doug and I had met four years back through working on the *Spurs Opus* and it seemed especially nice that a mate was interviewing me. He gave it a fantastic review, and while it's easy to say, 'Yeah, but that's what mates do,' you could tell it was genuine enthusiasm. Then the national papers came calling. More nice reviews. John Crace interviewed Mum, Mandy and me for the *Guardian*, and what really chuffed me was that later on he wrote about meeting us and what my dad meant to him in his book *Vertigo*.

I went on Radio 4, the *Today* programme. Twenty past eight, a prime-time slot. I was glad no one had told me before I went on that by that time of the morning it pulls an audience of 7–8 million and essentially what I was doing was addressing the nation. Then I really would have got stage fright. I might have got slightly carried away preaching Denis Laws's revisionist theory of how World Cup history might have been changed had the Ghost lived to play for Scotland in 1966. But I managed not to swear and also not to cry, so it went off OK, I think.

In fact, the only shit thing that happened was that I'd been looking forward to Tottenham stocking my book in their shop, but when I approached them they said they weren't going to because they were only selling licenced products from then on. This book was to be the first victim of this commercial decision, and no amount of emails, calls or pleas would change their minds. It left me wondering whether there was anyone left at THFC plc who valued heritage and history over profit and loss. Keith Burkinshaw was right . . .

Thing is, all my life I'd had to deal with the feeling I didn't belong at the club. I'd wanted some sort of recognition that I was the son of one of its greatest players and it never happened. Then when I wrote the book I thought, 'Now they'll acknowledge me at last, now I'll be accepted by the whole club.' And that still didn't come about.

I guess that feeling of not belonging originally came through indoctrination from my grandmother Alma, Harry Evans's wife, and even my mum. Jimmy Greaves has said publicly time and again that he didn't think the club did enough for us after Dad died, and certainly it always rankled with Alma and Mum that when a few months had gone by they asked us to move out of our house because they wanted to move another player into it. It was as if to them Dad was just another employee who had left.

I'm not saying any other club would have done it any differently – that was the way footballers and their families got treated back then. Even so, when I was a kid I kind of wished Bill Nicholson would come and talk to me about my dad, but I never got to meet him. Except for once, a few weeks after Dad died, when apparently Bill came round to our house with a bag of sweets for Mandy and me. Obviously I've no recollection of it, being six months old at the time, but somewhere there's a photo of the occasion. The whole thing had been set up by a photographer from one of the tabloids, who supplied the sweets too.

After that, as far as the club was concerned, we were pretty much left to get on with it. It was hard for Mum, not just financially. She'd been living the glamorous life of a footballer's wife: parties, dances, travelling. She was still very young, and suddenly she wasn't part of it all any more. So the years went by. Then in 2006, Bill died, and his daughter Linda rang up. After they'd spoken, Mum put the phone down. 'Bloody Bill Nicholson. All this time he's never invited us anywhere and now we've been invited to his funeral.'

I'm OK – more than OK – with the Bill Nick thing now. I've managed to rationalise it. It must have been one of the worst times in his life. He'd lost his potential new captain, he'd lost his linchpin, he'd lost the whole direction he was planning to take Spurs in. For Bill, who was the ultimate perfectionist planner, what happened must have been devastating. The glorious future he had visualised was snatched away in an instant. And when I talked about it to his daughter Jean while I was writing the book, she said his *own* family came second to Spurs. So our family were going to be way down the list.

But while we're on the subject of families, here's another thing. Once the book was out suddenly everyone wanted to talk to me about their dads. I was playing for an All Stars (loosely termed) charity side against Spurs Legends – Mark Falco, David Howells, Ian Walker, Garry Brook, they were all there. We were warming up on the eighteen-yard line when Paul Hawksbee, the TalkSport presenter, confided to me that his father had died when he was six months old, and how his mother had never talked about stuff to him, so he understood that aspect of the book perfectly. Belatedly discovering that I wasn't the only person that this had happened to was a kind of validation. I wasn't so strange, what happened in my family wasn't unique. This is the way some people deal with grief.

And because there is stuff in the book about losing a parent, there have been other people who talked to me about strange, closed stories in their own families. Some had been given the information once and then all the doors were shut. 'You've been told that. That's been passed on to you. But actually we'd rather you never talked about it again.' Some had come up against the elephant-in-the-room approach. The things I've been told would once have left me boggle-eyed. Things like: 'My big sister's actually my mother.' 'My auntie's actually my uncle.' To the extent that I'll never be amazed by anyone's revelations again.

Which brings me back to April 2011.

It was Sunday the 10th when it started. Cara and I were about to have dinner with a friend who'd come round to see us, and for some reason I decided to check my mobile for messages. I don't know why because I hardly ever get any (makes me sound kind of sad and lonely!). But this time there was one. So I thought I might as well listen to it.

It was from Jack Mathieson of the *Daily Record* in Scotland. I could only just about hear him down a very bad line, so not a lot of it made sense. But my head did that thing where it felt like it was being squeezed inwards. I knew full well what the call was about. I made my excuses from the dinner table and went outside to phone him back.

'I'm glad you called me,' he said. 'I'm just letting you know that there's a story running tomorrow in the *Record* by your father's other son.'

My heart was pounding by then and it was hard work to stay in control. All over my body it felt like klaxons were being sounded. It's going to be in the papers! Tomorrow!

'His mother is very upset by how she's been represented in the book. So he wanted the opportunity to put the record straight, and tell his side of the story.'

I finally managed to breathe. Stay calm, carry on. Act normal.

'OK, I'll read the story and get back to you for Stephen's number.'

I went back in from outside and sat at the table carrying on with dinner, while working out how to say what had happened without appearing weird. It felt that much more awkward because we had a friend there. I tried to play it down, as if it was the most ordinary thing in the world for me to get rung up by a journalist saying there was a story coming out tomorrow about my half-brother who I'd never met.

But I really wanted to keep it to myself. It was difficult to process it all in one go. And it wasn't just the standard panic and fear and excitement and nervousness. It was the embarrassment I felt for causing a fuss and putting the Whites in the spotlight.

Telling the world about the half-brother I'd never known was no accident. The reason I talked about it in the book was probably so he would come forward. But at that moment all I could think was, If only I'd just left that story hidden. It would have been so much easier all round. Which is, I guess, why so many people hide the truth.

The next day I had a meeting late on in the morning at Alexandra Palace, so I went on from there to my studio by train. Which is something that over the years I've done about as often as applauding an Arsenal goal; normally I cycle in from home in Crouch End. I'm only mentioning going in by train because it underlines how strange and unusual that whole twenty-four hours of my life was panning out.

Anyway, overground from Alexandra Palace to Moorgate, then tube to Farringdon. This is when things got really weird.

The Metropolitan Line trains have these old-fashioned seats that face each other and after I sat down I looked across at the seat opposite. And there lay a copy of that day's *Daily Record*.

Cue *Twilight Zone* music in my head. I'm still astounded because these days if there's a paper on a tube seat it's the *Metro* or the *Evening Standard*. For a short while it felt like something from a dream. It was as though nothing else was there. Only me and this Scottish paper, neatly folded in half, like it would be.

I got up slightly off my seat and reached out to grab it, and this voice said: 'Excuse me, pal, that's my paper.'

I registered that the voice was a deep, deep Scottish one and I wouldn't have been surprised to have discovered that it was the Ghost, just taking over some guy's body for the moment. But then I looked up at the owner of the voice. Which broke the dream, because he was dark-haired and wearing a suit and didn't look anything like my dad. More Bobby Smith-ish in a way.

I said: 'Sorry, mate, I've just got to look at something,' and hung on to the paper.

My eyes were riveted by a red strip across the top of the front cover. SCOTLAND SPURS SOCCER ACE'S SECRET SON, like they'd had a competition in the office to see who could fit the most *ss* into a sentence.

Even then it went on being bizarre. 'That bit on the cover, that's about you, isn't it?' he said, staring at me.

'Er, yes it is,' I said nervously.

'I've just been reading that. Go ahead, look at it. It's amazing.'

Full story, pages 5 & 6, it says, so I opened up the paper. This face seemed to leap out at me.

It was him all right. It had to be.

There'd never been a point when I'd felt cynical about some unknown guy coming forward to say he was my half-brother, but if I'd had any doubts at all about who Stephen was then they would have been totally wiped out in that split second of seeing at his picture. OK, you take any Scottish guy over forty who's lost his hair and doesn't weigh fifteen stone, and you've got a candidate for someone carrying 50 per cent of the same genes as me, but this was something else entirely.

The feeling of recognition I had as I looked at his photo was the very same I'd had as a kid when I first saw that footage of my dad playing in the '61 Cup Final. We had the same arms and hands, the same lines at the corners of the eyes.

The next thing I felt was relief that he didn't look more like my dad than I did. Well, a release from fear too. In that microsecond between opening the paper and finding the page I'd been frightened that he'd look exactly like the 27-year-old version of my dad and would still have a full head of hair. But he didn't. There was a photo of me on the page too. Anyone who saw them would know we just *had* to be related.

Then I tried to read some text that was just a mass of blurred letters scrolling past my eyes while a few words and phrases jumped out shrieking: 'a weak man . . . hurtful . . . she told John, and from that date he disappeared . . .'

But I did manage, finally, to take in the major points of the story and it didn't make my dad look very good, to be honest. It wasn't the story told to me by Tommy. In Stephen's family's version, my dad and Stephen's mum Helen had been going out together for more than a year. They were a proper courting couple. My dad had met Helen's parents in Berwick. She'd gone up to Musselburgh to meet Granny White. Then she'd told him she was pregnant and never got to speak to him again. The one time she saw him after that, he ignored her. Next thing he'd signed for Spurs and headed off to London. In our family history, Helen was the villain. In her family, it was my Dad.

It's back to that piece of writing by John Steinbeck that I quoted earlier. The story I'd been told by Tommy had just been one way of presenting the facts and here was a different storyteller telling it a different way.

I assume the reason why my uncle Tommy told it that way to me was that he wanted me to grow up thinking my dad couldn't do a thing wrong. Now I was pleased to have the extra information. I'd managed to straighten out the story a bit. It was really comforting to find out there was more to the story than I'd been told. Though I was uncomfortable with the way I'd had to find out, I came away feeling quite happy. I'd suspected there was more to it than Tommy had made out. I was right.

★ ★ ★

'I've felt nervous every time I thought about phoning you,' I say.

'I've been nervous every time the phone rang,' he says.

It's the end of third week of April 2011 and I'm on the phone to Stephen. I know a bit more about him now. The man Helen later married brought him up as his own son; he's got two younger brothers. He's a plumber, married with four kids of his own. He's always been a good footballer.

One thing really stood out. It's as though the elephant in my family's room was pretty much in two places at once. His mum never talked to him about our dad either. When he was growing up, everyone around seemed to know the story and he'd heard the rumours himself.

'But you never had that conversation with your mum,' I say.

'No, she never talked about it.'

It seems finding out I'd written the book was the catalyst. When Stephen arrived for his regular visit to her, it was the first thing she came out with. 'Do you know who your real dad is?' He told her it was no great surprise to him and that he didn't blame her. 'I was just more relieved than anything that we were having the conversation at last,' he says.

Stephen and I talk a bit more. 'Apparently one of my grandmas used to say our dad being killed by lightning was God's revenge,' he says.

'Oh yeah,' I say, 'like Glenn Hoddle saying disabled people deserved it, because they'd done bad things in a past life.'

And that's about it, really. It's good to talk to him, if a bit surreal. Like quite a lot of things in life, not what I've been expecting – although to be honest I'm not sure what I *was* expecting. When the call finishes, I'm left feeling happy that contact has been made. And relieved, too. I've done it, I've grasped the nettle. I don't think either of us possesses any burning desire to be best friends. But then again, maybe this is just the start. Maybe writing about him now in this extra chapter is my message in a bottle. And I'm waiting to see if he'll pick it up.

★   ★   ★

18 September 2011. It's Spurs v Liverpool and I'm on my way to White Hart Lane with Peter Baker. I've collected him as normal. We have this routine. I get to his block of flats, I phone Linda, and Linda sends him down.

I love seeing Peter. He's going to be eighty soon and he has this problem with forgetting things, but he's great. On the way to White Hart Lane, we have the same kind of conversation we always have.

'Who are we playing today, then?'

'Liverpool,' I say.

'How are they doing, then?'

'They're not bad.'

'They're always a good team, Liverpool, aren't they?'

'They've bought a couple of players. Carroll from Newcastle, and Suarez.'

'Oh!' says Peter. 'Been to many games this season?' All the while we're chatting, he's telling me which way to go. He might have mislaid a fair amount of stuff in his head, but he hasn't lost his directional sense. We get there with perfect timing, without any hassle.

'Where we parking, then? We got a car-park ticket?'

We go in through the Legends suite, which has been refurbished. My eyes are immediately drawn to something new. There's a big photo of my dad in the stairwell now. Cliff Jones walks across to greet us. 'You two just look the same,' he says to me and Peter. 'You look like father and son.' An unfamiliar sensation is starting to come over me. I feel almost . . . at home.

So anyway, the game. We've had, it must be said, a particularly crap beginning to the season. The postponement of the first game, at home to Everton, because of the riots in Tottenham, then getting stuffed by both the Manchesters, has left us just off the relegation places. It's been hard to believe that this time last year we'd finished just off the Champions League places. Spurs have conceded as many goals (fourteen) in their past six home matches as they did in the previous twenty-five at White Hart Lane. I'm wondering if it's going to be one of those seasons, like 2007–8 when we made that disastrous start under Juande Ramos, when every paper seemed to be running a Spurs Sackwatch Special and printing oh-so-funny Spurs jokes.

But it isn't, of course. We've got a game-changer now. Scott Parker, with his black boots – no logo – and his sixties haircut and his sixties running style, very straight and upright like Mr Cholmondeley-Warner from *Harry Enfield*, sends a little shiver down my spine: some sort of energy. Here's a proper player wearing the number 8 shirt. My dad's shirt.

Spurs 4, Liverpool 0 (Modric, 7 minutes. Defoe, 66. Adebayor 68, and 90+3).

No, it's most definitely not going to be 2007–8 all over again.

On the way back home, I think about this afternoon. Obviously, it doesn't take a lot of psychoanalysis to realise that in these Spurs situations Peter's my stand-in dad. If I can't have the reality, this is a pretty good substitute. It's the Dad feeling. He kind of belongs to me in a way.

And going with him today, seeing that photo of my dad in the stairwell, having Cliff there saying hallo – it's been the first time that I didn't feel out of place there or as if I didn't belong.

It's like I'm really accepted there, at last.